T0357511

Praise for *Feminine Intelligence*

"*Feminine Intelligence* is replete with rigorous research and sound advice. In these challenging times, to heal our homes, our communities, and our world, we desperately need the practical wisdom that Elina Teboul shares with us in *Feminine Intelligence*."

—Tal Ben-Shahar
Creator of Harvard University Happiness Course, New York Times
Bestselling Author of Happier

"I love this book! *Feminine Intelligence* is the kind of work that shifts perspectives on leadership forever. It's an inspiring and essential read for anyone seeking to create a more balanced and compassionate world."

—Poonacha Machaiah
CEO of The Chopra Foundation

"In *Feminine Intelligence,* Elina Teboul transcends traditional leadership paradigms, offering a holistic approach that aligns perfectly with the values of social and environmental responsibility championed by B Corps. This book not only provides invaluable insights into conscious leadership but also inspires readers to navigate the complexities of the twenty-first-century business landscape with integrity and purpose. It is truly a transformative guide for leaders committed to making a positive impact in the world."

—Ben Anderson
Former CEO and Co-Chairman of the Board of B Lab US and Canada

"An inspiring call to awaken your heart to take the lead. Feminine intelligence isn't about thinking outside the box, it is about reimagining a world that doesn't put you in a box in the first place."

—Dan Tomasulo, PhD
Author of Learned Hopefulness *and Academic Director of the Spirituality Mind Body Institute, Teachers College, Columbia University*

"Teboul boldly reminds us of what we have lost by overemphasizing the rational, linear and masculine side of capitalism, and invites us into the ultimate both/and that values the intuitive, holistic and feminine side in service of a better world. This book is a manifesto for the future of leadership."

—Wendy K. Smith, Dana J. Johnson
Professor of Management, Author of Both/And Thinking:
Embracing Creative Tensions to Solve Your Toughest Problems

"With a blend of pragmatic business acumen and bold idealism, Elina Teboul challenges readers to envision a new paradigm of capitalism. Prepare to rekindle your faith in a future whereby doing good and succeeding in business are not mutually exclusive."

—Jill Lublin
Author of The Profit of Kindness

"By challenging conventional notions of leadership dominated by masculine perspectives, Elina Teboul's book serves as a transformative resource for leaders striving to elevate their effectiveness. *Feminine Intelligence* is a must-read for anyone in a position of power seeking to cultivate inclusive and empathetic leadership skills."

—Elinor Stutz
Author of Hired!

"Elina Teboul takes readers on a meaningful, spiritual, and imaginative journey into the world of business leadership. This book stands as the quintessential leadership philosophy for the dynamic landscape of the modern era."

—Lorna Davis
Former Chief Manifesto Officer of Danone

"*Feminine Intelligence* is an eloquent guide on how businesses, governments, and the public can fulfill their moral and sacred obligation to protect nature. Packed full of wisdom, storytelling, and passion, this book tells the story of innovative leaders with win-win solutions that help address the environmental crisis."

—Grant Wilson
Executive Director, Earth Law Center

"Teboul's fascinating work on feminine intelligence offers valuable wisdom to all leaders who want to make a difference, by leading with the head and the heart."

—**Mauro Schnaidman**
Former President of Sara Lee in Europe, founder of Coaching Ventures and author of the book Who Said You Can't Change the World? Building a Career with Purpose

"One of the things I look for in a book is its ability to challenge my values and beliefs—to stretch my brain to look at things through a different lens. I found that in Teboul's '*Feminine Intelligence*'. As I journeyed through the chapters, I relished the chapters that resonated with my deepest beliefs; I was inspired by thought-provoking streams of wisdom; and finally, I was challenged to set aside my biases (at least temporarily) to consider new ways of looking at leadership and life. Yes … my brain was stretched and I enjoyed every minute of it."

—**D. Lynn Kelley**
Author of Change Questions

"Elina Teboul reveals how our beliefs about modern business leadership can be woefully misguided. She invites all of us to adopt a timeless, yet underappreciated approach to leadership based on authenticity, joy, and whole system perspectives rather than control, fear, and tribalism. *Feminine Intelligence* offers a roadmap for leaders to cultivate these qualities within themselves and create workplaces that foster genuine connection, creativity, fulfilment … and, importantly, sustainable results."

—**Gaurav Bhatnagar and Mark Minukas**
Authors of Unfear: Transform Your Organization to Create Breakthrough Performance and Employee Well-Being

"Through vivid storytelling, Teboul illustrates the untapped potential within each of us to revolutionize our leadership approach by embracing our human capacity, both masculine and feminine. Her persuasive argument that the cultivation of feminine intelligence is vital to the survival and thriving of our planet resonates deeply in a time of global uncertainty."

—**Dr. Sandro Formica**
Professor of Positive Organizations at Florida State University

"With *Feminine Intelligence*, Elina Teboul challenges the business world to enter a new era of conscious capitalism. Her approach to blending economic success with global well-being and environmental sustainability is innovative and essential. This book is a powerful guide for current and future leaders to create lasting, positive impact."

—Elisa Juarez
Bestselling Author of Sparkle On Changemaker: A Practical
Guide to Equitable Social Impact

"Elina Teboul offers a refreshing perspective on leadership that feels like a breath of fresh air. *Feminine Intelligence* is a must read. The ideas here will transform the way you think about leadership and your role in creating a happier world."

—Karen Guggenheim
Co-Founder of the World Happiness Summit and Author of
Captivating Happiness: Overcome Trauma and Positively
Transform Your Life

Feminine Intelligence

Feminine Intelligence

How Visionary Leaders can Reshape Business for Good

Elina Teboul

Foreword By RAJ SISODIA
Co-Founder, Conscious Capitalism Movement, FEMSA Distinguished
University Professor of Conscious Enterprise, Tecnológico de Monterrey

WILEY

Registered Office(s)
John Wiley & Sons, Inc., 111 River Street, Hoboken, NJ 07030, USA
John Wiley & Sons Ltd, The Atrium, Southern Gate, Chichester, West Sussex, PO19 8SQ, UK

For details of our global editorial offices, customer services, and more information about Wiley products visit us at www.wiley.com.

Wiley also publishes its books in a variety of electronic formats and by print-on-demand. Some content that appears in standard print versions of this book may not be available in other formats.

Library of Congress Cataloging-in-Publication Data

Names: Teboul, Elina, author.
Title: Hidden intelligence : how visionary leaders weave feminine and
  masculine intelligence to reshape business for good / Elina Teboul.
Description: First edition. | Hoboken, NJ : Wiley, 2025. | Includes index.
Identifiers: LCCN 2024050250 (print) | LCCN 2024050251 (ebook) | ISBN
  9781394330119 (hardback) | ISBN 9781394330133 (adobe pdf) | ISBN
  9781394330126 (epub)
Subjects: LCSH: Leadership. | Organizational behavior.
Classification: LCC HD57.7 .T434 2025 (print) | LCC HD57.7 (ebook) | DDC
  658.4/092—dc23/eng/20241228
LC record available at https://lccn.loc.gov/2024050250
LC ebook record available at https://lccn.loc.gov/2024050251

COVER DESIGN: PAUL MCCARTHY

Set in 11/14.5pt and BemboStd by Straive, Chennai, India

SKY10098085_020725

To my children, Philip and Annabelle

And to all our children, and children yet to come—the future
leaders, change makers, and visionaries. The future belongs to you.

To my husband, Jeremie.
Love is everything.

Contents

Foreword		*xv*
	Introduction	1
Chapter 1	**"Greed is Good"**	**9**
	The Money Trail	9
	The Legacy of Adam Smith	11
	Maximizing Profits	15
	The Man Who Broke Capitalism	19
	The Upside of Profits	21
	The Next Generation of Leaders	23
	Questions for Reflection	23
Chapter 2	**Feminine Intelligence**	**25**
	Unexpected Leadership	25
	Head and Heart	27
	The Power of the Feminine	34
	Questions for Reflection	39
Chapter 3	**Broken Open**	**41**
	Congruence is Power	46
	Power Shift	49
	Seeds of Change	52
	Questions for Reflection	56

Chapter 4   South Africa's First Unicorn   **57**
   Against the Odds   57
   Go1's Rise   61
   Propagating Prosperity   63
   Questions for Reflection   66

Chapter 5   The Heart of Courage   **67**
   The Courage to Connect   67
   The Courage to be Authentic   70
   The Courage to Lead   72
   Questions for Reflection   76

Chapter 6   Africa's Conscious Billionaire   **77**
   Allan Gray   77
   Anthony Farr   81
   The Letter   82
   Questions for Reflection   85

Chapter 7   Building Cathedrals   **87**
   The Architect   87
   The History of Why   89
   Lighting Purpose in Your People   92
   It's a Hero(ine)'s Journey   96
   Questions for Reflection   100

Chapter 8   Rebels *With* a Cause   **103**
   Gross National Happiness   103
   Business Reimagined   108
   Questions for Reflection   113

Chapter 9   "B" The Change   **115**
   Setting a New Course   116
   Bringing Love Back to Corporate America   119
   Movement Builders   120
   And Then He's Gone   124
   Questions for Reflection   128

Chapter 10   Tools of the Masters   **129**
   Honing Your Leadership   129
   Time Mastery   131

	Relationship Mastery	134
	Mastery of Uncertainty	139
	Emotional Mastery	145
	Tools to Get Started	147
	Questions for Reflection	150
Chapter 11	**Psychedelic Leadership**	**151**
	Beyond the Taboo	151
	A Brief History	153
	The Psychedelic Renaissance	157
	Psychedelics to Transform Leadership	160
	PowerTripp	162
	Questions for Reflection	164
Chapter 12	**Seeds of Conscious Leadership**	**167**
	The Earth Spoke, and I Listened	167
	Nature Mother	169
	The Creative Spark	171
	Connection with Others	175
	Connection to Self	176
	A Higher Connection	179
	Questions for Reflection	182
Chapter 13	**Awake Not "Woke" Capitalism**	**183**
	Leading with Wholeness	183
	The Inner Power of the Feminine	186
	Voices in Crescendo	189
	A New Era of Leadership	193
	Questions for Reflection	196
Notes		*197*
Acknowledgments		*213*
Index		*215*

Foreword

Raj Sisodia

When Elina Teboul approached me about writing the Foreword for her groundbreaking book *Feminine Intelligence*, I was immediately intrigued. As a longtime advocate for conscious business practices and the integration of traditionally "feminine" values into leadership, I knew this book would be an important contribution to the ongoing evolution of capitalism and organizational culture.

Business has long been driven by the ideals of competition, conquest, and control—values traditionally associated with the masculine. While these principles have helped shape the modern economy, they have also led to great imbalances, particularly in terms of human and environmental cost. In my work with Conscious Capitalism, I have been consistently reminded of the urgent need to elevate the feminine—the qualities of empathy, nurturing, collaboration, and love—into the heart of business leadership. It is not merely a moral imperative but a strategic necessity for the survival of our planet, our organizations, and our species.

This book is not simply a call for a shift in leadership style but a revolution in consciousness. It is about reclaiming the full spectrum of our humanity, integrating the power of the masculine with the wisdom of the feminine. It is about awakening a new paradigm for leadership that can heal the wounds inflicted by decades of exploitative practices and short-term thinking.

Feminine Intelligence builds on and extends many of the core ideas I've explored in my writing and speaking over the years. In *Shakti Leadership*, Nilima Bhat and I examined how leaders can tap into divine feminine energy (Shakti, in the Indic tradition) to become more conscious, compassionate, and creative in their roles. Elina takes this concept even further, offering a comprehensive framework for how feminine intelligence can be cultivated and applied to reshape organizational cultures and business practices from the ground up.

In *The Healing Organization*, Michael Gelb and I discussed how companies can transform themselves into forces of healing. Healing requires us to address the root causes of suffering, and this is where the feminine comes into play. Healing, after all, is an act of love. It requires tenderness, deep listening, and a commitment to the well-being of others—all hallmarks of feminine intelligence.

Love, the ultimate expression of the feminine, has often been considered out of place in the boardroom. Yet, as I wrote in *Everybody Matters*, co-authored with Bob Chapman, love is the most potent force available to business leaders. In that book, we examined Barry-Wehmiller's radical approach to leadership, which treats employees as whole people to be cared for, nurtured, and respected, rather than mere resources. By leading with love, Barry-Wehmiller has created a culture of deep connection, commitment, and purpose, achieving remarkable business results in the process. Love and care are not distractions from business—they are the very foundations of a sustainable and thriving enterprise.

Feminine Intelligence builds upon these lessons and extends them into the future of business leadership. The stories in this book highlight individuals and organizations that are awakening to the power of the feminine, challenging outdated notions of what leadership should look like. These stories show that success in today's world—where the challenges we face are global, interconnected, and unprecedented—requires a new kind of leadership, one that embraces vulnerability, emotional intelligence, and the strength that comes from empathy.

I admire Elina's nuanced exploration of how both men and women can cultivate and express feminine intelligence, moving beyond simplistic gender stereotypes to examine these qualities as innate human capacities we all possess. Her practical strategies for developing feminine intelligence offer a roadmap for leaders of all backgrounds to access more of their full potential.

Elina Teboul reminds us that leadership is not about dominance but about service. The feminine teaches us to lead from the heart, to care deeply for our people, and to value relationships over transactions. It shows us that true power lies in the ability to uplift others, to create spaces where people can thrive, and to nurture the ecosystems—both human and environmental—within which we operate.

As we face a world in crisis, where climate change, social inequality, and mental health issues are becoming ever more pressing, the time has come for a new kind of leadership. The integration of the feminine into business is not a luxury—it is a necessity. The wisdom of the feminine can guide us to new models of growth that prioritize sustainability, equity, and well-being over mere profit. It can help us create businesses that are not just successful, but healing.

This book is an essential guide for leaders who want to step into this new paradigm. It offers not only inspiring stories but practical tools for cultivating feminine intelligence in leadership. These tools are not about abandoning the masculine, but about balancing it with the feminine, creating a holistic approach to leadership that can truly transform business and society.

I believe this book will spark important conversations and inspire meaningful change in boardrooms, business schools, and beyond. Elina's voice is a welcome and necessary addition to the growing chorus calling for a more conscious, humane, and regenerative approach to business.

Feminine Intelligence is not just for women. The qualities of the feminine—love, empathy, intuition—reside in all of us, regardless of gender. The future of business depends on our ability to awaken these qualities in ourselves and our organizations. As we learn to lead with love, we will find that the path to prosperity, sustainability, and human flourishing is one and the same.

We stand at a pivotal moment in human history. The path we choose now will determine the future we create, not just for our organizations but for life on this planet. *Feminine Intelligence* illuminates a way forward—one of greater wholeness, wisdom, and positive impact. I'm deeply grateful to Elina for this important contribution and excited to see how it shapes the ongoing evolution of business and leadership in the years to come.

—Raj Sisodia
Co-founder, Conscious Capitalism Movement
FEMSA Distinguished University Professor of Conscious
Enterprise, Tecnológico de Monterrey

Introduction

I continue to be inspired by the power of capitalism, and I believe that within its DNA is the potential, means, and capacity to lay the foundations for an inspired, harmonious, and symbiotic world in which so many of us can thrive. But if the vision for capitalism has ever been to engender such a world, we have gotten severely, ominously, off-track.

Yet, demonizing capitalism is merely indulgent as well as futile. Over the past century, the economic system has spawned extraordinary benefits for billions of people around the globe. In a world where vilifying profit-seeking and growth has become a fashionable pastime, it's crucial to recognize that profits aren't just the lifeblood of business; they're the pulsating force driving innovation, sustaining livelihoods, and ultimately empowering businesses to serve society.

But the pursuit of profits should not be a myopic endeavor. We must ask ourselves: At what cost do we seek profits and expansion? Must we make a binary choice between economic growth and abundance on the one hand and the well-being of the natural world, our mental and spiritual health, and our joy on the other? Is it necessary to sacrifice one for the sake of the other?

No—absolutely not. It's just that, for too long, we've been suffering from a shortage of vision and an inadequate understanding of ourselves, which have prevented us from seeing how we can have both. And we can.

I believe the vital call of our time is to elevate the consciousness of our global business leaders. Why? Because who better to rein in the damaging practices, re-evaluate the values, and set us on a higher course toward a regenerative future than our business leaders? As economics is arguably the most

1

formidable driving force in today's world, businesses in particular are the power players in our global economic systems. With the resources, creativity, and capacity for innovation, businesses can champion a vital, thriving future for our world. And it's not merely individual businesses that wield this transformative potential; it is the potential of their being an integral part of an interconnected whole. When businesses collaborate and work together, acknowledging their shared responsibility, they have the capacity to address the degradation of conditions that the previous 50 years of profit-driven rational self-interest have created. Like it or hate it, it is the collective business community that is best positioned to resolve the mess we find ourselves in.

So, I welcome you in. Consider this an invitation, perhaps even a provocation. Whether you're at the helm as a CEO or navigating the early stages of managing your first employee, your title is inconsequential. What matters is your commitment to this journey—your quest to broaden and refine not just your leadership role but, fundamentally, yourself. Your presence here signifies an eagerness to evolve.

Thus, together, we stand at the proverbial crossroads. We must decide if today's capitalist paradigm will deliver us to a brighter future or destroy what matters most to us. The responsibility falls on leaders like you. Upgrade your leadership skills, transcend conventional ways of operating, and seek alignment—with your mind, heart, and soul. Embrace integrity as your guiding principle, especially when faced with challenges or temptations to deviate. (Trust me; there will be plenty.) These steps are crucial for solving the challenges we face today—and for ensuring we still have a tomorrow to enjoy at all.

Doing so, however, will require a tectonic shift in our perceptions and values. The insights trickling down from the ivory towers of higher education are insufficient to the monumental task at hand, and the influence absorbed through our cultural and societal biases falls short of fueling a pivot of direction. They simply don't impart the wisdom, methods, and perspectives needed to reverse the addicting and pervasive drive to rack up profits, outperform competitors, and relentlessly grab at power—an outdated definition of "success" that too often still defines our aspirations.

The good news is that there's a growing number of conscious leadership advocates today who are willing to venture into new territory. Many are opting to shift their organizations' visions and move beyond the conventional set of CEO responsibilities that include shareholder returns, profits, and the bottom line. Instead, they are embracing a broader perspective that incorporates more humanistic values.

As formidable as such a task sounds, it is within reach. For years, I have worked with entrepreneurs, executives, investors, and other high performers to ignite their influence and tackle big, hairy problems. By unlocking their feminine intelligence, shedding limiting assumptions, stress-testing ingrained narratives, and answering uncomfortable questions, they rewrote their personal leadership story. They engaged a newfound wholeness that optimized their decision-making, expanded their vision, fueled their creative genius, and allowed them to finally hear and respond to the callings of their hearts. As a result, they have become amplified, elevated, expanded, and more fulfilled than they had ever imagined was possible. They are also fueled with the resolve, strength, and courage they need to lead their organizations as a force for good in the world.

While more leaders seem willing to step up to the plate, it is not enough; it will take many more of us to get to a true inflection point. It will take many leaders—of organizations large and small, current and aspiring—to elevate the status quo of business practices worldwide. To get there, we need to reimagine what leadership is and can be, redefine why businesses exist in the first place, and step into a profound change in how we operate, think, feel, and breathe as leaders ourselves.

To get there, we need you. The call to conscious leadership is not a whisper; it's a clarion call. It seeks global leaders who are ready to step into their power and make a difference.

I repeat: Nothing is more important right now than elevating the consciousness in ourselves as leaders. Leadership, after all, is autobiographical. As we attune to our individual needs and cultivate wholeness within, a remarkable shift occurs. When our egos quiet down, we liberate ourselves from a focus on trivial grievances and limited perspectives. In this ascended state, we rise—aligned, courageous, and expanded—capable of working toward wholeness, not just within ourselves but on an organizational and world scale. This places us in a position of profound responsibility, allowing us to attend to the greater needs of the global economy, humanity at large, and the very planet we call home.

~ • ~

As a student of economics and politics at New York University, I did not question the premise that the sole purpose of an organization is to make money for its shareholders. At Columbia Law School, I dedicated myself to contributing meaningfully to discussions focused on ensuring the primacy of shareholder interests. I considered myself both prudent and logical, ready to embark on my career in corporate law and to serve "Corporate America" and the values that come with it.

But when I finally arrived at my dream job at a prestigious New York law firm, I was gravely disappointed by its soulless and disassociated culture, and I found I lacked purpose there. The "noble" profession I had envisioned turned out to be anything but. It wasn't until I found the courage to quit focusing on advancing social entrepreneurship that I learned that business can be at the heart of creating social and political change. I finally started to internalize how the societal and cultural values that we build our economy on are broken.

A few years later, I returned to Columbia University to study leadership and psychology. I wanted to understand what makes people tick. I realized that we can't simply transform the system without understanding the person, and we cannot help a person transform without understanding the system within which they live and work. The two are interdependent and intertwined.

After completing my studies, I began to coach startup founders and seasoned executives on how to excel and unlock business impact. I was motivated by helping people dig into their authentic power and shed confining assumptions and perspectives. I wanted my clients to unlock the highest version of themselves, and I soon discovered that their transformation was felt far beyond their personal and professional lives. Once they tapped into the peace and wholeness within themselves, their work resonated far beyond their personal space, bringing appreciable positive change to their organizations, their communities, and beyond.

At the same time, my friend and colleague Jordana Confino and I co-created a course for Fordham Law School in New York that we called "Positive Lawyering." The course applied positive psychology (the study of happiness) principles to the legal industry, guiding students to find their purpose, ignite their passion, and arm them with techniques around mindfulness and resilience so they can succeed, soul intact, in the corporate world. The students learned to recognize and draw from their own feminine intelligence—although we didn't call it that then.

It still astonishes me how much people are afraid of the "feminine," too—whether they're negotiating the word itself or talking about that part of our essential nature. When I was conducting research for this book, in fact, I received an enormous amount of resistance from scores of women. One prominent female UK politician I reached out to declined an interview with me, saying, "I don't agree with the concept of feminine intelligence," and many others echoed her sentiment. My conversations with many other female senior executives began with their denial of this part of themselves—they felt that focusing too much on such a "controversial" subject would threaten the equality and respect they had worked so hard for so long to achieve. The irony is that while we are groomed to be feminists, we are simultaneously conditioned to be afraid of our femininity.

Surprisingly, many of the men I spoke with jumped at the chance to have a conversation about it, not because they wanted to put women back in their "place," but because they wanted to tap into that side of *themselves*. Most conversations with men, be it young tech founders or grey-haired gents, turned into stories about how they led with purpose, values, and heart and wanted to be included. They weren't mansplaining, either; they longed to reconnect to their humanity. After all, masculinity has suffered under the patriarchy, too—just in a different way.

But women would often get quite upset when I asked to discuss feminine intelligence with them. I realized that their reactions were rooted in the way so many of us conceptualize what "feminine" means in ourselves and our culture. In the back of their minds—in the subconscious warehouse of their ideas—they pictured the classic pink-attired, blonde, ponytailed *Barbie*, who, for decades, had been as worldly and self-aware as a field mouse. Yet, Barbie the doll is a caricature of how the feminine actually shows up in us; it is an image fashioned by men in a male-dominant world, with no qualms about subverting and minimizing women. No wonder women were turned off.

But feminine *intelligence* is something of a very different order. It's not about eyelashes or fingernails. It's an essential quality of our deepest human nature that we have disassociated from, become uncomfortable with, put down, submerged, and misunderstood. It has been judged, dismissed, and gagged; nevertheless, it has persisted. And yet, today, it is a burgeoning and boundlessly powerful sensibility within all of us, irrespective of our gender, that has the capacity to restore our joy and save ourselves and our planet at the same time.

It also amazes me that people are surprised at the *power* of the feminine within themselves. What is feminine intelligence, anyway? It expresses itself as many things, including empathy, courage, and a sense of interconnection that energizes, supports, and yet inspires. It is the anchor for heart-centered decision-making. It's how to be comfortable in chaos, find hidden opportunities in conflict, and bring out the creativity and effectiveness in others. It embraces our personal humanity as well as the humanity of others, and it inspires us to push the boundaries of our imagination to envision more expansive possibilities than we've known before.

One of the most urgent issues of the day is the climate crisis; it is urgent because if we don't solve it, nothing else will matter because none of us will be here. Yet the very fact that we are on the brink of environmental disaster speaks to our relationship with the feminine. Nature has been associated with feminine qualities and has been represented by feminine symbolism in spiritual, religious, and cultural traditions throughout time. This association draws upon the nurturing, life-giving aspects attributed to both nature and the feminine. The feminine is the seed of our life force, like Mother Nature herself. Yet the capitalism we know today has disconnected us from nature, cutting us off from just about everything that makes us human. When we consciously reconnect with our feminine intelligence, we revive our profound interconnectedness to the natural world and awaken an innate desire to adopt an ecological worldview. Then, as we make decisions for our organizations that impact the natural world, we feel aligned with the regenerative pulse of the Earth.

This doesn't mean that masculine intelligence is any less important than feminine intelligence. It's just that we can't cut off *any* part of ourselves if we are to feel fulfilled, to make a difference, to succeed, and to achieve great things. Yet, the patriarchal fabric of our society has, by virtue of subverting the feminine, robbed people of all genders of the opportunity to exist in an expanded state of wholeness and consciousness. As a result, all of us have, to some degree, dissociated and distanced ourselves from a powerful energy that we have historically and wrongfully minimized and misidentified with the female form, with women. That practice has short-changed all of us.

As I wrote this book, I could have decided to steer clear of the word "feminine" to avoid controversy, misunderstanding, and charged reactions. I could have called this essential quality "yin" or "anima" or another fairly remote or exotic term that people are less familiar with—ones that evoke less emotional baggage and fewer preconceptions. But I soon realized that only the term "feminine" would yield enough emotional response to get the point across. Language is important, and honoring the word and being honest about the feminine within ourselves has been one of the most compelling motivations for writing this book in the first place. I didn't want to shy away from it; I wanted to bring it into the full light of day. It is time to be bold and to discover and own this extraordinary part of ourselves fully.

~ • ~

Until now, most of the world's leaders have been operating from a limited level of consciousness, a limited sense of their own being, and, as a result, a limited sense of their capacity to lead in such a way as to bring positive and powerful change in the world. They remain unaware of their potential for wholeness, but it is only from wholeness that true transformation can be generated. Within wholeness lies our true humanity; if we are going to have a future at all, we must begin to draw from its rich well of wisdom and wider vision to inform how we run our businesses. It is a part of us that we can no longer afford to ignore.

At the heart of our wholeness is a balanced integration of the feminine and masculine. Our feminine intelligence is ripe with ideas, energy, profound insights, and a felt, visceral connection to all of life. To balance the feminine, a healthy masculine energy contributes rigor, analytical prowess, logical thinking, assertiveness, clear direction, and autonomy. These are absolutely essential attributes for any leader. Toxic femininity, without the counterbalancing masculine, is the stereotype we run into—manipulative, overly dependent, emotionally fragile, and prone to sabotage. Conversely, toxic masculinity without the counterbalancing feminine is the status quo—suppressed, extractive, aggressive, dominant, rigid, and excessively controlling. The harmonious interplay between the two results in a synergy that inevitably brings us more internal harmony and the peace, love, and wisdom that result from it.

This book is dedicated to awakening the heart of business. It is for those who dare to dream, who long for a more beautiful and prosperous world. For those of us who want to see the healing of our economic ecosystems for the betterment of humanity and the planet, it's essential that we begin now, infusing it with beauty, power, and feminine intelligence as much as possible.

With this book, I hope to inspire you through stories spanning continents—from South Africa to Paris, London, New York, and even the Bermuda Triangle. Whether they spotlight philanthropists, unicorn founders, happiness gurus, pioneering scientists, multinational giants, or small startups, these stories share a common thread: the unwavering commitment to championing business as a force for good, irrespective of scale or geography.

With this book, I hope to equip you to become a pioneer in a new, conscious leadership philosophy. Within these pages, you'll find a framework and tools that those who have mastered leadership rely on. Accompanied by reflective questions, you'll be invited into radical self-inquiry. These resources aren't meant to be hurried. Allow them to settle. Their purpose is clear: to gently lead you to restore trust in business and to renew your sense of enchantment and wonder for life and its vast realm of possibilities.

Above all, my deepest wish is for you to become intimately acquainted with the extraordinary strengths, brilliance, and beauty deep inside you. Let these narratives guide you to lead an exceptional and fulfilling life—one that is filled with joy and purpose—and ignite a ripple effect of positive change in your world and beyond.

> *The future belongs to those who believe in the beauty of their dreams.*
> —*Franklin D. Roosevelt*

1 | "Greed is Good"

The Money Trail

We have inherited a cultural belief system that most of us don't ever think about. Like the air we breathe every day, we take it for granted and depend on it, and while it remains largely invisible, it also makes it possible for us to operate in the world. The problem is, as long as we remain unaware of it, it runs us—our choices, our values, our behaviors. So, it is time to acknowledge its presence. Then, once we take a closer look at it, we can find out if it is truly aligned with our aliveness and if it supports the larger vision we have for ourselves, our communities, and our world.

The belief system I'm referring to here is the economic system behind our Western capitalist societies. But let me be clear. I am not here to bash it. On the wings of Western capitalism, humanity has come a very long way over the past few hundred years. We have progressed first into the Industrial Age and now into the Digital Age, where driverless cars, robotic manufacturing, artificial intelligence, and other realities that were once the whimsy of mere fantasy and are now integral to our day-to-day human experience. We've constructed a civilization with complex social structures, unprecedented technology, and resources that are infinitely more abundant than humanity has ever dared to imagine in the past. We enjoy longer, healthier life spans, greater levels of literacy and education, and more freedom, leisure, and luxury than at any other time in history. In the West, at least, we are very much a prosperous world.

Yet our mesmerizing, sophisticated world is on fire. A tangle of damaging consequences has emerged from the unchecked exploitation, dominance, arrogance, transactional relationships, and short-term thinking that comprise our current system. Underneath our material achievements, we are drowning in an epidemic of stress and existential despair; we witness discrimination, inequality, and social injustice everywhere we look. This ecosystem of which we are a part is plagued by senseless, violent wars, food insecurity, desperate poverty, and an alarming deterioration of the biosphere. We are killing our own habitat—the very wellspring of resources upon which we depend to survive.

We are turning into boiling frogs. So, why aren't our business and political leaders marching us toward radical solutions or showing real determination to answer our most threatening issues? Because we have grown to harbor very narrow, impoverished views of what leadership is and what it can be. Leadership is not merely the harnessing of intellectual logic to drive economic growth. And it doesn't come into being by means of titles, status, financial wealth, or X (formerly known as Twitter) following. It doesn't materialize through the acquisition of a corner office, or—for the digital CEO—one with ocean views, or by the thrill of standing center stage with thousands of eager eyes looking up to hear our wisdom. Leadership is not synonymous with the power to command people. It can be so much more than any of these outdated trappings.

And how have we arrived at this juncture? How have we, as a collective, allowed ourselves to forget the highest promise of leadership? Full of hope, idealism, and zeal when we started, how have we just become another cog in the wheel, perpetuating the problems of old? If any of us want to see real progress—that is, a sea change in the priorities and values of our leadership—these are critical questions to think about.

Leadership has the potential to be a personally transformational experience as well as one that oversees organizations that operate as a force for good in the world. It can be a conscious endeavor that charts a new course to a healthier, more fertile, more equitable, and more mutually beneficial future for all of us. It can be based on a deeply authentic sense of purpose, be an expression of our whole, alive selves, and be informed by a profound sense of connection to each other in order to solve society's biggest problems. But to get there, we need to make a bold break from the mistakes of the past. We need to establish a new paradigm based on broader values and empowered by the wisdom of our full selves. To do that, we first need to take the time to delve into the foundations of our existing systems and paradigms and examine the lessons we can now learn from them. The future of leadership must begin now. And it begins with us.

The Legacy of Adam Smith

Let's examine our assumptions and presumptions about leadership. What have we been taught, and what have we adopted unconsciously from our culture? What implicit expectations do we harbor about running businesses or about being successful? Many believe that the original seeds of thought pertaining to "modern" leadership can be traced back to 1776, when Adam Smith, the economist and moral philosopher, published his groundbreaking treatise, *The Wealth of Nations*. Now standard reading throughout the halls of higher education, the book is largely an argument in favor of free market economics. Smith argued that division of labor was the most efficient way to produce goods and services for society, and his ideas laid the groundwork for classical liberal economic thought. Thanks to his writings, the concepts that would later be associated with capitalism gained a foothold in the public's mind, and the discourse on the topic has continued to grow ever since.

For economies to grow, Smith hypothesized, we should make our personal interests our priority. He argued that if we allow what he described as "rational self-interest"—our self-serving human nature—to guide our economic choices, then prosperity will readily follow. Further, he proposed that if both producers and consumers focused on taking care of themselves, then governments wouldn't be needed to centrally plan the allocation of societal resources. There's an "invisible hand," he claimed, that guides free markets and ensures fair and satisfactory outcomes for all involved. If individuals, and by extension, businesses, look after their own interests, he argued, supply and demand will be matched, and the invisible hand will keep everything in equilibrium.

These notions form the basis of Western economic thought, frequently earning Smith the honorary title of "father of modern capitalism." Yet, the world was very different in 1776 than it is today, and, like most authors, his writings reflected the times in which he lived. There were no big corporations then; the economy consisted of innumerable small merchants and traders operating under the whims of monarchs. It also seems safe to assume that he did not expect his theories to become a cornerstone of economic decision-making in the modern context of large multinational organizations. But they did.

What's more, knowledge about the mechanics and interplay of human behavior and motivation was limited in the eighteenth century compared to what we know now. And what was accepted as science was often quite inaccurate. Yet Smith, in all of his wisdom, positioned rational self-interest and the "invisible hand" as the engine and orchestration of economic prosperity. Quite simplistically, he believed that people will just know what's best for them—through rational thinking—and that they will act accordingly. He presumed that the motivations of man were selfish and rooted in a desire for material wealth. A somewhat more obscure fact about Smith is that he had published, 17 years prior, *The Theory of Moral Sentiments*, in which he observed that man was motivated by feelings and passions. But he believed that an outside voice, a rational and logical one, prevailed when man had to make economic choices. Smith concluded that we should trust our natural capacity for rational choice. Doing so would serve the economic needs of the many and create flourishing economies for nations.

Of course, today, in the twenty-first century, we are vastly more informed about the mechanisms of human behavior than even the most erudite scholars were in Smith's time. Our economic sciences have evolved a great deal from their classical liberal economic roots. In the 1970s, the field of behavioral economics emerged and then gained prominence in the 1980s and 1990s when economists began to collaborate with psychologists to study how biases and heuristics affected economic decision-making. They ousted "*homo economicus*"[1] and demonstrated that most of the decisions and choices people make are indeed far from rational. In fact, such decisions are often highly biased and irrational and influenced by factors the decision-maker wasn't even aware of.

In short, what often motivates us is *anything* but rational. As social animals, we are driven by hopes and dreams, fears, and the desire to be liked or to belong. Why? Because, as science now recognizes, we are so much more than just our rational capacities. We are so much more than thinking machines.

We are relational and interdependent; we seek meaning and purpose; we marvel at the mysteries of life; and we are guided and often driven by our instincts and emotions. Many of us are happiest when we serve others, and many of us have come to feel that our true human nature is collective rather than individual. Thus, we can see now that placing the classical rational choice economic theory as the basis of our economic system is an enormous miscalculation of the human disposition.

Adam Smith's "rational" man acknowledged no context, no relationships, no environment. He was a separate and singular solo actor. (It should be remembered, too, that Smith wrote only to and for men at the time.) His "rational" man has no past, no childhood, no story, and no parents to consider. He has the power to override triggers, fears, hopes, and dreams. He doesn't value relationships—even with his family. According to Smith's theory, the rational man only operates on rational self-interest and profit maximization. In today's Western world, such an approach to decision-making would be seen as little more than nonsense. Such a man would be a lunatic.

> The heart has its reasons, which reason does not know.
> —Blaise Pascal, French philosopher and economist

When Smith wrote freely about emotions and empathy in some of his other writings, he theorized that economies would function best if they were accompanied by "the adoption of moral standards" and the rule of law. Unfortunately, those other works didn't receive the same amount of press and visibility as *Wealth of Nations*. The lack of attention to moral principles—what matters to our hearts—has wrought some of the most detrimental damage to our economic systems. It foretold the dangers of ignoring our other forms of intelligence and engaging solely by virtue of our rational capacities when we make choices with far-reaching consequences.

Here we stand, heirs to a vast paradigm based on rational self-interest. This legacy has sculpted a culture that glorifies individualism and sown the seeds of egotism, self-centeredness, and indifference to what's beyond our personal boundaries. In the West, such a creed has helped fuel a culture of individuals who sport attitudes affirming that serving oneself is the way to succeed in the corporate world and in life. Beyond their own interests, leaders of organizations are incentivized to prioritize the interests of their organizations above all else. Nothing matters more than the heights of narrowly defined outcomes and robust profitability for the organization.

In this relentless pursuit of conquest, the broader system to which businesses belong is often disregarded, and the intricate web of interdependence that sustains them is overshadowed. Organizations routinely engage with the world as self-serving, isolated entities. Their workforce, the environment, and other stakeholders are viewed merely as resources to be exploited for self-centered "success." The impact of a business's practices on people, on the environment, and on vulnerable communities in societal, cultural, and political contexts is given minimal considerations by those who have the power to effect change.

The self-centered model puts at risk many of the very facets that are most important to us, including our personal and financial health, our need for connection and community, our compassion, and our desire for a better world. As humans, we seek out the satisfaction of our fundamental needs for belonging, security, and love—and even more so for fulfillment, self-expression, and making a meaningful contribution. These needs are truly what motivate our choices and actions—not simply a motivation to serve our own self-interests. We are not merely economic units. Thus, if we want to transform our leadership and our world, these values, too, need to be factored into what we build and how we build it.

What is equally heartbreaking is the sacrifice we're frequently compelled to make of our authentic selves if we want to ascend to leadership positions. Our journey of dissociation has taken a devastating toll on our individual and collective psyches. As we doggedly pursue achievement, we often detach from our humanity and suppress any emotions that might impede the ascent to that imagined summit. Here lies the fallout of the "rational" self-interest narrative. A relentless fixation on accomplishments forces many to conceal a clandestine shame and profound self-loathing, a consequence of betraying the inner calls for authenticity and the yearning for a holistic connection with the world. Our individual anguish can also be understood to be a kind of systemic imbalance—not just a personal one. It is a collective crisis of spirituality and disconnection brought on by a lifestyle and set of values that have sprung from our capitalistic sensibilities.

Compounding these grave costs are grim statistics revealing rising rates of burnout, anxiety, depression, and suicide, particularly within high-pressure professional spheres. The price paid for the unyielding pursuit of "success" is reflected not only in personal suffering but also in broader societal consequences.

> *The alternative is unconsciousness, the default setting,*
> *the rat race, the constant gnawing sense of having had,*
> *and lost, some infinite thing.*
> —David Foster Wallace, novelist

For his time, Smith's ideas were advanced and innovative, yet they could not fully anticipate the negative consequences of unfettered capitalism. The complexities and scale of our global economy and our own existential despair have forced us to finally see the perilous cracks in the paradigm, imploring us to question the limitations, assumptions, and outdated perspectives of such an approach. Political and economic instability, income inequality, mental health crises, and environmental degradation are escalating at a faster pace than ever before, compelling us to question the sustainability of the system that has benefitted us so richly.

Maximizing Profits

Fast forward to the 1960s, when neoclassical economists decided to bring fresh attention to Adam Smith's ideas of rational self-interest and expand upon them even further. The most notorious among these financial leaders was the US economist and statistician Milton Friedman, who focused his spotlight on the "interests" of shareholders, namely, shareholder profits.

"Corporations have no higher purpose than maximizing profits for their shareholders," he famously wrote in *Capitalism and Freedom*. Friedman believed Smith's emphasis on individual freedoms coupled with the self-regulating nature of markets supported the premise that a corporation's primary responsibility is to maximize profits for its shareholders. Nothing is more important than shareholder interests and the value of the company's stock, he argued; they need to be prioritized over and above the interests of all other stakeholders, including employees, customers, partners, the community, and the planet. While not all scholars agreed with Friedman's interpretation of Smith's ideas, his views took root in the world's economic consciousness.

Friedman specifically advocated for Smith's notion of self-interest, quoting Smith's famous passage from *The Wealth of Nations*: "It is not from the benevolence of the butcher, the brewer, or the baker that we expect our dinner, but from their regard to their own interest."

As a result of Friedman's writings, corporations started focusing more of their attention on stock price as a metric of a company's worth in the market than they had in the past. Over time, a higher stock price became the de facto "purpose" and goal of a business, and corporate missions, whether officially stated or not, increasingly fixated on generating profits for the corporation and its shareholders.

In 1970, Friedman hammered these ideas home even further in a now-infamous *New York Times* article, "The Social Responsibility of Business Is to Increase Its Profits." In it, Friedman railed against any business executives who concern themselves with anything beyond profits, accusing them of being "unwitting puppets" who are "undermining the basis of a free society."

Importantly, Milton's tirade was written in response to the "principal-agent" problem that was prevalent at the time. Motivated by their unquench-able materialism and a singular focus on how much they could acquire, many business executives began to manage companies with an eye for their own personal gain. They found ways to optimize business operations to maximize benefits for themselves much more than for their shareholders. Self-declared "masters of the universe" gifted themselves with lavish perks and made extensive use of corporate jets and expense accounts.

Eventually, shareholders revolted. Institutional investors, in particular, demanded accountability from overpaid executives. The tension between executives and shareholders intensified further when both sides vied for control over the direction and management of their companies. Ultimately, public outrage over executive compensation paid off, and organizations were forced to increase their scrutiny of and accountability for such actions.

In response to such excesses, regulators took action to limit business executives' unbridled pursuit of personal wealth. For example, they created fiduciary duty requirements for directors, which legally obligated senior executives to act in the best interests of the company and its shareholders; they were no longer able to make decisions that resulted solely in their own personal gain. To help management align their interests with those of shareholders and not just themselves, many organizations also began to include issuing company stock in management compensation plans. This incentivized managers to prioritize the firm's profitability, as it would also facilitate financial gains for them personally.

Still, motivated by self-serving interests—some would call it greed—with little concern for creating value for society or prosperity for their workforce, managers and owners fought and won their wealth in those earlier decades. To a large degree, their tactics worked—and wrought dramatic consequences for the rest of us. Overinflated CEO compensation packages proliferated, resulting in extreme pay inequities—after all, the incentives were aligned with enriching business executives.

We see evidence of this same self-interest ethic today. Thanks to these tactics, combined with Friedman's promotion of the shareholder primacy model, we see the rampant upsurge of enrichment for senior executives. In 2020, surveys revealed that CEO compensation had increased 1,322% from the reported levels in 1978, while typical worker compensation only increased 18% in real terms.[2] Even more shocking is the fact that today, the fiduciary duties that prioritize shareholder primacy in some jurisdictions might prevent directors from considering a multistakeholder approach at all, as it can arguably conflict with their obligations to shareholders.

Friedman had so many admirers and followers that many referred to his assertions about shareholder primacy as "the school of Milton Friedman." They recognized no other purpose for a company than to make money for itself. The doctrine even got Hollywood's attention, inspiring the 1987 movie *Wall Street*, in which the corporate raider, cultural hero, and lead character, Gordon Gekko, proclaims to a room full of followers: "Greed is good."[3]

Gekko embodied the philosophy of putting shareholder profits above all else, even if it's motivated by a desire to protect shareholders from the greed of their own business executives. Notice that any discussions of virtues, moral objectives, and the social good didn't warrant taking up any oxygen in the boardroom at all.

The trend continues even today. We have been led to believe that maximizing profits is the primary purpose of business and the optimal path to economic prosperity. Friedman and others like him saw shareholder primacy as a means to promote individual freedom, economic efficiency, and prosperity—but in actuality, it has led to increased pay inequality, environmental degradation, and systemic financial instability.

To some extent, we have all been duped. We have been tricked into a quest for consumerism, materialism, and individualism that have become the cornerstones of deep unhappiness and anguish in our Western world. To turn it around, we need to unlearn what has been ingrained and indoctrinated in us. We need to take a fresh look at the larger picture of how these assumptions are breaking our world. As a new generation inherits a system in need of repair, serious reflection on the future of capitalism is required.

In the meantime, while businesses naturally have to manage and utilize their resources to produce economic profit, their definition of "resources" has now expanded beyond capital, property, and equipment to include the company's "human" resources—its people—and its "natural" resources— the environment. And, lacking a more generous credo, the vast majority of businesses have come to exploit their "soft resources" as much as any hard resource. When it comes to employees, few companies *actually* create positive work cultures, contrary to what leadership gurus might suggest on social media. Goals to meaningfully support employee wellness or provide a sense of belonging or purpose rarely get included in business planning. Countless organizations have successfully ignored the environmental "resources" they exploit, as well. And why not? They often didn't have to pay for any consequences of their access to them. For decades, they released noxious emissions into the air and dumped toxins into waterways without taking any responsibility for their effects on ecosystems, wildlife, or human health. Today, greenwashing has replaced sheer indifference with calculated deception.

> *Modern capitalism has the potential to lift us all to unprecedented prosperity, but it is morally bankrupt and on track for tragedy.*
> *—Paul Collier, influential development economist*

The self-obsessed, short-term-minded, unbridled version of capitalism doesn't serve the world anymore. It is a kind of capitalism that seeks to use and manipulate all of its resources to achieve a higher stock price, regardless of the cost to anyone outside its shareholders and senior management. While customers are sometimes alienated, and while some businesses falter or fail in the long term, their short-term interests are satisfied. The status quo is maintained.

Of course, some companies have chosen the road less traveled, seeing themselves as stewards of a greater good. However, the shareholder profit approach to capitalism has become so firmly embedded in corporate America that the ethos has spread far beyond US borders and, to various degrees, has become idealized around the world.

The Man Who Broke Capitalism

For Adam Smith and Milton Friedman, these ideas of economic vitality were theoretical. For one of the clearest displays of how they played out in the world, though, look no further than the leadership of Jack Welch at General Electric (GE). Glorified in business circles, Welch's vision of capitalism was one in which the unchecked pursuit of profit was seen as virtuous and necessary. Welch stepped in as CEO of General Electric in 1981, when GE was worth US$14 billion, and, under his watch over the next two decades, the company's value grew to US$600 billion.[4] For all of his achievements, he became a "captain of industry," the first celebrity CEO, and was lionized for growing GE into the world's most valuable company.

Welch's success was forged through the unceasing push for an ever-climbing stock price for the company. He acquired companies, slashed jobs, and cut costs wherever they could be cut. He focused relentlessly on efficiency and on doing everything he could to raise the price of GE stock.

New York Times reporter and author of *The Man Who Broke Capitalism*, David Gelles, wrote, "Welch was the personification of American alpha-male capitalism, a pin-striped conquistador with the spoils to prove it."[5]

But are these the values we want to aspire to? Think about what this ethic says about our societal values when our business leaders glorify rapacious behaviors and promote ruthless efficiency as a leadership philosophy. Why did countless magazines put Welch on their front covers? Why did the greatest minds of our generation study his strategies as case studies in business schools worldwide?

Welch pursued the goal of shareholder primacy fanatically. In his rubric, employees didn't matter. On the contrary, a leaner workforce meant higher profits—at least in the near term. So, in addition to offshoring and outsourcing thousands of jobs, Welch devised an unambiguous, transactional relationship between employer and employee to slim down the size of his workforce. Each year, GE managers were instructed to rate their employees, and those who ranked in the bottom 10% were axed. He even earned the nickname "Neutron Jack" for his tactics—a reference to the neutron bomb, known for annihilating the people in a city while leaving its buildings standing.[6]

Then, in 2001, not long after Welch retired, the company fell under the pressure of its debts and unsustainable practices. The value of its stock plummeted. There were huge numbers of lost jobs, the effects of which were felt across the manufacturing sector and the overall economy. In the meantime, many of his followers went on to adopt his techniques and follow his playbook at other large corporations—Home Depot,[7] Albertson's, Chrysler, and Boeing. Ultimately, most of those companies faced failure, yet his tactics became the norm for corporate America.

Then 2008 happened. The global financial system came near collapse. The ensuing "Great Recession" brought a massive decline in economic activity in the United States and around the world, and carnage followed. Banks saw themselves as above the law and sold what author Michael Lewis colorfully—but accurately—called "dog shit." In his widely acclaimed book about the global financial crises, *The Big Short*, Lewis exposed the consequences of greed and disconnected incentives. The failure of banks was a direct result of the subprime mortgage crisis that had been building for years. Short-term shareholder profits were the name of the game, with little consideration for long-term consequences to the company, its customers, or the world at large. GE happened to be a major holder of subprime mortgages. As a result, their stock price plummeted, their credit rating downgraded, and a major re-evaluation of the business model and financial practices followed. As Warren Buffett so aptly put it: "Only when the tide goes out do you discover who's been swimming naked."

So, what happened? Why couldn't any of our economists, financial gurus, and genius bankers read the tea leaves? What blinded them from recognizing the inevitable ripple effects on the entire global financial system that would send the world into a recession? Chuck Prince, the CEO of Citigroup at the time, said, "As long as the music is playing, you've got to get up and dance." It was sheer, reckless greed.

The 2008 crisis finally forced the global business community to begin to question many of its underlying assumptions. The events of the day might have even shaken Neutron Jack, who, in an interview for the *Financial Times* in March 2009, seemed to have completely reversed his position, declaring, "On the face of it, shareholder value is the dumbest idea in the world."[8] He added, "Shareholder value is a result, not a strategy... Your main constituencies are your employees, your customers, and your products."[9] That's different. In the meantime, the lives of innumerable employees and customers of organizations holding shareholder primacy as the Holy Grail were ruined, their dreams shattered, thanks to the self-interest of the financial sector.

> *I believe that all good things taken to an extreme can be self-destructive and that everything must evolve or die.*
> *This is now true for capitalism.*
> —*Ray Dalio, Co-Chief Investment Officer of Bridgewater Associates,*
> *the world's largest hedge fund*

The Upside of Profits

To be clear, free markets that encourage businesses to earn healthy profits are a good thing when they are awake to the realities of human nature, when they are ecological- and climate-conscious, and when they are built on a foundation of principles and values. Free markets encourage entrepreneurship and investment, which lead to increased economic growth and technological innovation. The competitive nature of markets incentivizes businesses to develop new products and services and improve efficiency. Free markets can provide opportunities for individuals to improve their economic and social status through hard work and ingenuity, which in turn promote social mobility and reduce economic inequality.

Profits, after all, are the lifeblood of businesses. Without profits, businesses cannot keep the lights on, let alone invest in communities and social impact programs, champion environmental initiatives, take care of their employees, or develop great products for consumers. Besides, many of us in the Western world are shareholders in one way or another—whether we've purposefully invested in the stock market or whether our retirement funds are comprised of stocks—and we'd like to see a healthy return on them as much as anyone else. However, there is a large difference between short-term self-centered profit and long-term sustainable retirement planning and investment.

Through the economic turmoil of the Great Recession, all of us players on the global economic playing field had an opportunity to learn something new: when we pursue the greatest possible returns, focus exclusively on profit, and ignore all negative externalities, the system will eventually fail, and people will be hurt. We had an opportunity to finally understand that if we continue to operate a global economic system that's steeped in an age-old self-interest paradigm, we should expect the associated economic and social fallout.

> *We have subsidized buoyant shareholder returns by fraying the fabric of our societies and using up the planet we live on. We all know this is happening—the world is literally on fire.*
> —*Yvon Chouinard, founder of Patagonia*

The year 2008 *could* have marked a turning point. Some business leaders started to question the long-held assumptions of the traditional economic model and the ideologies that disregard our human values and environmental concerns. They had a chance to reflect on the ramifications of such philosophies. And for a *brief* moment, they did. However, the momentum toward a more humane and sustainable approach didn't last long. The bold and transformative notion of prioritizing the well-being of our people, communities, countries, and the planet itself was quickly overshadowed by the pressures of profit-driven capitalism and the allure of short-term gains.

Then, in the first quarter of 2023, the collapse of several major US banks sent shockwaves throughout the global financial sector, and its ripple effects were felt by businesses of all sizes. As I write, 2024 is already being filled with the same headlines of unabated financial greed, audacious maneuvers of unscrupulous corporations, and the fall from grace of leaders once deemed invincible. While politicians and economists point to interest rates and other technical factors, the matter is more soundly grounded in psychology.

> *Whoever wishes to foresee the future must consult the past, for human events ever resemble those of preceding times. This arises from the fact that they are produced by men who ever have been, and ever shall be, animated by the same passions and thus necessarily have the same results.*
> —*Niccolo Machiavelli*

The Next Generation of Leaders

We are in a fragile moment of transition and transformation, with ecological and social collapse knocking at the door, and we urgently need to establish a new foundation for business and capitalism that is built around purpose and humanity. We need to find new ways for all of us to lead so that we can create a better future, a more sustainable future. Our lens has been too narrow; we must open our eyes and awaken to our own as well as the wider global story. And we must expand our cognitive, emotional, and spiritual capacities to do so.

The world is changing rapidly, and we must change with it. The current conditions of society require a new generation of courageous leaders who are willing to step up and lead us into a fresh era of regeneration, innovation, and transformative workplaces. The current state of the world demands action, and we cannot afford to sit back and wait. We must all take responsibility for our part in creating a better world. It's time to unlearn the conditioning that has brought us to this point and awaken to a new way of being.

A transformation of our global economic system will require the flowering of a new kind of leader, one who is willing to ignite their own personal power, dare to create change within and without, and embody a holistic and humane approach to leadership that embraces the value of people and planet as much as profits. One who is willing to reject old assumptions, ask more of their organizations, and become a force for good in the world. One who is ready to have their own life enriched with more purpose, authentic power, aliveness, and joy. Are you ready to usher in an enduring paradigm of conscious leadership?

Questions for Reflection

1. Who are you as a leader today?
2. What unquestioned assumptions and socially conditioned ways of seeing and acting do you need to let go of to step into conscious leadership?
3. How do you want to contribute? What legacy do you want to leave behind?

2

Feminine Intelligence

Unexpected Leadership

In 2003, shortly after the United States invaded Iraq, Lieutenant Colonel Chris Hughes was leading his armed squad down a street in a city about 100 miles south of Baghdad, when the town's residents started pouring out of their homes. They swarmed out, lined the streets, and surrounded the troops, agitated and angry. The air was thick with tension. Hughes knew that any one of his men could easily interpret a single slight hand gesture, a hint of a knife, or some too-quick movement from one of the townspeople as a sign of aggression and fire their weapons. More fire would follow. It could be a bloodbath.

"Kneel!!!"

Hughes shouted the command to his troops, surprising everyone within earshot, and, almost as one, his men immediately fell to a knee on the ground. For two full minutes, they sat motionless, the crowd watching, still, uncertain. Then, slowly, the townspeople began to disperse, and within a few minutes, the normal bustle of the town had returned. There had been no confrontation. There had been no bloodbath.

No doubt, Hughes' actions were unconventional. The typical military response to such a show of aggression would be to assert dominance and force the angry crowd to abandon their protest. As we see throughout the West, the customary approach to managing a power struggle is to establish control, dominate, and, if necessary, conquer. It's a muscular, linear approach to confronting situations, a zero-sum game that requires winners on the one side, losers on the other, and not much in between.

But Hughes did something extraordinary. Instead of using force and showing off his weaponry to gain power, he had his troops come to an immediate halt. Then kneel. Then get quiet. In the stillness and, with a gesture of respect, he offered the villagers a moment of choice to leave the troops in peace. Holding steadfast to the humane possibility of preventing violence, injury, and death, he took a road less traveled to get his result.

Of course, Hughes' actions weren't the usual macho, masculine ones we usually associate with the military. As he took control of the situation, he embodied patience, compassion, and respect for human life, and yet, he exhibited no signs of weakness. He stood with great power, effecting change, and successfully achieved the result he wanted—a return to peace and routine.

Forget the military. Hughes' approach didn't mirror the kind of leadership we're used to seeing in our corporations, our politics, and in Hollywood movies. There was no ego there. He didn't need to show off his strength or assert his dominance, although he easily could have since his troops had firearms and the villagers had none. He didn't put his company first or prioritize his "team" by acting in the interest of their safety alone at the possible expense of the villagers clamoring around them.

Hughes tapped into a very different paradigm for leadership—one that is a far cry from the typical leadership we see today. He drew his inspiration from the softer side of himself, the *feeling* side, the part that houses our feminine nature. And with it, he brought about the best possible outcome.

Of course, Hughes was by no means the first male leader to enlist a more "feminine" leadership model. He's not the only one to consider kindness, peace, and understanding a higher priority than winning. Many male icons throughout history have drawn on more conscious expressions of leadership than the norm, choosing nonviolence, collaboration, and inspiration to guide a movement to succeed for as many parties as possible.

Mahatma Gandhi, Nelson Mandela, and Martin Luther King are just three who have tapped into emotion and led with heart. They were unifying, not divisive. They didn't lead by creating fear and discord; they led by creating healing. Gandhi's leadership was characterized by his commitment to nonviolence, moral and ethical principles, empathy, and compassion. Mandela had a relentless vision to free the disenfranchised in his country, and King devoted himself to building an equitable, inclusive, and peaceful world. These men acted as servants of their purpose; they weren't in power to enrich themselves but to do the right thing for their people. Their approach was conspicuously different. They led with their hearts.

But these men are undoubtedly the exception to the norm. Throughout the world, and decidedly in the West, we simply expect, even demand, that those in command perpetuate the energetically masculine paradigm of leadership that we're born into in this culture. We continue to love the Jack Welches of the world, even if we're reluctant to admit it. We love leaders who are forceful, emphatic, and, often, narcissistic. It is the winner-take-all, linear, and single-minded style of leadership and power that gets applauded so much more than any other. The patriarchy has been sewn into the foundation of economic and commercial leadership as we know it, and we can easily see it expressed in the rational self-interest and shareholder primacy values we reviewed in Chapter 1.

Head and Heart

> *A good head and a good heart are always a formidable combination.*
> —*Nelson Mandela*

Harvard neuroscientist and author Jill Bolte Taylor lost most of the function of the left hemisphere of her brain when she suffered a massive stroke in 1996 at the age of 37. It took her eight years to recover all that she had lost—her ability to walk, talk, read, and write, as well as her memories of her past and her sense of identity. But in those years, she got to directly experience the power, wisdom, and profundity of the right hemisphere of the brain. In those early days of her recovery, she "stepped into the awe-inspiring experiential sensations of the present moment, and it was beautiful there," she wrote later. "I ... shifted into this consciousness of my right brain, I perceived the essence of myself as enormous and expansive, and my spirit soared free."[1]

Through the eyes of a neuroscientist, she watched her left brain slowly come back online, gradually heal, and bring with it that disciplined, punctual, well-organized, analytical side of her personality. The stroke had temporarily washed away the boundaries of her individuality and separateness, imparting an indelible sense of oneness with all of life. With the return of her left-brain functions, her sense of identity and the chattering of her internal dialog were also reinstated.

Before discussing the import of Taylor's revelations, it's necessary to point out that it's easy and tempting to oversimplify the extremely complex, elaborate, and interconnected functions of the left and right hemispheres of the brain. A great deal about the brain is still unknown, and neuroscientists continue to discover more about it. Still, for the purpose of educating ourselves, it helps to see the bigger picture. Each hemisphere has its predominant set of functions. The right hemisphere of the brain provides feeling and experiential functions, body awareness, nonlinear thinking, and holistic and intuitive perceptions. The left hemisphere, on the other hand, is recognized for providing language, logic, and linear thinking; it allows us to make plans and predictions about the future based on past experiences. It is good at analyzing information, categorizing it, and helping us arrive at logical conclusions. Clearly, both hemispheres serve us well.

While the brain's two hemispheres are separate and distinct, they are connected (you could say "interconnected") by a bundle of nerve fibers called the corpus callosum. This arrangement supports communication and coordination between the two hemispheres and allows the brain to function as a whole.

What does this have to do with leadership? For the leaders among us to guide us toward a prosperous and healthy global landscape, we must recognize the genius within both hemispheres. More importantly, we must recognize when and how to use each one best. We must take a look at how these aspects of ourselves further or impede the realization of our highest visions. As Albert Einstein once said, "The intuitive mind is a sacred gift, and the rational mind is a faithful servant. We have created a society that honors the servant and has forgotten the gift." And a gift it is.

Unfortunately, ours is a culture that chooses to elevate Einstein's "servant"—the rational, linear, goal-oriented mind—rather than the gift. We are blindly submissive to the rational mind and have learned to close off receptivity to our intuition and imagination, our physical bodies, and our humanity. We've been indoctrinated into a masculine mindset and attitude, and we assume that the perspective we have been raised with since birth is the only way to go. Our linear, rational, masculine attitudes create a collective blind spot, preventing us from seeing that a more gracious, holistic, encompassing, and inclusive approach—one that brings with it more encompassing perspectives and higher solutions—is also possible.

From Bolte Taylor's experience, we learn that by intentionally accessing the right brain, we have the ability to free ourselves from being limited to the analytical, rational self-interest of the left brain—that which ultimately drives us to measure ourselves by quantifiable external factors such as bank accounts, profit margins, and titles. It frees us leaders from being so obsessed with the metrics of winning that we can only see so far as the next quarter to keep shareholders happy. Accessing our right-brain functions allows us to flow with intuition, connect with our physical bodies, and experience the aliveness of the moment. It allows us to tap into the collective consciousness where we are not completely alone, disconnected, and ego-driven. Moreover, it holds within it a sense of oneness that cares about our collective humanity—in addition to ourselves individually—which motivates us to make a difference instead of driving us to succeed while others fail.

Yet, the win–lose masculine archetype is so pervasive, so dominant, and so ubiquitous that we barely see it. We are indoctrinated into it as soon as we're born; it has become the air we breathe, permeating virtually every aspect of Western culture. The masculine mindset is embedded in our subconscious minds, affecting our education, molding our relationships, dictating our parenting styles, determining our career paths, influencing our work habits, and even shaping our self-images.

In our educational systems, analytical thinking, logic, and memorization are prioritized much more than artistic expression, collaborative activities, and getting out and connecting with nature. For most of us, the career choices we make, our drive to rise up the corporate ladder, and our relationship to our future come from our masculine mindset—they are cerebral, linear, and goal-oriented. Yet that masculine mindset has its shortcomings: as we strategize our career path with logic and reason alone, we inevitably run into feelings of failure and inadequacy when our unrealistic expectations for success and status aren't met. Disconnected and self-serving, we enter the world of work feeling confused and wounded. We have not engaged all of ourselves to get where we want to be. Only our masculine aspects.

In our relationships, too, we see the masculine archetype in the power dynamics we fall prey to; they are essentially a concern for domination and control—a characteristic expression of the masculine archetype. And within ourselves, we focus on external validation, neglecting personal values—true to the masculine mentality.

It is visible in our parenting. More often than not, parents in Western cultures raise their boys to be "masculine" in a variety of ways, based upon a limited and narrow definition of the term. Boys are told not to cry; they are told that showing fear, emotions, or any kind of vulnerability is an expression of weakness. They are trained to mask their emotions and to "man up." And while these are the obvious ways in which we train them, other, more subtle messages are absorbed as well. They learn that their manhood is dependent on their ability to provide financially, and their relationships with masculinity and money become psychologically intertwined.

By the time these boys grow up to become leaders in the world of commerce, education, and politics—estimates are that roughly three-quarters of the world's political and business leaders are still men—most are predominantly well-trained to focus on facts, logical correctness, power, data analysis, objectivity, and bottom-line profit. Many see themselves as separate from their employees, their neighbors, their communities, and the planet. They just want to succeed on their own, caring mostly about their own career, seeking power and followers. They don't consider themselves in service to anything or anyone outside their own ambitions. Yet, despite all of the socialization that occurs right before our eyes and in which we all unwittingly participate, we are still surprised when those running our politics and businesses put profits over purpose and dismiss environmental and humanitarian efforts as distractions that reduce productivity or as inconsequential costs of doing business.

But this is not just a problem with our boys and our men. Girls and women are caught up in the net of conditioning and cultural beliefs as well. I admit—I was one of them. As a corporate lawyer, I was functioning almost exclusively on masculine values, principles, and thought patterns. The leaders I idolized were all men; I defined success by what I saw in them. I leaned into my hyper-rational, over-achiever side and never had a thought that my intuition or my feminine side might have a place at the negotiating table or in the courtroom.

And I witnessed the same dynamic in so many of the women around me. Some of the women I interacted with then were the embodiment of the masculine mindset; they just happened to be walking around in women's bodies. Of course, at that time, few women were in executive suites, much less at the helm of law firms; those that did make it to the C-suite were the trailblazers. Walking and talking like a man was virtually the only way they could get their low-heel pumps in the door and hope to make it as partners.

One senior attorney I worked for exemplified this. She once told me to "hop like a little bunny" and go take care of something. I was astounded by her cold, demeaning attitude. I met many women like her. She embodied masculine aggression, ambition, and headstrong behaviors; she was cold and insulated, unwilling to collaborate, and was perhaps incapable of kindness. Hiding behind their titles and status, they embraced the hierarchy so they didn't have to lead with empathy, connection, or vulnerability.

James MacGregor Burns, a Pulitzer Prize-winning historian and political scientist, alludes to this masculine mentality when he described the leadership style of the twentieth century as "transactional" and "autocratic." It is focused on hitting targets, clarifying responsibilities, and establishing relationships based on trading one thing for another. These leaders rely on their own authority—their power, charisma, connections, and influence—to get what they're after; they're rarely interested in accord and consensus. This is easily characterized as an analytical, left-brained, dominance-and-submission game of wealth and prosperity.

Of course, since the beginning of recorded Western history—long before Adam Smith's time—those who owned capital, ran businesses, and published economic theories were almost always men, so it's no surprise their approaches were muscular and masculine. And since that masculine style of leadership is deeply embedded into our history and culture, most of us equate it with leadership itself.

As an alternative to the transactional style, Burns introduced transformational leadership, which is based on gaining followers' trust and confidence by mentoring and empowering them. Transformational leaders trust and support others to deliver, and they make decisions factoring in diverse perspectives. They celebrate success through positive feedback and learn from failure instead of punishing it. Transformational leaders build collaborative relationships to get things done, and through their empathy and ability to consider the whole environment, they create loyal followership. Burns began describing a different leadership paradigm—one that embraces feminine intelligence.

What would it mean to bring our whole selves to our leadership roles— our rational, strategic masculine intelligence along with the intuitive, connected, and emotionally aware inner world of the feminine? What future could we envision and achieve together?

The Forgotten Treasure

By now, we're well aware that for thousands of years, women have been relentlessly oppressed by patriarchal systems around the world, systems that are premised on the superiority of masculinity and the repression of all things feminine. There are countless books, articles, media programs, podcasts, and more that seek to bring to light the many ways the female half of the population has been controlled, denigrated, overlooked, and treated as a threat to the patriarchal order. They document and raise our awareness of what women have endured over the years as embodiments of the spirited, often wild and chaotic, intuitive, and feeling nature of the feminine.

And, of course, women have long been seen as the weaker sex, a judgment sustained by stories from our religions, played out in our histories, and supported in our education systems, where our leaders are nurtured and created. Gender stereotypes persist, beginning with the assumption that leaders come in male bodies.[2] By association and osmosis, feminine behaviors and characteristics, including showing emotion, expressing vulnerability, and demonstrating generosity, are considered weak, frivolous, and of little consequence. Surely not the stuff that leaders are made of. Yet, when they show up like leaders and exhibit ambition, independence, assertiveness, or unreservedness, they are, by and large, overtly or covertly punished for it.

For many women, the struggle for gender equality has often stirred up a complex relationship with femininity within themselves. Working with clients around the world, I've witnessed first-hand how the word "feminine" itself has become radioactive; mentioning it in a room full of women can incite an explosion of fear and misconception. Women of all kinds— particularly educated women of means—continue to believe in the myth of the weakness of the feminine and believe that leadership and power are inherently masculine. Most conclude that if they want to be in positions of power themselves, they must reject their femininity and, for the most part, act like a man. "Man up," you could say. A prominent female politician declined an interview for this book because of her own judgments and fears around concepts of feminine intelligence.

Both men and women bring these preconceptions of masculine and feminine, of power and weakness, into the work world and, with left-brain thinking and self-interest at the heart of it, create the strategies, policies, and systems that stoke our entire financial world. The status quo is maintained.

And we're surprised we are in the dire position we're in?

If we look closely and impartially, we can see that the world's patriarchal attitudes and practices have been deeply costly to us, both individually and collectively. The repression in boys and men closes them off from the world of feelings, and they have lost access to their softer side, kindness, and holistic perspectives that touch their hearts. And women, having suffered the archetypal wounding of the feminine, have closed themselves off from their authentic power, their unique gifts, and their alignment with and trust in themselves.

> *The more manly you are, the more remote from you is what woman really is since the feminine in yourself is alien and contemptuous.*
> —Carl Jung

The costs have been great for all of us. Regardless of the gender of our body, we have lost access to the treasure of wisdom and power that is sourced in our feminine intelligence. We have disconnected from the internal life force, from what makes us human. In the process of developing our civilization economically and flexing our muscles in the world through competition, self-interest, and profits-over-people, we have left our hearts and our values behind along the way, eroding our spiritual vibrancy as well as the well-being of our employees, communities, and the planet. We have forfeited our humanity, failing to safeguard each other and our habitat. This can no longer be sustained.

Times of crisis beg for reflection and re-evaluation. If we choose to prioritize macho attitudes and embrace the ideals of power over others, winning at all costs, self-reliance, and self-interest—as we have for millennia—where's the place for empathy, humility, collaboration, and the desire to raise up everyone involved? To be able to birth the solutions we need today, we need to strive for wholeness and bridge the gap between masculine and feminine. We need to embrace and respect both logic and sensitivity. Surely, we are learning that we cannot survive in a world without both.

To be clear, this book is not about a "battle of the sexes." I'm not recommending that we swing the pendulum all the way to the other end of the spectrum to the hyper-feminine, overriding the brilliance of our masculine intelligence. It's not about having one sex win dominion over another—that would be just one more example of the winner-take-all attitude we've been living with for centuries. The focus here is on discovering how we can shift out of the rut of hyper-masculine leadership styles—taking the singular emphasis off strict logic, profits, efficiencies, and finances—and embrace the feminine intelligence within us. That part of ourselves that encourages us to ask how we might collectively thrive. It is about moving the pendulum from the extreme of zero-sum profit maximization leadership to leadership that is driven forward with the head-smart efficiency of our inner masculine along with the compassionate wisdom of our inner feminine. It is about finding an equilibrium between the strengths and capacities of both parts of ourselves so we can serve with the greatest positive effect.

Social theorist and bestselling author John Gerzema went to 13 countries and interviewed more than 64,000 people about what qualities make good leaders. He asked them to rank which qualities were masculine and which were feminine. To everyone's surprise, his research revealed that the most important leadership traits are the ones we'd consider feminine. "Codes of control, aggression, black-and-white thinking have led to many of the problems we are facing today," he wrote. "I fundamentally believe that femininity is the operating system of 21st-century progress."[3]

Imagine the extent of our power if we could find inner peace amid the chaos, disarm our enemies, and realize a positive, mutually enriching, sustainable future. To achieve this, we must embrace both our masculine and feminine intelligence and integrate both of them into our actions.

The Power of the Feminine

The idea that freeing up the feminine within those of us in leadership roles is necessary to see critical change in the world is not just conjecture.

Research shows that when women are involved in global projects, they improve outcomes significantly and "outshine men in most of the leadership dimensions."[4]

Why is that? Statistically, women embody and express feminine traits more frequently than men. When put into action, those dispositions help break down barriers and open opportunities. They have a more participative and collaborative style than men, inviting more ideas, creativity, and solutions.[5] Yet it is not because of their gender or their female form that these women have made a profound impact. It's because they have been successful at drawing on their feminine intelligence—their heightened listening skills, compassion, drive for inclusion, and their willingness to seek outcomes that benefit the whole.

> *I hope I leave New Zealanders with a belief that you can be kind but strong, empathetic but decisive, optimistic but focused. And that you can be your own kind of leader.*
> —*Prime Minister Jacinda Ardern's 2023 resignation speech*

Women are also more likely to be driven by social impact and purpose than men; again, Western cultures allow and condone the expression of caring, compassion, and purpose by women. In 1982, three-time Nobel Peace Prize nominee and peace-builder Dr. Scilla Elworthy founded the Oxford Research Group, a non-governmental organization to develop effective dialogue between nuclear weapons policy-makers worldwide and their critics. When I interviewed her, she explained that women involved in peace agreements improve outcomes because they consider the long-term consequences of displacement, resentment, humiliation, and dignity and are more likely to use nonviolent means.[6]

Women's presence in discussions of import makes a difference. In 2016, The Council of Foreign Relations reported that "women's participation in conflict prevention and resolution advances security interests. One study found that substantial inclusion of women and civil society groups in a peace negotiation makes the resulting agreement 64% less likely to fail and, according to another study, 35% more likely to last at least 15 years."[7]

There are now quite a few women who are in leadership positions who have been able to hone that power and breathe care into the most important issues facing our world—environmental action, a future of work that is equitable and inclusive, and a focus on collective well-being. In 2022, the top three happiest countries in the world, according to the United Nations' annual World Happiness Report, were Finland, Denmark, and Iceland. All were previously led by women. While the data didn't necessarily show causality, the report pointed out that these countries have high-performing social systems and fairness and accessibility for all as fundamental principles.[8] The latest 2024 research shows that these countries remain the leaders in global happiness.[9] Angela Merkel, the first woman to hold the position of Chancellor in Germany, which she occupied from 2005 to 2021, has been credited with pragmatism and economic stability for Germany. Her deep commitment to democracy, human rights, and tackling climate change has earned her widespread respect and admiration.

> *If it had been Lehman Sisters rather than Lehman Brothers, the world might well look a lot different today.*
> —*Christine Lagarde, former Managing Director, International Monetary Fund*

Whether they're leading small companies or large corporations or they're acting on the world stage, trailblazing women have been outstanding examples of bringing feminine intelligence into leadership roles and putting it to work for the greater good. They are laudable examples for all of us to learn from.

An Evolution of Consciousness

For thousands of years, many traditions of the East have considered masculine and feminine forces as underlying principles in the existence and creation of the universe. The concepts of yin and yang originated in China, representing opposite but interconnected forces, one feminine, the other masculine. Yin, the feminine principle, is associated with darkness, earth, water, and passivity; yang, the masculine principle, is associated with light, sky, fire, and activity. The relationship between the two is dynamic, constantly changing and adapting to the circumstances of the universe.

And while it might be easy for us Westerners to emphasize their opposing nature, they actually coexist in harmony and balance.

Several of India's most popular spiritual traditions see Shakti and Shiva—considered the sacred feminine and sacred masculine, respectively, within all of life—as the cosmic energies that created our universe. Shakti is often described as the creative and nurturing energy of the universe, while Shiva is considered the destructive and transformative force of the universe. In some yogic philosophies, the whole universe is understood to be created, penetrated, and sustained by these two cosmic forces.

In the West, Carl Jung, the father of analytical psychology, based much of his teachings on discussions of the feminine and masculine principles within us. Jung believed that the ideal state of psychological development was one in which individuals integrated both their masculine and feminine aspects; men need to integrate their feminine aspect, their "anima," and women need to integrate their masculine aspect, their "animus." According to Jung, feminine qualities include emotionality, intuition, and creativity, and masculine qualities include logic, rationality, and assertiveness.

Jung believed that in order to reach a state of wholeness, we must acknowledge and embrace all parts of ourselves, including those parts traditionally associated with the opposite gender. He believed that *individuation*—the development of a unified and fully realized sense of self—requires the integration of these two aspects of our psyches. By doing so, we'd reach a sort of spiritual androgyny, a balance of masculine and feminine qualities within the psyche. According to Jung, this is essential for personal growth and the realization of our full potential.

It's important to remember that we can choose which aspect of ourselves we want to express in a given situation. We can choose to embrace more masculine energy when we need it, and we can choose to express our feminine energy when that is called for. But to be able to master such nuance and finesse, we first have to give ourselves permission to be both—to value both.

It's striking that in the cosmologies of the East and in the psychological theories of the West, neither the masculine nor the feminine is considered superior to the other. There is no hierarchy. They are complementary qualities; both are necessary for us to function in the world. And if we reject one half of ourselves, we become fragmented; we cannot be whole. As the yin/yang symbol so clearly illustrates, the masculine and feminine are fully interconnected and interdependent; they are harmonious and balanced. When courageous leaders of any gender learn to embrace the feminine principle and call on its wisdom and power along with the masculine, we might actually be able to heal our world and even restore our Mother Earth.

> *The world is suffering from hyper-masculinity . . . from a world of doing rather than feminine qualities such as nurturing creativity, playfulness, beauty, and empathy.*
> *—Mo Gawdat, happiness expert and former Chief Business Officer at Google X*

The tumultuous times we live in are an invitation to unleash the feminine intelligence we are born with and to get in touch with the other half of who we are as humans. We're up against the wall; it's time to explore the empathetic, inclusive, inspiring, holistic, and creative sides of ourselves and upgrade the manner in which we lead. Where the masculine hero might want to slay the dragon, the feminine heroine tames it, brings out its unique gifts, and gathers allies for battle against real enemies. We don't have to choose one or the other; we have both.

To accomplish our ambitious goals, we can bring the feminine qualities—intuition, stillness, compassion—to inform the masculine that is in action. We want to engage the two to energize a new future for ourselves.

How do we recognize this feminine energy within us? Our feminine side gives us access to a powerful, magical inner world. It is the seat of creativity, intuition, flow, and, yes, life. It is the channel through which we experience our spiritual connection to something greater than ourselves. Through our feminine intelligence, we experience our connection to nature—to Mother Earth. Where the masculine intelligence within us demands order and hierarchy, our feminine intelligence can find presence—and inner personal power—in the chaos of the modern world. While the left brain loves to analyze, compartmentalize, and examine things intellectually in order to make sense of the world and control it, our feminine intelligence—informed by our right brain, our body, and our hearts—sees and feels relationships and sees and feels the unity and interconnectedness of the multiplicity. While our masculine side is driven to achieve, rule, compete, and dominate, our feminine side reaps the rewards of collaboration, elevates the whole through a felt sense of interconnection, and aims for the highest outcome for all.

In their book, *Both/And Thinking: Embracing Creative Tensions to Solve Your Toughest Problems*, authors Wendy K. Smith and Marianne W. Lewis propose that builders of great companies reject "either/or" thinking and embrace "both/and" thinking. They can hold in their thoughts several seemingly contradictory dimensions simultaneously. Rather than seeing rigor, practicality, and financial prosperity as incompatible with love, imagination, empathy, and kindness, they allow them to coexist. We are not being asked to choose. Through integrating the feminine and the masculine, we can find wholeness.

What we are seeking is integration, balance, and wholeness that ultimately empowers us to see the forest *and* the trees, to make broader, higher judgment calls, and to serve ourselves, our families, our communities, our countries, and the entire world. Without embracing, owning, and expressing our feminine intelligence, we will continue to miss opportunities for greater peace and prosperity.

In the next chapters, we begin to discover, hone, and ultimately unleash our feminine intelligence. It will pay off in ways we can't even imagine.

Questions for Reflection

1. What associations do you have with the concept of "the feminine"? What are they based on?
2. What would it look like to open yourself up to your intuition and imagination? To allow in chaos and mystery?
3. What gives you pause to unleash your feminine intelligence?

3

Broken Open

What does it take to break free from the confines of the "matrix"? To awaken, to truly see, and to commit wholeheartedly to the advancement of the greater good? How can we, entrenched in societal norms, having been consumed by our prevailing masculine culture, shift our focus toward a vision that champions business as a force for good?

We must break open.

Time and time again, I find that people who are rooted in purpose and committed to people and the planet have had some sort of pivotal experience. It tends to be something intense enough to shift the tectonic plates of their consciousness into something much bigger, more meaningful, and more inclusive. For many, the experience was spiritual in nature, opening them up to a higher level of consciousness that puts everything else in perspective. Such peak experiences—in whatever form they come in—offer up another incredibly valuable gift: a window into our authentic selves.

Such events happen to more people than we realize.

When he was in his 30s, former Google X Chief Business Officer Mo Gawdat had already achieved impressive success through his work at IBM and Microsoft. But when he lost Ali, his 21-year-old son, during a routine appendectomy in 2014, his world turned upside down. He wondered how he could honor his son's legacy. How could he possibly give himself permission to be happy if his child had died? Within the depth of those questions, he found his purpose.

In the wake of the tragedy, Mo made happiness his personal and professional mission. He vowed to help "a billion" people become happier by spreading the message that happiness can be learned and shared. His #OneBillionHappy movement was launched at the World Happiness Summit (a.k.a. "WOHASU") in Miami in 2018.

WOHASU is the brainchild of my dear friend Karen Guggenheim. When her husband died in 2013 from the flu, something deep within her was shaken awake. At first, she wasn't sure if she wanted to live or die herself. Then she went into what she often described to me as "analysis and introspection and awareness and what I wanted my life to look like." Four months later, her "transformation toward happiness" began.

Ironically, like many of the world's most prominent happiness advocates, Mo and Karen drew their passion and purpose from painful and poignant personal experiences.

One of my clients, Samantha Duncan, experienced a profound shift when she worked in Peru, helping women in poverty get microfinance loans to launch new businesses. Witnessing the structural inequality and the inability of these women to access even the smallest amounts of capital, which crippled their livelihood and families, was her breaking point. Sam has since leveraged that experience to create and lead Net Purpose, a platform to help investors with sustainable and ethical investing.

Executive director of the Earth Law Center (ELC), Grant Wilson, found his calling unexpectedly. Prior to starting law school, he volunteered to work for a nonprofit wolf conservation organization. A month into his volunteer work, a disturbing incident shook him to his core. Reports surfaced of a local post office clerk receiving a box that was "bleeding." Blood was seeping out of the seams. Upon opening the box, a wolf carcass was discovered inside, evidently an attempt to ship it through the mail. This shocking event left Grant deeply affected. He realized that the wolves his organization sought to protect were in desperate need of safety and advocacy. From that moment on, he knew in his bones he needed to dedicate his life to making that a reality.

~ • ~

I had my own experience that tore down the walls around my heart and broke me open enough to see more deeply within myself. I never saw it coming. At Columbia Law School, I was a hard-working and ambitious student.

I didn't just clerk for one judge; I clerked for two—one at the New York State Court and one at the Second Circuit Federal Court. I got straight As, was published in the Columbia Business Law Review, and was accepted as an editor for it. Was I strategic? Sure. To succeed in law school, what matters are journal publication, clerking for a judge, getting As, and getting a top-ranking job. Check. Check. Check.

When I graduated, I landed a coveted job as a corporate lawyer at Davis Polk & Wardwell LLP—dubbed the "Tiffany's" of law firms because it counts federal judges, presidential candidates, and Fortune 100 CEOs among its alumni. (Check.) And while I had a heavy caseload working with hedge funds and private equity funds, I felt drawn to do some pro bono work and help African women who had suffered from female genital mutilation (FGM) and forced marriages to obtain asylum in the United States. It was rewarding and exhausting work, but I felt I was making a difference.

My achievements were the essence of my identity. You couldn't tell me that I wasn't the most important person in the room because, by law firm metrics, I certainly was.

A few years later, billionaire investor and philanthropist Allan Gray, founder of the Allan & Gill Gray Foundation, offered me a job. The primary objective of his foundation was to attack poverty and unemployment in South Africa "by educating and nurturing high impact entrepreneurs" in the country. I found myself in the fortunate position of being a part of something that was helping to make the world a better place on a much larger scale than I had been before.

Allan was a prince among princes and larger than life. A brilliant and kind visionary, he had a purpose, a *raison d'etre*, as he often called it, that I'd never come across before. He had built a global investment management firm with assets under management reaching some US$100 billion. The African part of the business alone is now the largest private investment manager in Africa. With extraordinary insight, he placed a philanthropic foundation as the principal shareholder of the business, ensuring that all future profits would fund philanthropic initiatives and influence all future strategic business decisions.

Unlike other philanthropic efforts, this wasn't just charitable giving or the fulfillment of some sense of corporate social responsibility. Allan designed it to be both sustainable and strategic: empowering and creating economic opportunity for otherwise disenfranchised youth to seed and nurture their own long-term success. He fundamentally believed that it would be entrepreneurs—and their drive to create ventures that are forces for social good—that could uplift the African continent out of poverty. He called it "active strategic philanthropy" because instead of setting himself up to dictate how charitable money should be spent, he empowered entrepreneurs who understood what their communities needed and allowed *them* to decide what businesses to build. It is a self-sustaining, self-nourishing, long-term strategy whose positive impact and reach has and will continue to compound well into the future.

My immersion in Allan's magnanimous world was an initiation of sorts into the exceptional world of what has recently come to be known as "conscious capitalism."[1] But as I look back, I recognize that it was only an intellectual initiation on my part. At the time, I was still embodying the masculine values and mindset of my Western culture. Sure, charitable work was a good thing, and it would be good for my career, too. My generosity was typical for those of us in the West—it was largely conceptual, and it was seeded by my own ego. I wanted to make the world a better place because it was the "right thing to do." I wasn't truly and fully embodying my altruism, although I would never have admitted it at the time. I didn't quite have a wholehearted belief in what we were doing.

And, I hate to admit it, but as Allan worked tirelessly and gave unreservedly, I didn't quite buy it. I couldn't understand why he would give away his fortune to philanthropy; in fact, it was shocking to me that someone would do that. How could anybody be *that* altruistic, creating a US$100 billion firm and just giving their wealth away? Part of me held back. And when Allan died at his desk in 2019—literally working until his last breath to make the world a better place—I still didn't understand it. Why didn't he take his billions and do whatever he wanted to do? Why wasn't he off on his yacht somewhere? He even convinced his children that giving up their inheritance in furtherance of the social good was the noble and moral course of action. I couldn't even understand why it was so hard for me to understand.

It wasn't until I returned to Columbia University for my master's degree in psychology that my journey into expansiveness and awakening truly began. It was then that I had a chance to explore consciousness, spirituality, and psychospiritual states induced by various breathing techniques—some of which were practiced in the university basement, cocooned in a sleeping bag, in the dark, with very loud music! These experiences sparked my curiosity and prompted me to, over the years, delve deeper into the therapeutic and spiritual applications of psychedelic medicines, such as sacred plants, MDMA (also known as ecstasy), and LSD, which expanded my mind, body, and spirit even further. As a result of these teachings, I experienced a life-altering relationship with the natural world and came to know, deeply within myself, that I was part of a larger collective energy. I felt more connected to myself and the world around me than I'd even known was possible. It was the culmination of my years of exploration, and it was life-changing.

Finally. Everything that Allan was doing made sense to me. Even though I'd had such a hard time grasping the why and how of his philanthropy, I ultimately grasped it on an emotional and even spiritual level. I reconnected with a sense of knowing and wisdom that elevated my understanding. I could tune out the chatter, judgment, and limitations of the masculine-infused mindset that had been dominating me. My heart was open. I felt expansion. I uncovered the feminine intelligence inside me.

> *The way to recover the meaning of life and the worthwhileness of life is to recover the power of experience, to have impulse voices from within, and to be able to hear these impulse voices from within—and make the point:*
> *This can be done.*
> —*Abraham Maslow*

These experiences awakened a very beautiful "feminine" quality in me. I knew as truth that we are all connected and intertwined, that we cannot function—much less succeed—if we're merely driven by our own personal success, our own self-interests. But perhaps just as importantly, the shift inside me drove home the power of congruence. I finally understood the potency of energy that awakens when one's heart, mind, and spirit are aligned with one's purpose. I came to see what drove Allan to share so generously. And I learned that through congruence, authentic leadership "presence" is achieved.

Congruence Is Power

If you are reading this book, it is likely that, at least intellectually, you appreciate the importance of reshaping capitalism as we know it today. But an intellectual understanding is just a starting point. The engine that will drive us forward sustainably is a felt connection with our values and our inner drive. This congruence within ourselves activates passion and desire for action.

It's intoxicating to be around people who feel aligned and have inner power and courage, isn't it? They give themselves permission to stand in their truth, and they don't waver. Powerful leadership isn't about being efficient machines; it's about engaging our hearts, our souls, and our vision to create a better way of doing business. It's about redefining what "success" means to us. Beyond personal wealth and organizational victories, it means contributing to a thriving global economic ecosystem. That can only be done with the power of congruence.

Many who've come to me over the years have wanted to build the skills and get the training they needed to be more effective, more powerful leaders. But powerful leadership isn't just a matter of learning new skills and understanding body language. It's not just about building confidence and getting assertiveness training, although those have their benefit and value. Essentially, the people that came to me wanted to develop more of a *presence* of leadership, an executive *presence*. They wanted to exude that power from within, not have it come across as learned behavior. Anyone paying attention can tell the difference. And that is achieved through congruence.

I experienced a deficit of congruence when I went to Turkey in 2022 to co-present a workshop in front of a 60-person leadership team for a company that was getting ready to go public. I wasn't there as the lead coach; I was there mostly to support my colleague, who had a long-standing relationship with the CEO. Perhaps because it was "her people" and not mine, I felt out of touch with the group. I soon realized their values were deeply different from mine. Since our values are very much a part of who we are and how we express ourselves, I felt somewhat out of place. I started to feel very uncomfortable—which is rare for me—as I stood before the group. I felt disconnected from my message; I couldn't be myself.

At one point, the group was guided into an exercise and instructed to come up with a quick ESG (Environmental, Social, and Governance) storyline. They were told to find some way to represent their company to please their customer base and give the impression that they are committed to ESG efforts. But I saw it for what it was: just a story. I knew that a true and meaningful ESG narrative cannot be created out of thin air. There wouldn't be heart and commitment and value behind it. There wouldn't be truth and congruence behind it. So, as I stood there, in a leadership position, I felt incongruent and inauthentic. My energy felt zapped. I felt horrible.

From that experience, I knew that if we're not congruent, if we're not standing in our truth and expressing our truth, we can't be exceptional leaders. We won't be able to perform at the level we're capable of—part of us will be held back, taking with it valuable energy and, yes, power.

After all, intellectually, we know what we need to do—yet we don't necessarily do it. As business leaders, we know, theoretically, we shouldn't just focus on making money. Inwardly, a desire to contribute positively to society resonates with many of us. But our priorities are often monopolized by conventional metrics—the bottom line, personal accolades, our standing among competitors—and we can't fit anything more into our agendas and checklists. Besides, perhaps a lot of what has driven our desire to do good in the world up until now is more of an egocentric drive stemming from fear and shame. Fueled by a need for validation, we find ourselves compelled to adopt certain roles to affirm our worthiness in the eyes of others.

We know from the research on intrinsic and extrinsic motivation that if these subconscious fears and ego-driven ambitions are all that we rely on to motivate us, they will eventually run out of steam. As Daniel Pink highlights in his book *Drive: The Surprising Truth About What Motivates Us,* "human beings are not merely smaller, slower, better-smelling donkeys trudging after that day's carrot."

In a time when simple punishment and reward have become outdated and ineffective, it is personal congruent power that motivates us as well as those we want to inspire. Instead of constantly pursuing external rewards, Pink proposes three essential elements of true motivation: the desire to direct our own lives (autonomy), the desire to expand our abilities (mastery), and the desire to contribute to something greater than ourselves (purpose).[2]

Think about the people you know who ooze aggression, insist on dominating, or are subtly abusive. From your perspective, how congruent are they? Do they say one thing but do another? Have you lost respect for them? Do they seem to be overcompensating? How effective are they as leaders when their actions and words are fractured and not aligned?

More often than not, underlying personal challenges, often from child-hood, have shaped such behavior. Unless they go on a journey of introspection and self-discovery, they'll show up as the bastard everyone secretly has contempt for without even realizing it. We *all* have a lot of unprocessed anger, sadness, fear, guilt, and shame, and most of us, most of the time, aren't able to articulate, let alone release, these emotions. Yet these feelings magnify our insecurities, influence our behaviors, and even control us if we don't properly investigate them.

~ • ~

While it's true that going through an extraordinary life experience—whether it be losing a child or confronting a bleeding wolf carcass—is often necessary to break someone open to their innate desire to contribute to the greater good, it's not the only way there. Lacking peak experiences—or, for many, in addition to them—a journey of inner discovery and inner work is necessary to clear away unhelpful, habitual ways of seeing and knowing. It is a quest to open a channel of congruence within oneself.

When we do the so-called "inner work," we can unlock the stories and patterns hiding in the back of our minds, find out what our narratives are, and learn what false stories we're telling ourselves. With trepidation, we become aware of our filters, our triggers, and our worldview. Carefully, slowly, mindfully, we begin to unpack the limitations of our unexamined perspectives. Through doing inner work, we can take our blinders off and lead consciously, trusting who we are and what we are, knowing what makes us tick. Knowing ourselves. How could we lead powerfully without those insights? Only then can we break free from our cultural conditioning, unleash the feminine power and wisdom within us, and become the leader we want to be. The time is now to have the courage to shed the mask and be our true selves.

Doing inner work also frees up our inner *feeling* self—those sensitive parts we've suppressed and hidden away within us for fear of revealing our weaknesses or feeling that we're not good enough. They are *feelings*—part of the mysterious world of our feminine side. We usually ignore them because we can't perceive them with our five senses. But these are components of our feminine psyche, containing our hurts and sadness, our anger and traumas, and aloneness. Therein lies our spirituality as well.

It takes a great deal of energy to ignore these parts of ourselves; even worse, doing so suppresses our natural instincts, our creative self-expression, and even our joy. You can't close a door without preventing entry from either side. Opening the door to our emotions and feelings, on the other hand, opens us up to resources of tremendous power within us that can give us a broader vision, more sensitive intuition, and the genuine motivation to be of service. It is the door to our feminine intelligence. And by bringing it to bear in our leadership, we empower ourselves as conscious leaders.

> *The most important lesson I've learned is that inner work is a prerequisite for outer effectiveness, for the simple reason that the quality of our awareness directly affects the quality of results produced.*
> —Dr. Scilla Elworthy

A foundational principle of leadership psychology is that leadership is autobiographical. In other words, your desire to go into the world and lead others is deeply connected to who you are, what you feel, and what you value. That's why self-inquiry is fundamental to leadership.

Power Shift

But what kind of power is it? The deeply transformative pivotal experiences I've described above—such as those of Karen, Sam, Grant, and myself—also seem to be accompanied by a surprising, profound, and pervasive humility. The journey of self-discovery and healing that gets us to the place of opening our hearts and building inner congruence often shrinks the ego as we disarm ourselves. This diminishment of self-importance liberates us and creates a space for self-inquiry, evaluation, and alignment.

But a pressing question arises: can that egolessness be harnessed as a source of power? How can we exert positive power and instigate meaningful change if we don't have a big ego to drive the show? Navigating these questions prompts a re-evaluation of how we see power dynamics in the first place.

I had the privilege of speaking to Lorna Davis, former CEO and chairwoman of Danone North America (Danone NA), about her experience of tapping into her own feminine intelligence and the results that came from it. She had started early in her career when she was running a program designed to improve sharing of best practices. First, she selected the 10 best business units in the organization, based on a variety of metrics, with the intention of learning what they were doing that was so much more productive than the rest. Then, she set her "manager" hat aside and shadowed people, sat in meetings, watched, and learned. "I listened for gold instead of listening for coal," she told me, looking for what people were great at. She complimented them abundantly and got them to trust her. All of these are feminine principles at work.

Later, as CEO of Danone NA, Lorna brought creativity, collaboration, and even fun and whimsy to the company's annual General Manager's conference in Evian, France, in order to inspire a higher level of sharing of ideas. Lorna picked 10 rockstar influencers in the company and asked them to speak to the crowd and share their stories. But there was a catch. They needed to dress up as fairy tale characters; Disney princesses, pink boas, and fake mustaches could be seen everywhere. Improv actors were also hired to help create a light-hearted environment. The results? The participants started to feel good about sharing ideas and being inspired by each other. The conversations they had were more authentic, more probing, more honest, and more productive than they had ever experienced before, and countless new ideas for new products and distribution systems came out of it. The usual top-down, hierarchically structured approach to conferencing was dramatically outdone by a setting that invited debate, reflection, individual creativity, and collaboration. All of them—powerful expressions of feminine intelligence.

I asked Lorna for her opinion about why it went so well. "I think the reason it worked so well is that, generally, people are too dismissive of the difficulties they have during the execution of something because they have forgotten about the inevitable twists and turns. So they ignore the real lessons along the way—which are the most valuable to others. Either that or they are too shy to share their great ideas for fear of looking arrogant, so they pretend it wasn't great. This system made it fun and silly and everyone got vulnerable and honest. This leads to 'side by side' instead of 'power over'."

Well-infused with her own personal power, Lorna didn't need to set herself up as the master/leader to influence, empower, motivate, and fuel innovation and solutions. She told me about the first day of her promotion to CEO of Kraft Foods, when she put on a big pink suit—to leave a lasting impression—and felt, she admits, pretty full of herself. And when she stepped onto huge stages to speak to huge audiences thereafter, she felt powerful and sure that she had all the answers.

But, over time, something about that rang false in her. As time went by, she realized that such ego-saturated hero treatment wasn't actually going to allow people—on any level of the organization—to authentically share and collaborate and to come up with the best possible solutions and ideas. So she got creative.

She didn't need to stand on a stage and win big applause to validate her superiority and power. She recognized that what's best for a business is to create an environment where ideas are freely exchanged, where people are free to raise their hand and ask a question without shame or hierarchical pressure. Lorna's congruence with her inner beliefs and desires was strong; she didn't need external validation to bolster her sense of power. On the contrary, she created a thriving business environment for growth and innovation through collaboration and exchange. An environment that didn't need to revolve around her ego.

Yet, in our hyper-masculine Western society, "business as usual" means to grab a situation by the throat and to try to dominate it and control it in order to achieve the desired outcome. In an atmosphere of a zero-sum game, the typical way to gain power over something is to wrestle it to the ground until it is tamed and less problematic. Governments take this muscular tack by default. The US government, for example, has a history of going to war with its problems—as in its "war on terror" and "war on poverty"—to galvanize resources and show its commitment to handling the problems of the day. Richard Nixon's "War on Drugs" ultimately led to mass incarceration and hindered vital medical research into potentially life-saving treatments. Yet, not ironically, even with such formidable-sounding names, these ambitious agendas rarely succeed at accomplishing anything meaningful, effective, or sustainable in the long run. In fact, most have failed desperately and brought on worse outcomes than they started with.

A different approach is desperately warranted—and available. One of the unexpected gifts of life-changing experiences and deep inner work is that leaders find that their need to exert *power over* others wanes as they begin to prefer to engage in a *power with* mode of getting things done. This is emblematic of switching from a predominantly masculine mindset to one that encompasses and activates the feminine side of the psyche as well. Conscious leaders pull back from being enchanted with ego gratification and the dominance they can potentially yield. They're okay with not having all the answers, and they become much more willing to solicit the opinions of others, collaborate, and build a vision for much bolder and more impactful outcomes.

> *"All CEOs either lead with profit, process, or people. You have to do all three well, but you have to decide which one you will lead with. And as soon as I started running the business, I obviously knew that I was always going to lead with people. And process and profit would take care of themselves."*
> —*Lorna Davis*

Allan Gray took a similar approach. Wanting to help build prosperity in South Africa, he could have set in stone a strategy for South African entrepreneurs to follow to reach their goals. But he didn't go that route. Over many early morning cups of coffee, he shared with me how he wanted to fund social entrepreneurs because *they're* the ones who live in their communities, and *they're* the ones who have the answers for those communities. They're the ones that are going to be able to come up with the great ideas. By supporting the ideas and creativity of social entrepreneurs and letting them drive, he seeded opportunities for them to create the businesses that would best serve their communities.

The approaches of Lorna Davis, Allan Gray, and others exemplify collaboration, compassion, inclusiveness, and holistic ideas that recognize how interrelated and interdependent life really is. Their far-reaching achievements demonstrated the feminine principle at work in leadership and are models of conscious leadership.

It takes a lot of deep personal congruence to be able to lead in this fashion. Congruence makes it possible for us to feel secure enough to give up power and stop pretending that we have all the answers. Congruence makes it possible to envision and work for the best outcomes—not only for ourselves and our companies but for society and the world.

Seeds of Change

Faith in Nature is a UK-based startup that makes soaps and other beauty and household items. In 2022, it became the first company in the world to nominate a director to their board specifically to speak on behalf of the natural world.[3]

The company considered nature to have enough standing and enough meaning to warrant a seat at the table. And with this one simple action—although it took a great effort to get there—the company effectively did something no one else in the world had done at the time—it gave the Earth a voice and a formal vote in company decisions.

> *And in the meadows, my spirit becomes so quiet that if I put my cheek*
> *against the earth's body, I feel the pulse of God.*
> —*St. Thomas Aquinas*

I had to ask myself: What does it take to fuel such a commitment and act so vigorously in nature's defense? Why would someone decide to put such a director on their company board and give them a voice in company decisions if they didn't feel vitally connected to the environment? Do they experience, as I do, a sense of wonder, reverence, and awe when they see the beauty of the flowers, trees, and mountaintops? When they think about their children and grandchildren, as I do, does it inspire a deep sense of commitment to nature's preservation? If they weren't deeply and fully alive around nature, why would they go and do that in their company?

When it comes to advocating for nature, the business world has played it safe, establishing a track record of putting profits over the environment and money above our home planet. The consequence of these choices is that our own human survival has gotten caught in the balance. In the spirit of the patriarchal mindset, prioritizing domination and control over nature and feminine expression, tremendous damage has been and continues to be done.

Faith in Nature's bold choice was a momentous act. Keep in mind that, in the United States such an action would be considered illegal unless a company has special legal status, such as public benefit corporation status, allowing them to do so. Otherwise, US laws require that directors of corporations abide by fiduciary duties and act in the interests of "shareholder value." And while there is great debate as to the meaning of "value" in such laws, in the United States, it is interpreted as referring specifically to shareholder returns. Not surprisingly, that means—once again—that shareholder interests *must* be prioritized over and above all other stakeholders.

Laws in the United Kingdom are framed somewhat differently than in the United States, and as such, Faith in Nature was able to take their unprecedented steps. Still, the company was forced to engage in a huge legal battle to allow representation of nature in the boardroom. What's important here is that the achievement isn't merely a breakthrough for the company and for the natural world; it is a pivotal event in the way business gets done around the globe.[4]

Another organization helping to shift the business world's prevailing legal relationship with the natural world is the ELC, which advocates for the legal rights of the Earth, arguing in court that nature is more than just personal property and should have legal standing of its own. Along with UK partners like Lawyers for Nature (LFN), a collective of lawyers and advocates working on behalf of nature in the United Kingdom, ELC helped Faith in Nature navigate the hostile legal terrain and win their right to place a representative of nature on their board. By doing so, ELC set a legal precedent for other companies to do the same. This victory even seemed to have inspired Apple, which, in late 2023, unveiled a short film in which Oscar-winner Octavia Spencer stars as Mother Earth confronting CEO Tim Cook about Apple's sustainability agenda.[5] (Tellingly, a number of critics slammed the video for being everything from "cringeworthy" to "paganistic." They clearly don't find it viable to give the Earth a voice in the boardroom.)

ELC is securing new laws and landmark court decisions to protect biodiversity and ocean health, and its advocacy has resulted in the granting of legal rights for rivers, which are the lifeblood of communities around the globe, including the United States, Columbia, New Zealand, Pakistan, and Serbia. It has even gone as far as to advocate to get Earth a seat at the United Nations (UN).

With an eye on the future, ELC has also instituted educational initiatives to groom tomorrow's leaders to seek environmental solutions that value nature as a partner instead of property—creating long-term, sustainable progress for our world.

I've been fortunate to be part of ELC's mission through my work with their board of directors and their executive director, Grant Wilson. Their philosophy, namely, that we humans should consider ourselves stewards, not owners, of lands, has been profoundly inspiring to me. The perspective stands in striking contrast to the patriarchal mindset, which prioritizes domination and control over nature and feminine principles in general. It reflects an important aspect of conscious leadership.

ELC's work also has the potential to dramatically shift the paradigm of property rights. Shifting from the centuries-old *power-over* approach to the Earth, ELC proposes that we are symbiotic with nature, and our focus should be to work *with* it—a true expression of feminine intelligence—for mutually beneficial outcomes so that, ultimately, we can thrive together for a long time.

> *The natural world is the larger sacred community to which we belong. To be alienated from this community is to become destitute in all that makes us human. To damage this community is to diminish our own existence.*
> —Thomas Berry, philosopher

The intrepid steps of Faith in Nature and ELC exhibit the brilliance of bringing feminine intelligence to the issues of the day.

The Measure of Ourselves

In the West, growing up within a masculine-dominant culture, we're used to evaluating our businesses as well as our own work and worth from the linear perspective of the left brain, that is, numerically. We add it up, calculating how much money we make, how high we can go in a corporation, how much value we bring our shareholders, the square footage of our homes, and so on. And now that the world has learned to digitize virtually everything, it has never been easier to quantify, collate, analyze, aggregate, forecast—and otherwise measure—whatever is at hand.

Numbers and data are perfect measuring sticks for people like Jack Welch, who could look at his "numbers" and easily conclude that, as the guy with the most profitable company in the world, he was, well, king of the hill. But as useful and functional as it is, such a means of evaluation is myopic and blind to many other important factors. For example, while GE's numbers were great under Welch's rule, he remained blind to the fact that his employees were feeling marginalized and alienated at the time and that he was losing customers due to their dissatisfaction with GE's products. He was blind to the impending collapse of the company and all the ways financial engineering and other unfair business tactics were contributing to that collapse. His lack of awareness resulted in great losses, grief, and pain for thousands of people. Ultimately, it came at a great cost to the company and to the countless entities it engaged with. The collapse of GE may have served as Welch's personal breaking point, prompting a shift in his perspective on profit maximization.

As conscious leaders adopt and embrace the feminine mindset, their perspective on their companies and their relationships to external factors and parties widens and broadens. They don't simply measure the success of their company by the numbers on the balance sheet or the stock price. There are many factors that can't be documented or quantified, such as mitigating environmental costs and increasing employee health and well-being. Plus, there are benefits that, like seeds in the ground, aren't visible and don't yet produce a crop, but over time, can produce profound gains.

Leaders with a whole-brain mindset, intent on forging a conscious leadership model of their own, don't limit themselves to the tyranny of the left brain. They recognize that quarterly reports and other numeric snapshots of a company's valuation don't come close to telling the whole story of the company's value in the context of its engagement with the world. And, whether they've experienced a mind-bending, pivotal experience or they've traveled a journey of self-discovery, they are congruent with their inner values. Those values, then, can be brought front and center into their business, helping to shift the focus from short-term wins for the few to long-term gains for many, many more.

Questions for Reflection

1. What pivotal life experiences shape your narrative of self and business?
2. Are you speaking your truth? If not, what limiting beliefs might be hindering you from fully embracing and expressing your authentic self?
3. What is your relationship with nature? How can nature have a seat at the table in your business?

4

South Africa's First Unicorn

Against the Odds

Money and opportunity were rare visitors in the small South African village where Melvyn Lubega was born and raised. His family tree was extensive and complex; his grandfather wedded multiple wives, giving his mother 35 siblings. When he was still a child, Melvyn lost his father in a car accident. The family tragedy thrust his mother into the demanding role of being both the sole provider and protector for Melvyn and his siblings. Apartheid had ended just three short years before Melvyn was born, but tension and anxiety still hung heavy in the air. It was a period of slow transition from the tremendous suffering that had been endured due to systemic oppression and a pervasive stripping away of dignity.

An industrious student, when he was a teenager, Melvyn decided to attend a job fair taking place at his high school. The fair was brimming with companies, all actively seeking to engage with bright young people who were driven to shape a brighter future for themselves. But something about one booth and its energy drew him in. He was attracted to the colors in the company's logo, which were somewhat reminiscent of the iconic South African flag. The visual aesthetic had an undeniable coolness and even a little swag. But it was the ethos and passion of those who manned the booth and their genuine support of budding entrepreneurs that resonated with him. When he discovered the Allan Gray Orbis Foundation (AGOF), Melvyn realized he had an opportunity to turn his dreams into reality.

Allan Gray and his wife Gill founded AGOF back in 2005 as a reflection of Allan's ongoing commitment to nurturing responsible entrepreneurship in Southern Africa. An exceptional investor and business strategist, Allan believed that through entrepreneurship, he could tackle unemployment and make a meaningful dent in the pervasive poverty in his home country. Under his direction, AGOF committed itself to investing in, nurturing, and empowering responsible entrepreneurial leaders who help accelerate the creation of meaningful employment and who embody the values and behaviors of ethical leadership. It remains an extraordinarily ambitious vision.

Driven by a profound sense of purpose, Allan's commitment to philanthropy transcended the bounds of passive charitable giving. He understood that a more dynamic and sustainable strategy would be necessary for his country to thrive. So, he launched a fellowship program under the AGOF umbrella. It would be a sophisticated, immersive educational program to give future entrepreneurs the education, mentorship, and support they need to launch and run a conscious startup of their own successfully. With success, these businesses would create jobs and economic opportunities for others. The organization had originally planned to take a simpler route to financing conscious businesses in South Africa, but they ran into a problem. There was no pipeline of young South Africans with the education and entrepreneurial mindset needed to start a business—let alone one that embraced social issues and healthy profits. They realized they had to start much earlier in people's lives to see the change they were aiming for.

Today, AGOF identifies and selects students as young as 11 who exhibit remarkable instincts, passion, intelligence, and vision. Looking to find candidates demonstrating the potential to make a lasting and positive impact on their local communities' economic well-being, AGOF recruiters comb through African villages far and wide to find qualified youth for its prestigious scholarship program. By the time these aspiring young people complete their education, they will have acquired valuable insights into entrepreneurship and a deep appreciation for the values of community and collaboration.

Upon successfully passing a barrage of candidate tests, successful candidates in the program are awarded comprehensive scholarships that cover all of their school and university expenses, including accommodations, meals, and books. They also receive a tutor allowance, a monthly living stipend, academic support, and access to a program focused on entrepreneurial and personal growth. And exceptional graduates, known as "fellows," may have the opportunity to secure seed funding to launch their own ventures.

> *Do your little bit of good where you are;*
> *It's those little bits of good put together that*
> *overwhelm the world.*
> *—Desmond Tutu*

AGOF was a strategic initiative designed to have a long, meaningful, and sustainable impact. Its long-term vision, long-term risks, and long-term investments would defy the patience of the most strategic of donors. Can you imagine investing in a young person 11, 12, or even 15 years old? Can you imagine seeing some entrepreneurial skillsets and capabilities in some kids and deciding that you could educate, nurture, and support them sufficiently so that, at some time in the future—maybe decades later—they *might* start a business that *might* employ people, that *might* succeed, and that *might* possibly help their community begin to pull itself out of poverty?

It takes tremendous courage and conviction for leaders to withstand the pressure of short-term results in favor of long-term success, much more so when what's at stake is to build positive change in our societies and communities well into the future. But AGOF, with Allan Gray as its lead visionary, has been doing that since 2005.

When Melvyn discovered AGOF, he saw an opportunity to turn his dreams into reality. He felt that AGOF offered more than just financial support—it would give him a platform for personal growth and an opportunity to make a genuine impact on his own terms. He was intrigued by the vast possibilities.

As he filled out the application, Melvyn was struck by its thought-provoking questions, further reinforcing his sense that this was an extraordinary opportunity for him. The depth of its inquiry pulled him out of his everyday high school mentality and asked him to think beyond his own career.

It asked him to think *long-term* about the impact he might want to have on his country. It was powerful stuff for a young kid, and it excited him.

Then came the selection camp. Finalists were given puzzles, tested on creativity, and asked to describe how they would approach a variety of problems. "Spaghetti Tower Marshmallow Challenge" kind of stuff.

I spoke to Melvyn about his experiences there in early 2023. He remembered the atmosphere of that weekend was all very new to him. There was a diversity of representation among the candidates; some were intellectuals, some were jocks, some had already started a business. "Yet even as a young, poor, Black kid in South Africa, I didn't feel invisible," he said. "It didn't seem to matter who you were or that you came from nothing."[1]

> *Your time is limited, so don't waste it living someone else's life.*
> —*Steve Jobs*

That's very different from what so many in corporate America and much of the Western world experience, where, research shows, people from diverse backgrounds—whether by race, gender, sexual orientation, or socioeconomic status—are often fearful of expressing their perspective, thinking they will be shot down or their ideas won't be considered valuable. "When you're in the numerical minority or different from everybody else, then you're going to feel pressure to self-censor. Just by nature of being one of the only makes an environment feel less psychologically safe," writes Modupe Akinola, associate professor of management at Columbia Business School.

AGOF created psychological safety for Melvyn—a concept popularized by Harvard Business School professor Amy Edmondson in her book, *The Fearless Organization: Creating Psychological Safety in the Workplace for Learning, Innovation, and Growth*—allowing him to shine. AGOF is in the business of creating entrepreneurs, impressing them with the idea that the very nature of innovation requires courage—enough courage to suggest half-baked ideas, take risks, or propose solutions that just might lack supporting data. Google's famed Project Aristotle found that psychological safety was "far and away the most important" of all the dynamics identified for high-performing teams; creativity and innovation require supportive environments to thrive.

Melvyn felt empowered by the experience, and that self-acceptance would turn out to be a superpower for him just a few years in the future when, as co-founder of the first billion-dollar company to come out of South Africa, he would interact with seasoned executives in corporate boardrooms around the world.

Recognizing Melvyn's potential, AGOF accepted him into the program and awarded him a fellowship at the University of Cape Town, where he would graduate with a bachelor's degree in Business Science. In addition to his university classes, on the weekends, he and other program fellows participated in AGOF's events and classes that were uniquely geared to prepare them for social entrepreneurship and to give them the tools to flourish in creating a conscious business. They even offered classes in self-awareness, leadership, and the basics of building a startup—topics that are rarely, if ever, taught at schools and universities, although they should be.

During his time at AGOF, Melvyn formed deep connections and friendships with a few fellow aspiring entrepreneurs with whom he shared the common dream of making a lasting impact in their communities. Inspired by their passion, they pooled their money together to invest in stocks. They raised about US$1,000—a fortune to them at the time. They also tried their hand at investing small stakes in companies run by their friends. It was a way to genuinely support and share resources with others in the fellowship network, people who shared their intentions and values to help their communities and their country through their entrepreneurial endeavors. Their teamwork and efforts embodied AGOF's values of collaboration, investment, and community building.

Melvyn's instincts for investing served him well. One of his friends, another AGOF fellow, had started Yoco, an online payments platform for entrepreneurs, and Melvyn jumped in as a pre-seed investor. The company has since become the second biggest success story to come out of South Africa. Melvyn's investment proved lucrative, and his confidence grew.

Go1's Rise

Like so many good tech startups, Go1's origins started with a few friends in a garage. Andrew Barnes and his high school friends, Chris Eigeland, Chris Hood, and Vu Tran, had been building a web development company in Australia. A few years later, Andrew met Melvyn when they were students at Oxford University. A bond quickly took root between them, and they found themselves deep in conversations about business and leadership. Just as some steer clear of political debates at the dinner table, Andrew and Melvyn also agreed to shelve any mention of the impassioned rugby rivalry between their respective homelands—South Africa and Australia—a topic near and dear to their hearts—for some time in the future.[2]

The two shared a frustration with the huge gap between what they saw as the skills employees needed to thrive and the training they actually received from their employers. By 2015, Andrew brought Melvyn into the fold, and together with the original team, they co-founded Go1, an innovative digital learning library; its name was inspired by the encouraging phrase to "Go one better."

It wasn't long before Go1 clinched a spot at Y Combinator, a startup accelerator that's been a pivotal launchpad for many superstar companies, including DropBox, AirBnB, and InstaCart. It was a turning point for Go1. The five co-founders set up shop in a two-bedroom apartment in Mountain View, California, and the dream quickly began to take shape.

As the new venture gained traction, it began to attract high-profile customers such as Microsoft, Suzuki, and Thrifty. Melvyn's passion for creating thriving work environments aligned perfectly with Go1's mission to unlock positive potential through a love for learning. So, through partnerships with several of the world's leading content providers, Go1 began offering an array of enriching courses that would help workers enhance their skills, nurture their personal growth, and find more fulfillment at work.

The year 2018 was a good one. Go1 raised US$10 million in a Series A funding round that allowed its co-founders to expand its reach and invest in technology that would improve the user experience. In 2019, the company raised an additional US$30 million in a Series B funding round led by M12, Microsoft's venture fund. With subsequent funding rounds attracting big players like Softbank and other respected investors, their growing financial support solidified their position of influence and garnered widespread recognition in the industry.

By 2023, Go1 had established offices across the globe to become one of the world's largest learning and development platforms. Their extensive course catalogue and innovative proprietary technology attracted millions of learners from thousands of organizations. The scale is huge; every 1.2 seconds, someone in the world starts learning a new skill on the Go1 platform.[3]

Thanks to the brilliant minds and visionary hearts of its founders, Go1 will hold a place in the history books: it is the very first unicorn—a startup company with a valuation of more than US$1 billion—to rise from the soil of South Africa.

But Melvyn's isn't the only success to come from AGOF's programs; the organization has nurtured many South African entrepreneurs to enter the marketplace, succeed, and be a force for good. In 2023, the number of young people participating in AGOF's fellowship program reached 1,339; 216 scholarships were awarded across a range of age groups. AGOF continues to support, educate, empower, and inspire new entrepreneurs, accelerate the South African business economic infrastructure, transform the country's business economy, and elevate the lives of its people in diverse and meaningful ways. It is extraordinarily inspiring and exemplifies the power of a business as a force for good.

Propagating Prosperity

It would be a mistake to think that Go1 is Melvyn's only vehicle to support, nourish, and enrich Africa's future. He also looks for other South African social entrepreneurs to invest in, rejecting the old-school values of assumed competition and winner-take-all at all costs. He is driven by the intention to build a sustainable future through collaboration and good works, finding that those works replicate and propagate.

Melvyn's gratitude for Allan and Gill Gray is humbling and infectious. And it wasn't just their good works that made an impression on him, he says. It was their principles that inspired and motivated him the most. "They literally enable the next generation of leaders and change agents to further society," he told me. Inspired by Allan's philosophy of business and philanthropy in action, Melvyn's personal mission is to create 100,000 jobs in Africa in his lifetime. To do this, he continues to innovate, founding the Future Logistics Company (FLC) to address the long-standing coordination and logistics problems in Africa. E Squared, the venture capital (VC) arm within AGOF, participated as FLC's first external institutional partner.

E Squared was very consciously set up to invest in young South African social entrepreneurs and their startup enterprises. Its ethos is to build a business's value over time, invest in entrepreneurs over the long haul, and not get trapped by a short-term mindset. It's a unique approach, especially among venture capitalist investors, who are notorious for putting a lot of pressure on companies to scale as quickly as possible. But that typical VC approach can interfere with decision-making, especially for purpose-driven companies. New entrepreneurs often feel the pressure of short-term demands for rapid growth, which can conflict with the founders' long-term vision. It often leads to an emphasis on short-term metrics—a core obsession when raising more funds—at the expense of other important objectives, such as building a strong foundation and a healthy company culture.

Unrealistic growth expectations can also strain resources, lead to aggressive expansion strategies, and potentially compromise the long-term viability of the business. Achieving rapid growth often requires substantial financial resources, so VC-backed entrepreneurs often find themselves in constant need of raising additional funding to fuel expansion, which can be a time-consuming and challenging process. Short-term pressure is often Kryptonite to efforts to build a healthy and sustainable business. Being deeply dependent on external funding can also limit a company's flexibility and increase its vulnerability to market downturns or changes in investor sentiment. In turn, it can force founders to give up more of their equity.

But E Squared has become a model of conscious investing, and Melvyn is inspired by it. He loves that E Squared cares about the success of the entrepreneurs it invests in—not just the investment returns they win for it. As an investor, E Squared demonstrates that in two key ways. First, it doesn't require liquidation preferences in its favor. Traditionally, most VCs invest in a company by acquiring preferred shares of stock, while founders and early employees typically hold common shares. Under that arrangement, if the business fails or is sold in a fire sale, the VC generally recoups any assets left in the company, while the entrepreneurs who started the company are left with nothing. Nada. They have nothing to show for all the blood, sweat, time, and tears they've poured into the business to get it launched.

This is where E Squared takes a different tack. Demonstrating the degree to which it supports its entrepreneurs, it offers them participation via the same share class—which effectively puts them together in the same boat. The approach sends a very different message and gives a very different vibe to the entrepreneur, conveying that it is truly a collaborative venture and that everyone can share in the spoils. It's just one more example of the value of putting long-term interests ahead of short-term stakes—placing the interests of the entrepreneur above immediate financial considerations brings the highest rewards for all in the long run.

The second way that E Squared does things differently is that it co-invests back into the business with the entrepreneur so that the entrepreneur doesn't have to give up their equity stake. By creating a special purpose vehicle (SPV) structure, the founder can manage dilution more effectively. The SPV acts as the equity stakeholder, representing the interests of E Squared, while the founder retains ownership of their business. This structure can allow the founder to maintain a larger percentage of ownership and control compared to directly raising funds from traditional VC sources.

Even more, as E Squared is a philanthropic venture, the profits are not distributed to any limited partners. Instead, the windfalls go back into the system to educate and sponsor the future generation of entrepreneurs. What is created is an evergreen, self-sustaining philanthropic circle of giving, reinvigorating Africa with new businesses owned by conscious African entrepreneurs.

"E Squared literally exists to back the entrepreneur," Melvyn told me, "and I think that's unheard of anywhere else."[4]

There are a few other venture capitalists out there who are defying the conventional notion of relentless scaling by adopting a more sustainable, more long-term-focused approach to entrepreneurship. It's not necessary to be a philanthropically oriented investor to recognize that success isn't solely defined by rapid growth; it lies in building enduring businesses with strong foundations. Conscious venture capitalists prioritize patient partnerships with entrepreneurs, offering guidance and support to help them achieve their long-term vision. By emphasizing the quality of growth over speed, these investors aim to create value and deliver exceptional products and services while ensuring the well-being and sustainability of the companies they support.

Inspired by AGOF's ethos of collaboration, Melvyn has brought a purpose-driven and sustainable approach to the for-profit world of investing by becoming a partner at Breega, a European VC company that helps African entrepreneurs get access to European money. At Go1, he had learned how critical a large network of support and access is; Breega is helping to create that network for entrepreneurs. He told me, "I want to bridge the gap between international capital and African entrepreneurs. How do

I make sure that international investors are able to get access to the best entrepreneurs and that the best entrepreneurs are able to get access to international capital and expertise?"[5]

> *Most of the important things in the world have been accomplished by people who have kept trying when there seemed to be no hope at all.*
> —Dale Carnegie

Melvyn balances his masculine intelligence of drive and efficiency with feminine intelligence—finding new ways to nurture growth, collaborate with colleagues, and envision a better future for his community, his country, and the world. Fortunately, Allan Gray had the foresight and courage to imagine that a young Black man from a small village in South Africa would make such a positive global impact, and he laid the foundations to make it possible for him to do so. And now, Melvyn is carrying on that tradition, opening doors for others to succeed in their own right while being an instrument for the greater good.

Questions for Reflection

1. Melvyn's story demonstrates that, with courage and conviction, people can launch a conscious enterprise in spite of the difficult conditions they might have grown up with. What does his story inspire in you?
2. Are there any role models or organizations that resonate with you and inspire you to make a positive impact?
3. How can you turn competition into collaboration for mutual benefit in your own business?

5

The Heart of Courage

As an advisor to business leaders across a variety of industries, I am always coming back to the same fundamental question: What stops them from having the courage to stand up for an approach that doesn't harm the environment, doesn't devalue their employees, and doesn't short-change their customers? What prevents them from calling on their courage to serve their organization as well as the world that sustains it?

Change can only begin with courage. After all, it isn't easy to make deep and lasting changes in a global corporate ecosystem that you've gotten quite comfortable with and perhaps even gotten rich from. The ones that do catalyze changes that reverberate deeply and broadly are willing to take risks. It's personal for them, and they are driven to put aside their conceptual boundaries and conventional ideas in order to advance the envelope of progress. And that kind of energy needs to be sourced from a place deep inside for it to be powerful and sustainable enough to succeed.

The Courage to Connect

In 2019, Lindsay Kaplan and Carolyn Childers decided to launch a new company with an innovative vision: they wanted to build a small private network of senior executive women, enabling them to gather—not just for support—but to cultivate a sense of belonging and create an environment for mutual enrichment. They called their venture Chief and hoped to provide a safe, engaging space for powerful women leaders to share their challenges and their wisdom with others who had faced similar situations and harbored similar questions and ambitions.

To do so, they harnessed the archetypal "gathering around the fire." They built a platform that brings together what they call "Core Groups"—eight to twelve members with matched seniority to talk, share, and learn—much like our ancestors convened around the flames to share stories and wisdom. Under the guidance of a facilitator, these monthly gatherings become a space where members openly discuss their challenges, seek advice, and learn from the experiences of their peers. Having led Core Groups for Chief for several years, I can attest to the profound transformation it has sparked in countless senior executive women—and in me. The experience is enlightening, intimate, and visceral.

Lindsay and Carolyn designed the company around a unique intention: to nurture authenticity and vulnerability in their members even as they strive to climb to the highest tiers of their industries. In other words, the company's mission isn't just to help professional women thrive in leadership positions; it is committed to helping them get there with their authentic selves intact.

This foundational objective of the company spoke to the intrinsic desire we all have for authentic connection, and it struck a profound chord at just the right time. In 2019 and 2020, the topic of authenticity was echoing on radio, in cyberspace, and in popular books, yet practical pathways to uncover and unleash it remained elusive. Chief's timely and intuitive response to the growing concern proved to be a powerful catalyst for its extraordinary growth.

After an initial seed round, Chief secured Series A funding, led by General Catalyst and Inspired Capital, that raised US$22 million. Months later, in the midst of the 2020 pandemic, it raised an additional US$15 million and announced its expansion into several other cities around the United States. Then its growth blew wide open. In 2021, Chief closed another round, this time a US$100 million Series B round led by CapitalG, the independent growth fund of Google's parent company Alphabet. From that massive infusion of capital, Chief was catapulted into the rarefied company of businesses with a valuation of US$1 billion or more. It had taken them just two years to become a unicorn. It was a record for a female-led team.

Chief's growth continues to impress. *Time Magazine* included Chief in its list of 100 Most Influential Companies of 2023. Being the only private membership network focused on connecting and supporting women executive leaders, membership in 2023 grew to include women from 10,000 organizations and representing 77% of Fortune 100 companies. These numbers are especially admirable when you consider that only a limited number of senior executive women would even be eligible to join.

Not surprisingly, the success of Chief and its membership consists of an unprecedented reliance on modes of expression of feminine intelligence. Members are collaborating, supporting, and empowering each other; they are listening to and contributing to each other; they are helping each other discover the courage they seek to lead a life of alignment and purpose.

In action, Chief's Core Groups carve out a sanctuary where women in leadership can probe into deeply personal issues such as their strengths, stumbling blocks, values, and personal definitions of power and success. That level of rapport allows them to weave deep, enduring connections with other women and create a powerful collective journey. Within the fabric of this cherished community, members find the strength to be their true selves, fully and fearlessly.

When I interviewed co-founder Lindsay, she described it this way: "When you think about what fuels business today, it is individualism. People often get ahead in business because of individualism. You don't hear a lot about 'the collective' and 'the community' in business. [But] I think true success is about rejecting that individualism. It is about knowing as a leader that your role is to build and forge connections and pathways forward."[1] Yes. Individualism—so emblematic of the masculine mindset—may have gotten us to where we are today. But it will take collaboration, a sense of community, and other expressions of feminine intelligence to lead us to a prosperous, humane, and healthy future.

Through our societal conditioning, we typically think that successful people got where they are thanks to their own hard work. We often miss what's not so obvious—that it might have taken "a village" to help them get there. That it was the fruits of a collective. "In America, we often associate courage with the ability to take risks," Lindsay said. "But I don't think we see the full picture. We don't see the scaffolding around the person taking the leap." We don't see the vast support network behind the person; we don't see the village that acted behind the scenes to make it possible.

Eschewing individualism, Chief's community is about "co-mentoring one another" and "cross-pollinating power," says Lindsay. Sharing their trove of expertise, navigating each other around sand traps, engaging in real, human, nurturing relationships—they learn to unleash their superpowers of feminine intelligence beyond what they could accomplish by themselves. "One-to-one relationships are great," Lindsay told me. "But a core group of 10 to one is really powerful. And a network of thousands to one is life-changing if you use it correctly."[2]

> *We belong to a bundle of life. A person is a person through other persons. I am human because I belong.*
> —*Archbishop Desmond Tutu*

Chief was the first of its kind, and Chief's founders were trailblazers. They could see the far-reaching benefits of providing female senior executives with a means to connect with each other and to be engaged in community—deeply, personally, and authentically. Further, they hoped that what they had created would help transform the existing paradigm of leadership around the world.

The Courage to be Authentic

In the Chief Core Groups I've led as a facilitator, conversations inevitably began somewhat superficially but ultimately evolved into a much deeper, more personal, intimate, and real exchange. As each person introduced themselves, most would hide behind their successful resume, their doctorates, their high-level positions. Their masks were securely in place as they described their professional lives, and I knew that I needed to invite them to take down their guard and reveal more about what's *really* going on for them. For that, I introduced the Life Map exercise, in which each person was asked to share the peaks and valleys of their life journey.

I started things off. I was the first to strip back my own facade. I admitted to them that I realized I hadn't been truly authentic when I was working with Allan Gray. I confessed to the group that it took me years to go beyond an intellectual alignment with the principles of social impact at the heart of his work. I acknowledged that it was only through my inner work and my journey with psychedelic medicines that I fully connected to myself and started to genuinely embody Allan's teachings and values.

As I spoke, the women in the group would show surprise; they weren't expecting such a degree of openness in a setting among peers and other professionals. But once the door had been opened, they softened, and walls came down—at first, somewhat reluctantly and then gratefully and passionately. Opening up is cathartic, and it wasn't long before a sense of relief was palpable.

Then they'd begin to talk about what it's like to be a woman in the workplace. They spoke of the echoes of being persistently talked over in boardrooms, and the weight of being the sole female voice in a sea of male colleagues. They revealed their struggles with the subtleties of workplace discrimination, and the dual burdens of expectation and invisibility that challenged them.

Of course, it has to be said that while Chief's conversations were inherently about women's issues, such honest discussions are critical to leaders of all genders. Men's groups, for example, will have many topics to discuss around masculinity in the workplace, such as gender-related expectations and assumptions, the environment of competition, and the wielding of authority and dominance tactics.

In the safe space carved out by vulnerability, the women in Chief's Core Groups dug into the "smush"—the vexing demand to tread a razor's edge of expectations. They described the contortions required of such a high-wire act: They needed to be authoritative yet not domineering, nurturing but not meek, ambitious without appearing threatening. They shared with each other poignant stories of shrinking themselves to fit into the narrow confines of acceptability, of amplifying their voices only to be labeled as too assertive. The narrative unfolds in a chorus of contradictions—they simultaneously need to be resilient, receptive, decisive—and demure. It is the complex tapestry of their daily existence.

In our groups, they realized they didn't have to show up as "a very important, polished person." Quite the opposite—they were invited to take off their masks and show up as who they were. They were promised that they would be supported no matter what. They could be themselves; they didn't have to hide.

As we journeyed together, month after month, we talked about values, strengths, who they really wanted to be, and how they could turn the parts of themselves that bring shame and pain into assets. It was a journey of awakening and discovery of their truest, most authentic selves.

> *Bringing your whole self and knowing that you are flawed, to me, is authentic. Being real about who you are, your strengths and weaknesses, and being open to sharing that with others is courageous.*
> —Lindsay Kaplan

The Courage to Lead

Yes, leadership requires courage. But what kind of courage is it? For millennia, we've had a singularly masculine perspective and set of assumptions, interpretations, and associations with what it means to be courageous. And it makes sense why. In many cultures, there is a historical emphasis on masculine bravery in the context of warfare, where physical strength and the ability to protect and provide for others were highly valued. It's a traditional view of courage that often focuses on acts of heroism, risk-taking, and overcoming obstacles through force, determination, and strength. It's a grit-your-teeth, "just do it" approach that often confuses courage with recklessness or overconfidence.

For centuries, business and governmental cultures have been deeply influenced and shaped by this traditional set of values, too, adopting and perpetuating top-down organizational structures and chains of command (hierarchies) used in the military. Martial metaphors proliferate—the boardroom is a "war room," competitors want to "conquer the market," and new ideas are "run up the flagpole." Competition, hierarchy, and aggression are prioritized throughout Western cultures, reinforcing the belief that leadership and success require a drive for dominance, single-minded assertiveness, well-armored toughness, and a fairly narcissistic macho masculinity. This archetype, once idealized as the stoic, fearless hero, no longer serves even the military. The numerous conflicts raging across the globe today are stark testimonials to the failure of the rigid, binary thinking that tends to exacerbate rather than resolve disputes.

Courage is being scared to death but saddling up anyway.
—*John Wayne*

This ancient attitude has infiltrated and deeply shaped our societal expectations around masculinity and influenced how we approach courage within ourselves. It has seeped into our relationships as well as our politics. Courage has become inextricably associated with a dualistic, us-versus-them, zero-sum game mentality, offering us only two possible outcomes: either you're a winner or you're a loser. It's a binary, black-and-white choice in a world made up of infinite color.

The prevailing, masculine narrative of courage overshadows any nuanced forms of bravery that embrace all the shades of grey between winning and losing that we humans usually experience. It's a sad fact that any expression of fear, doubt, or emotional transparency is often not just discouraged in our Western culture but seen as undermining one's strength or disappointing society's expectations. This limited perspective warps our understanding of courage and diminishes our ability to engage it fully despite its deep roots within us as a primal force.

We are used to seeing courage evoked when someone is battling *external* forces, and it's a very masculine energy. But courage also has the potential to be an expression of *internal* strength and congruence if and when we choose to express ourselves unadorned, unguarded, honestly, and truly. Courage from within is a characteristic of feminine energy. By embracing both feminine and masculine aspects of courage, we can have both the heroism of the masculine and the inner strength of the feminine. We can recognize that courage is not a fixed state but a dynamic process that evolves through the harmonious interplay of opposing forces—the feminine and the masculine.

Challenging many cultural norms, celebrated author and researcher Brené Brown spent several years studying courage and vulnerability in the context of success and empowerment. In her book, *The Gifts of Imperfection,* Brown defines courage in a way that we all can embrace.

"Courage is a heart word," she writes, immediately casting the powerful inner force in the realm of feelings and sensitivity. "The root of the word courage is *cor*—the Latin word for heart. In one of its earliest forms, the word courage meant 'to speak one's mind by telling all one's heart'."[3] And, at the core of courage, says Brown, is vulnerability—the willingness to be transparent and authentic and to unabashedly "tell all one's heart." To Brown, vulnerability is power, and the willingness to accept this truth takes courage.

But being transparent, authentic, and vulnerable is not the norm in our world. Societal pressures mold us, press us into conformity, and compel us to don masks that obscure our true selves. These are not mere disguises but armors, crafted from the expectations of others, that we wrap around ourselves to navigate a world that feels adversarial. Devoid of other tools or unaware of alternative paths, we clad ourselves with protective identities as we face the world. We opt for partial truths, curated openness, and cautious vulnerability, preferring to remain guarded and somewhat hidden. Essentially, we are navigating from behind our constructed facade in order to survive.

Further, for many of us, perfectionism sabotages our intent to be vulnerable. Societal expectations press us toward excellence, while fear of rejection taps into our most basic human needs for belonging. Some defend against low self-esteem by adopting perfectionism as a shield, while others chase the elusive "ideal" to secure acceptance and gain approval. So, we curate a polished persona—a carefully constructed version of ourselves for the public eye. This facade intentionally hides our wounded, dark, and broken aspects, concealing them from the scrutiny of others—and even from ourselves—as much as possible.

The great irony and loss in all this is that the more perfect we try to be, the less congruent and thus less powerful we become. When we hide, we contract into ourselves, and our influence, energy, and impact ultimately shrink.

It's time to consider a different kind of relationship with our imperfections. Accepting them fosters wholeness; embracing them puts us in touch with our humanity. When we choose to let down our walls in spite of our fears, we are more available to others, we are more open to opportunity, and we are more receptive to our inner guidance systems. We are more honest and true to ourselves. That, ultimately, empowers us.

Vulnerability is the birthplace of innovation, creativity,
and change.
—*Brené Brown*

As we express ourselves more authentically and accept that we're not perfect, we become more congruent and aligned within ourselves. Internal harmony liberates energy previously entangled by inner conflicts, enabling us to feel more inwardly connected, unified, and grounded. As a result of this internal harmony, our thoughts and emotions are clarified, laying the foundation for deeper self-trust.

Shedding our masks requires courage, but the dance between authenticity and courage is reciprocal. While finding and embracing our true selves demands bravery, the very act of vulnerability builds within us even greater courage.

What does all this have to do with leadership? Leadership requires being anchored in one's own elements of truth. It demands a quiet introspection, an intimate familiarity with one's inner landscape, fueling passion and conviction. A clarity of thoughts, feelings, and beliefs that endures even in the face of criticism, judgment, and rejection. It takes courage to embrace our imperfections while championing our cause. It takes courage to interrogate our hearts for our truth before we step into our assertive masculine energy and turn our attention outward to advocate for what we believe in.

Once again, true power is found in the interplay between the two extremes. The extraordinary demands of today's complex and troubled world require our leaders to recognize that courage can be multifaceted. Embodying the bold and risk-taking spirit of Sir Richard Branson is a compelling, exhilarating, and sometimes even necessary quality to fuel our drive to success. He was even knighted for his "services to entrepreneurship." The ethos of "move fast and break things" may get things done swiftly, but it is the integration of feminine intelligence that equips us with ease, confidence, congruence, and even grace. The inner alignment is what truly emboldens us to become disruptors. It allows us to navigate risks and opposing forces and remain true to our choices with integrity.

> *There are a lot of incentives to not be courageous, to not be authentic, and to 'play the game'.*
> *But I think the people who are able to break free from that and be their true self will find more success. And more people will gravitate to work with them, to believe in them, and allow them to lead.*
> —*Lindsay Kaplan*

This isn't mere speculation. Chief's unicorn status stands as a testament to Lindsay's words. "What's made a difference for me is being very clear about who I am, what I'm good at, what my strengths are, and being okay with acknowledging my weaknesses rather than trying to repair them," Lindsay told me. "I know that there are amazing people around me who have their strengths that can balance me out."[4] While, at first, it might be incredibly scary to choose to be vulnerable and let your authentic voice be heard, eventually, it is liberating and the cornerstone of impactful leadership.

Questions for Reflection

1. To uncover and affirm your strengths, reflect on three stories from your life that you're proud of and share them with 10 people. Then, invite them to "strength spot" for you by pointing out the strengths they hear in these stories.

2. What do you consider your imperfections? Are they traits that can be changed or improved upon? Or are they inherent qualities that you need to accept? Are they a source of shame? Or do you embrace them as part of your unique character? Your mindset here is crucial.

    Reflect on this from your own perspective and then from the perspective of how you feel society perceives those traits. Are you imposing an external standard on yourself? How have these imperfections affected your actions and decisions? Do you think they are impeding your journey toward fulfilling your purpose? Are there patterns in your behavior that are tied to these imperfections? This requires a deep dive into specific instances where you feel your perceived flaws have held you back.

3. What does vulnerability mean to you? Consider the facade you present to the world. What aspects of yourself do you feel the need to conceal? What might happen if you were to show your true self? What fears come up? How might this openness transform your relationships and opportunities?

6

Africa's Conscious Billionaire

Allan Gray

As a young boy growing up in South Africa under Apartheid, Allan Gray witnessed the great oppression, poverty, and cruelty suffered by South Africans every day. As a White male, he was deeply struck by the unfairness and suffering of so many innocent people around him. As he tried to make sense of it—while it was inherently impossible to understand—he concluded that a happy, affluent South African society would never be able to emerge unless extreme racism and unequal and unfair conditions were eradicated from his country. Profound change was needed, and it had to start at the grassroots level. It would need to be driven by the people of South Africa themselves. Still quite young, deep within his heart, a fire was lit, and a purpose was born, never to be extinguished for as long as he lived.

Allan stood tall, his commanding stature accentuated by a mane of silver hair and eyes that bore both kindness and an uncanny ability to penetrate you to the core. Engaging with him felt like having one's soul laid bare. I felt that almost every day—his presence was magnetic. And even though I only knew him in his later years, he was still very animated, very powerful, and driven to make a difference in the world. At his age, he was still very much in love with Gill, his wife of over 50 years, and referred to her as his "soulmate." While Allan was the creative and organizational force behind his philanthropic, investment, and business works, Gill was the cornerstone and foundation underneath him. He often described their unique relationship as "symbiotic," and I felt they were role models of conscious marriage as much as conscious leadership.

Prior to his involvement with philanthropy, Allan was, first and foremost, an entrepreneur and a "conscious capitalist." As an investor, he held a very personal commitment to getting the highest long-term returns for his clients—not only to ensure their financial stability but to open avenues of opportunity for them. But it was never at the expense of other stakeholders. It was Allan who introduced me to the principles of multistakeholder free market economics and instilled in me my own passion for catalyzing conscious leadership.

With a dream of creating the first asset management firm in his country, Allan studied at Rhodes University and then traveled to the United States to earn an MBA at Harvard Business School. After eight years of honing his investment skills at Fidelity, he returned to Africa in 1973 and set up a sole proprietorship there. His intentional ethics and business philosophy were already etched in his mind, and he envisioned a future of building long-term wealth for his clients and having the opportunity to serve the common good and uplift the African continent. While many see these two commitments as contradictory, the Allan Gray Orbis Foundation (AGOF) has since given millions of dollars to South African entrepreneurs, and the investment firms have grown into a global institution with offices in 11 countries and some US$100 billion in assets under management.

In 1973, Allan founded a privately run investment management company, which was initially called the Allan Gray Investment Counsel and was later renamed Allan Gray. In 1979, he began his philanthropic work, setting up a charitable trust to support organizations working on social and economic needs in South Africa. By 1989, he expanded outside Africa to create Orbis Investment Management, operating in the United States, Europe, and Asia.

Great companies start because the founders want to change the world,
not make a fast buck.
—Reid Hoffman, co-founder of LinkedIn

But, creating a global asset manager and setting up charitable trusts wasn't enough for him. Something more drastic had to be done. I spoke with Anthony Farr for an insider's perspective on that decision. Anthony had devoted decades of his career—along with his heart and soul—to AGOF in South Africa as its CEO and now heads Allan & Gill Gray Philanthropy Africa.

Anthony explained that in 1984, as South African Apartheid was committing some of its worst atrocities, Allan wrote a letter to South Africa's Ministry of Finance at the time with an unheard-of, incredibly bold proposal. He was seeking to donate 20% of his investment business to a trust whose purpose would be to support Black entrepreneurs. Even in those early days, Allan was aware that if the country didn't adopt a more inclusive perspective of itself—if it continued to exclude the vast majority of its population—it would never flourish. Progress would not happen.

Allan's offer was shot down, of course. There was no way the South African government of 1984 would allow a sanctioned means to support Black entrepreneurs.

In 1994, Apartheid officially ended, and to advance its Black population's participation in the South African economy, the country enacted the Black Economic Empowerment (BEE) Act. The legislation was then relaunched in 2003 in a more comprehensive and less ownership-focused format and retitled the Broad-Based Black Economic Empowerment (BBBEE).

In response to the government's first attempts to repair the cultural damage of Apartheid with the BBBEE, Allan saw an opportunity to contribute to his country meaningfully and sustainably. In 2005, he transferred 20% of his personal holdings in the Allan Gray asset manager to launch E Squared, a venture capital entity. E Squared's venture funding was designed to be directed toward Black social entrepreneurs, and that resonated with the government's ambition to champion economic transformation and facilitate meaningful participation of Black individuals in the economy.[1]

We might never be able to just have equality. But equal opportunity is
what will allow people to make progress.
—Allan Gray

But Allan's mission transcended mere compliance with new regulations. Armed with empathy, creativity, and foresight, he sought to sculpt a regenerative solution that would have a lasting impact. Thanks to his revolutionary approach, an additional US$2 billion—attributable to the valuation of the ventures created by fellowship program graduates, including Go1 founder Melvyn Lubega—has benefited the South African economy.

Many now recognize that Allan and his vision were ahead of their time. He built an interdependent and symbiotic web of business and philanthropic entities around a conscious business philosophy that was committed to being a profound force for good in the world. Even as the investment firm grew and became tremendously profitable, it remained firm in its unprecedented approach. Rather than merely making charitable donations as part of a corporate social responsibility initiative—which, for many companies, is a superficial display of generosity—the firm was committed to looking beyond its own interests and making a genuinely impactful contribution to the world. The solution? The investment firm's corporate structure would be controlled by a single philanthropic shareholder, ensuring that its long-term investment philosophy is never jeopardized by fickle shareholders in the public markets. Thus, it would forever be committed to active, strategic philanthropy so it could generate opportunities for people in the communities in which it operates.

That is precisely why Allan made the unusual choice not to list his South African asset management company on the South African Stock Exchange—doing so would interfere with the company's strategic and philanthropic goals. Keeping it privately owned, on the other hand, would allow it to contribute to the world for the duration of its existence.

"If the company was listed," Anthony said, "there would be very destructive pressure to make sure that there was short-term profitability and to make short-term decisions around the investments. And what's interesting about the Allan & Gill Gray Foundation is its dual purpose. It exists to improve humanity and the world through philanthropic resources, and, it has an equally important objective of providing perpetual succession to the business. In other words, it's always intended that the heirs of the Gray family maintain a controlling share, a majority share, in the business. And the reason for that is to ensure that they fully subscribe to the vision and fully understand the business model, which requires this long-term decision-making model, allowing the business to operate philanthropically, unencumbered, indefinitely."[2]

I can't help but be astounded by the inefficiency of our public market systems, burdened by innumerable agency problems and short-term incentives.

Anthony Farr

In 2002, Anthony Farr was working in the corporate finance team at Standard Bank London. Finance had been a passion of his for a long time; he considered it a significant enabler of progress, especially for a country like South Africa. His team focused on South African companies, so he went to Johannesburg to meet clients in the region.

While there, he was invited to visit a Salvation Army orphanage in downtown Johannesburg. At first, he hesitated to go, wondering what good such a short visit could do for anyone. But he agreed and spent an afternoon playing with, talking with, and listening to many of the young children who lived there. He'd never experienced anything like it before. Something deep within him broke open, and he would never be the same.

"I wondered what I could do as a banker," he told me later. "This one needed medical care, that one needed counseling, and I wasn't a nurse or doctor and didn't have any of that training. And yet, from the little bit of time I spent with them and the little bit of attention I gave them, I could see the difference in their faces. You know, they had so little. And I could no longer say to myself, 'Well, I'm just a banker. There's nothing else I can do'."

So when Anthony got back to London, he gathered a few like-minded people and launched the Starfish Greathearts Foundation, which has worked with communities to help orphans and other vulnerable kids in South Africa.

Word got around, and in 2004, Allan Gray asked to meet with him. Hoping that the billionaire investor and philanthropist would make a sizable contribution to his organization, Anthony launched into his pitch for Starfish almost as soon as he sat down to talk, but Allan stopped him. He wasn't there to vet the company for charitable contributions; he was there to find the right people to work on his vision of supporting entrepreneurs in South Africa.

Anthony realized Allan wanted to hire him as CEO, and he was excited by the prospect. Even though Starfish had been making a difference in the lives of youth in several South African communities, Anthony couldn't shake off a sense of restlessness. While providing immediate necessities like food, shelter, psychological support, and basic education was meaningful and helpful, he sensed it fell short of addressing the systemic issues plaguing these communities. He believed in the old adage that, if you truly want to serve others, it's not enough to give them a single fish for their dinner. When you teach them to fish, they are empowered to take care of themselves for years to come. As far as South Africa was concerned, Anthony saw that to make an enduring change in his country, a deeper and more strategic approach would be necessary—one that aims to tackle the roots of poverty and inequality. He told Allan he'd be honored to get on board with AGOF. The organization's long-term vision and its precedent-setting strategy to dovetail business and philanthropy could actually begin to dismantle the cycles of poverty in South Africa and empower people to materialize their own healthy financial futures.[3]

> *It is this holistic view of business entrepreneurship and the symbiotic relationship amongst all stakeholders— clients, employees, owners, and society—that the Foundation seeks to preserve.*
> —*Allan Gray*

The Letter

It was 2015 when Allan, his wife Gill, and their family established the Allan & Gill Gray Foundation (the "Foundation"), which would be endowed with the family's controlling interests in the Orbis and Allan Gray groups of asset managers and would extend the Gray family's philanthropic reach far beyond Africa to the rest of the world. It was about that time, too, that Allan offered me the opportunity to find my own path to meaning and purpose by leaving the law practice I'd been working for in New York and moving to Bermuda to join the nascent Foundation.

On December 31, 2015, at the age of 78, Allan publicly announced his decision to step down as chairman of the investment management business. After more than 40 years of hard work, he decided it was finally time for him to devote all of his time to the Foundation. Soon after, he wrote a letter to his clients,[4] describing important changes to the structure of the investment company that he wanted them to know about.

The letter started with a bold statement:

> To ensure that control will remain indefinitely in the hands of those who best exemplify the ethos that has served our clients so well in the past, the newly established Allan and Gill Gray Foundation has been endowed with our family's controlling interests in the Orbis and Allan Gray group.

Then, he called for everyone's values to be aligned with what he was up to.

> In particular, we believe it is absolutely essential for the firm's owners and key decision-makers to share the conviction necessary to stand behind our investment philosophy.

He revealed that their track record has proven that the long-term approach brings quantifiably improved returns for their clients.

> For more than 40 years, our experience has shown that taking a long-term perspective with a contrarian stance can produce demonstrably superior results

And then he underscored the commitment required to do so:

> —but only if it can withstand uncomfortably long periods of underperformance.

Of course, underperformance is inevitable from time to time, so if your priority is only the quarterly bottom line, you can figure out how to make short-term profits even in a bad market through financial engineering and decisions that are lacking in integrity. (In other words, somebody will get hurt.)

> The perpetual nature of the Foundation empowers the executives to focus entirely on doing what is in the best long-term interests of clients, free from the short-term pressures that third-party ownership can bring.

Long-term strategies prioritize stability and consistent returns over time and minimize the volatility that inevitably comes with short-term trading. So, the organization's new structure keeps decision-makers focused on serving their clients' interests well into the future.

Finally, Allan revealed the Foundation's ultimate commitment to ensure that the riches made through equity investments will be dedicated to its philanthropic interests:

> Another equally important purpose of the Foundation is to ensure that the fruits from its controlling interests in Orbis and Allan Gray are ultimately devoted entirely and exclusively to philanthropy in keeping with the family's long-held intentions. We consider this both the right thing to do and a small but necessary contribution toward a society full of hope for all humanity.

This brings us to my favorite part, a groundbreakingly holistic relationship for a multi-billion-dollar enterprise to have with the other members of its ecosystem:

> It is this holistic view of business entrepreneurship and the symbiotic relationship amongst all stakeholders—clients, employees, owners, and society—that the Foundation seeks to preserve.

Allan was adamant about safeguarding the investment management businesses from ever going public—even after his death. He wanted to guarantee that future generations would be unable to sell the business or take it public, thereby ensuring its continued commitment to philanthropy without interruption. His solution? He set up the Foundation as the main shareholder of the investment businesses. Distributable profits go to the Foundation, which is devoted exclusively to philanthropy, now with an even greater impact beyond the initial efforts of AGOF in South Africa. As the primary shareholder, the Foundation has the deciding vote on business decisions and is steadfast in its commitment to keeping the business private.

Allan was intent on democratizing the Foundation's giving, too. I worked closely with him to create the Philanthropy Initiative, an employee-directed collective giving program that allows employees from the investment business to choose local charities to receive significant financial grants. The Initiative enables employees to uplift their communities by providing them with a pool of resources they can distribute as grants according to their own judgment and discretion. Allan felt that it helped facilitate employee engagement with philanthropy while building excitement around giving for those working in the investment business every day. One year, for example, employees at the Bermuda office chose to focus on early education—a topic Allan and I discussed at great lengths as something critical for Bermuda's prosperity. They chose a local charity that provided educational programs and services for children. For nurseries on the island, they also designed tools and props to help children develop their fine motor control, hand–eye coordination, and other skills.

Thanks to Allan Gray's compassion, foresight, boldness, and brilliance, hundreds of millions of dollars a year are nurturing South African social entrepreneurs—like Melvyn Lubega—who are helping to sow new seeds of abundance and prosperity across the entire African continent. But Allan's impact has reached even further—around the globe—to empower businesses and the people working for them to bring about positive change in their own communities.

Questions for Reflection

1. Allan placed the Foundation as the primary shareholder of his investment management companies. Faith in Nature puts a director on their board to represent the interests of nature. What practical, legal, and/or structural changes could help your business be a force for good?
2. Who are your shareholders? Are your (and society's) interests aligned with them? If not, what can you do?
3. Allan's early childhood experiences under Apartheid triggered the development of his values around equal opportunity and economic empowerment. For Anthony, it was his visit to an orphanage. What early life experiences influenced your values and your worldview?

7 | Building Cathedrals

The Architect

Not everyone knows the name Christopher Wren, but many would recognize his greatest masterpiece: St. Paul's Cathedral in London. Wren was the English architect who designed the majestic cathedral in the late seventeenth century. Legend holds that one day, Wren decided to take a walk around the cathedral while construction was still underway. The workers, busy building the massive church, didn't recognize him as he pulled aside a few of them to ask a simple question.

"What are you doing?"

"I'm cutting a piece of stone," the first man answered.

"I'm earning five shillings two pence a day," the second man responded.

Turning to a third man, the architect asked his question once more.

"I'm helping Sir Christopher Wren build a beautiful cathedral," the third man said.

What is it that distinguishes the third man from his two companions? The perspectives of the first two men were, of course, valid. Cutting stone. Making a living. Good answers. But the third man saw himself within a larger context; he felt he was a part of something bigger than himself. Through his eyes, he was contributing to the super-human task of creating a great work of art out of stone. That third worker's expanded sense of purpose would serve him well. It would elevate his spirit and energize him. It would cause his work to be more precise, his patience more steady, and his fingers more careful as he helped build something extraordinary. And those things, in turn, would serve the great vision of the architect himself. With that larger purpose etched in the worker's mind, his contribution to the enormous undertaking was refined and deepened, and he felt himself a part of something bigger and more meaningful than just the chores at hand. His outlook would ultimately serve practically anyone walking past the historic church long into the future.

As a leader, some of the most important questions you can ask are: *How can you create conditions that encourage people to see their work as more than just "a job"? How can you inspire them to reimagine their work and find purpose in it? In what ways can you help them aspire to larger goals and align their roles with a greater purpose? How will you cultivate meaning and motivation to ignite collaboration, excellence, and a relentless pursuit of your shared mission? And importantly, how can you accomplish these actions in a way that fosters a cohesive, shared, united vision?*

The answer begins with *you*. As a leader, you cannot instill purpose in others until you have tapped the vein of purpose within your own mind and heart. As the architect of whatever cathedral you're building, to lead, you must first find your deepest "why" and embody it so effortlessly and honestly that it inspires and empowers others around you to help you build it. Leadership has to start with your own condition of purpose and power.

> *When soul force awakens, it becomes irresistible and conquers the world. This power is inherent in every human being.*
> —*Mahatma Gandhi*

Purpose is a soul force; it is a profound part of us that can shimmer with clarity, animate our spirit, and invigorate our energy. Purpose is soul-affirming, and more, it is absolutely contagious. When we are inspired with purpose, others can feel our light and see our sparkle. When aligned with our purpose, we are grounded and authentic yet full of life and drive.

Purpose is not so much about what we do or how we act—which are masculine expressions of ourselves—as much as it is about cultivating—which is a feminine sensibility—an inner life force and accessing a deep vein of power within ourselves.

The leaders we've discussed so far—those that are forging their enterprises into forces for good—those spearheading ecocentric legal battles and conscious capitalism and happiness movements, for example—are *inspired* leaders. They access that deep resource of power that is fueled by a greater purpose. That lights them up.

You, too, have that resource. You, too, can change the world. But you must first unlock and reconnect with your personal, passionate, soul-force awakening—your purpose—before others will be truly inspired to follow your lead.

The History of Why

We have long recognized that having a purpose helps us move forward to create progress, transformation, and change. And each of us harbors a need to get in touch with our individual purpose, although it might be deeply buried, dormant, quietly waiting to be actualized.

The quest to discover purpose got renewed attention when author and leadership expert Simon Sinek popularized the concept of "Finding your Why" in the early 2000s. He offered a set of replicable steps to help people identify and understand their deepest inner purpose, whether it pertains to work, career, or life. The concept resonated deeply with individuals and organizations around the world thanks to its elegance and simplicity. After all, it speaks directly to our innate, instinctive desire to connect with our purpose and foster meaning in what we do.

Research has also confirmed that organizations of all kinds perform better when their people have a clear, inspiring purpose—sometimes showing up in the form of a brand identity—to unify them. A company's well-defined purpose can help it accomplish many valued objectives, such as staying relevant and increasing productivity and innovation.[1] Research by Deloitte, the international professional services network, showed that purpose-driven companies experience higher market share gains and higher workforce retention, and they average a growth rate three times faster than their competitors.[2] "The ability of [an organization's] managers and leaders to inspire and help employees find purpose and meaning in the workplace are critical factors for attraction and retention," wrote McKinsey & Company in its 2023 "State of Organizations" report. Research finds time and time again that the key to a successful organization is to have a culture based on a strongly held and widely shared set of beliefs that are supported by strategy and structure.

When it's clearly crafted and meaningful to the market, a business purpose can, in fact, become its soul, its identity, as it motivates its people to share a vision and ultimately resonates in the hearts and minds of the public.

On an individual level, many highly accomplished leaders find they hit a wall if they haven't embraced a sense of purpose as their driving force. In our Western cultures, achievement often stems from a place of woundedness or scarcity or from subconscious beliefs that insist we must achieve certain goals to validate our sense of belonging and acceptance. But, almost universally, once we make our dreams come true, we find out we're still not truly fulfilled. Why not? Because we tried to fabricate a purpose—and that never works. Only an authentic purpose has the power to light up hearts and minds.

We might have taken a lot of steps and even congratulated ourselves for what we've achieved to create a certain kind of life for ourselves. Still, if those steps were unconsciously motivated and aren't in alignment with who we really are, ultimately, even our grandest accomplishments won't satisfy us. If we aren't connected to our life force, we won't be in touch with numerous possibilities that lie beyond the limits of our expectations. We just settle for lesser outcomes.

> *Success without fulfillment is the ultimate failure.*
> —*Tony Robbins*

In 2023, I began a close collaboration with the three co-founders of The Beam Network, a small and exclusive global network of high-networth women. Through the company's platform, members gain access to personalized and thoughtful financial literacy. Many Beam members have inherited or married into wealth, and The Beam's array of classes, events, and experiences empower them to navigate their financial choices with greater confidence and impact. Even those members who have amassed their own fortunes benefit from the financial education offered. Some have given away assets inadvisably; others have made choices they later regretted. After all, the skill set required to build a successful business differs profoundly from what's needed to effectively manage, invest—and often give away—your wealth.

When I first met the co-founders, their idea of the company's purpose centered around providing top-notch financial education. After all, that's the service they were actually delivering. Yet, they also recognized that the idea wasn't lighting a fire in anyone's belly. It lacked resonance. Something was off.

I walked them through a number of questions using a Sinek exercise as a starting point, and together, we started to dig deep. After an intimate and lengthy discussion, soul searching, and probing into a few sensitive issues, we began to understand the reason their corporate "why" had missed the mark. We asked ourselves, "Why are the affluent women in The Beam network so tremendously eager to gain mastery over their financial matters?" The answer came to us resoundingly: They want *community.*

While the whole world might look on with envy at those who are financially independent, enjoying a high-net-worth lifestyle comes with many challenging responsibilities and obligations. Beyond financial advice, the women seek a sense of belonging, a sanctuary where they can be themselves, and a place where they can have nuanced conversations with peers who understand their position and won't judge them for it. Beyond strategies, tips, and data, they seek empowerment and a sense of self. They yearn for a place where they can be honest and unguarded, sharing their true selves. We had unearthed the gleaming gem: the purpose behind all of The Beam's endeavors was to foster community.

We knew it in our bones. It resonated and lit us up. And it would do the same for the entire network. Inspired by our new insight, we created the Cornerstone Coaching program, which, reminiscent of Chief's Core Groups, brings women together monthly to grow, connect, and even invest together.

The journey of The Beam's co-founders underscores the importance of integrating purpose into any business model. It not only enriches the customer experience and ignites passion in its employees, it also lays the foundation for long-term success and societal contribution.

People don't buy what you do; they buy why you do it.
—*Simon Sinek*

Lighting Purpose in Your People

As profound and impactful as it is to define and discover your organization's purpose, it is equally essential to rally your people behind that purpose and bring them on board. How can you inspire them to think beyond their individual roles and recognize the greater significance of their work? What strategies can you employ to encourage them to connect with a unifying purpose that not only aligns them but also mobilizes their efforts to contribute to the building of your cathedral?

> *If you want to build a ship, don't drum up the men to gather wood, divide the work and give orders. Instead, teach them to yearn for the vast and endless sea.*
> —*Antoine de Saint-Exupéry in* The Little Prince

One way to encourage those in your company to "yearn for the sea" and kindle an authentic drive to forward the vision of your organization is to empower them to rethink and redesign their jobs to align with their personal passions and strengths. You might not even need to tell them it will improve their performance, increase their engagement, and boost their satisfaction. The beauty of this approach lies in the fact that management doesn't have to dictate job identity through rigid job descriptions; employees are encouraged to craft and shape their jobs and take control of their own professional lives.

It's called "job crafting," and it's often associated with research by Amy Wrzesniewski, now a professor at The Wharton School. The practice is comprised of three possible "crafting" dimensions, but the third one—cognitive crafting—is particularly relevant to instilling purpose at work. Cognitive crafting involves actively reshaping an employee's *mindset* about their role to discover greater meaning and purpose in their work. It might involve reframing the way they view their tasks or recognizing the significance their role plays within the company's overall mission. Stonecutters who choose to see that they're not just cutting stone, they're building a cathedral, are doing cognitive crafting.

How effective can cognitive crafting really be? Wrzesniewski and her colleagues tested their theory at a university hospital—not on doctors, nurses, or other highly paid professionals, as you'd expect—but on janitors. Initially, she assumed that these individuals would have little to say that was positive about their traditionally labeled "dirty job." As expected, some of the janitors she interviewed saw their work as simply a response to their job descriptions; they didn't experience much joy in what they did other than clocking hours and earning their daily wage. Many said they hated what they did.

But then some others saw their jobs in a radically different light. They didn't even describe their jobs in the same language; they went above and beyond to create more meaning and value out of what they did. Some of them fostered relationships with patients, families, and colleagues. Some guided elderly visitors who were lost in the maze of facilities. Others chatted with patients who seemed particularly vulnerable. One woman who cleaned the rooms of comatose patients even took it upon herself to rearrange the artwork on the walls each day, hoping to "spark something in their awareness" that might help them wake up.

The latter group chose to adopt a new perception of their jobs. They weren't "just" janitors—they were ambassadors and healers—and they were engaged, challenged, and fulfilled by their work. They successfully reframed the narrative of their work to create a deeper sense of purpose.[3]

Wrzesniewski's work shows us that a person's *perception* of their job can dramatically influence how they experience their work each day and the degree of satisfaction they experience when the day is done. Cognitive crafting teaches us that the stories we tell ourselves about our jobs are just as important as the jobs themselves.

Each of us holds the power to define our purpose by "re-storying" our lives and reframing the narratives we tell ourselves every day. As we learned from the COVID era, a restaurant deliveryman can become a superhero when the purpose of his job is reframed as bringing essential sustenance to someone too vulnerable to leave her home. People can craft their purpose, seeing the value in their work and daily lives by connecting them to something greater than themselves.

> *As soon as we see ourselves as part of a broader purpose, we behave like humans do—we listen to others, we're generous of spirit, we think about the consequences of our actions. So it's actually kind of a losing of an artificial overlay rather than an adding of a new thing called purpose.*
> —Lorna Davis

~ • ~

When I was a graduate student at Columbia University, I had the privilege of meeting regularly at a campus café with Tal Ben-Shahar, a lecturer, author, and leading scholar of positive psychology and leadership. He may be best known for creating Harvard University's most popular course on the science of happiness. Our conversations went beyond nerdy academic discourse; they delved into the very essence of what brings happiness to life for individuals, ignites passion within organizations, and fosters harmony in society. To be honest, Tal's insights helped to shape my perspective of human behavior to such a degree that simply calling him a "mentor" doesn't do him justice.

Tal often mentioned Wrzesniewski's research when he discussed the place of purpose and happiness in the workplace. He liked to emphasize the differences between a "job," a "career," and a "calling." A *job*, he said, is a chore we perform to make an income. A *career* focuses on gaining skills, influence, and prestige so we can climb some ladder of achievement. But a *calling* is driven by our unique passion. It's personal, and it forms a part of who we are. Tal pressed the point that the work we do as a calling goes way beyond promising us profit or promotion; it overflows with inherent meaning and value for us. It has a purpose.

Leaders who are called to create meaningful societal impact and transformation typically enjoy a much greater sense of reward and personal happiness in what they do than those who are just performing a job or pursuing a career. And purpose-driven leaders who make it a priority to cultivate purpose-driven cultures and foster happiness among their teams tend to lead the most successful organizations. Purpose can light our way.

~ • ~

When Paul Polman was CEO of Unilever, a company renowned for being purpose-driven, he began thinking about how he might spark a sense of purpose in people throughout his organization. The answer he came up with was far from the typical solution at large organizations. It wasn't about calling for company-wide conferences and getting employees to rally around the company's stated purpose, vision, and goals. Quite the opposite:

Polman created a leadership development program to help his employees explore their purpose themselves. The Unilever Leadership Development Program (ULDP) was a deeply personal process that encouraged each individual to unlock their own truth and discover their own purpose so they could connect with what they do at Unilever personally and meaningfully.

They tested a pilot ULDP program on 15 senior executives, and once it proved itself a success, they launched it with the top 100 executives. While the program received a lot of positive responses in its own right, Polman also chose to involve himself personally to further inspire his employees to explore what purpose they might find to be more meaningful for them at work.

In a case study by Harvard Business School, the creator of the ULDP, Jonathon Donner, said he felt that Polman's involvement was key to the program's success.[4] Polman spoke directly to his employees at those training sessions with passion and vulnerability, letting his feminine intelligence lead. He talked about the poignant events in his life that fueled his personal purpose. He shared about having a father who worked himself to death holding down two jobs and about climbing Mount Kilimanjaro with eight blind people from all over the world. He shared about surviving a terrifying terrorist attack in Mumbai. And then he shared how those life experiences lit up in him a desire to be a revolutionary CEO doing great things in the world.[5] People were deeply moved, and many were inspired to find ways to generate purpose for themselves in their work.

Unilever continued to fine-tune the training and then offered a condensed version of it to all employees at the company—more than 60,000 as of 2022.[6] It has become an important part of the culture so that "the company becomes an amalgamation of individuals with their own purpose. They can put their own twist on it, but they still need to align with the company's overall purpose and have a commitment to serving the world."[7]

As leaders, we have to inspire our people to "yearn for the sea," as Saint-Exupéry laments, and to do that, we must ignite our own purpose first. If, as leaders, we understand our true purpose and are honest about it, as Polman was, we help others unlock purpose within themselves. When executed skillfully, this interplay of purpose at various levels—individual, team, and organizational—creates a powerful synergy, each layer reinforcing and amplifying the others.

> *Unlocking the company's soul has to start*
> *with baring your own.*
> —*Paul Polman, former CEO, Unilever*

It's a Hero(ine)'s Journey

Joseph Campbell, the celebrated mythologist and author, gave the world a gift in the form of a storytelling framework he called "the Hero's Journey." It describes 10–12 typical stages of the protagonist's journey that reflect many of the archetypal patterns and aspects of myths and legends in history that Campbell had studied. Since its publication in 1987, the Hero's Journey has resonated deeply within the hearts and minds of millions, and it continues to guide and inspire writers, filmmakers, and countless other creatives worldwide.

Yet the Hero's Journey is also a powerful analogy to what we leaders go through as we strive to discover what drives us, as we attempt to unearth our purpose—alive with soul force—and the ways it can be expressed in the world. Like the hero(ine) of a great story, we are ultimately forced out of our comfort zones. We have to confront the inner demons/monsters that block our way forward. We must find friends and allies and cast aside toxic relationships that weigh us down. We have to wind our way through dark, unfamiliar caves, often chaotic and threatening, unsure when we'll ever see light again. We have to examine and bring to awareness so much of what has shaped us so we can deeply and viscerally know our truth rather than superficially contrive some facade based in fear and shame. Only then are we transformed into true leaders with a purpose that resonates and inspires. Only then can we lead authentically and powerfully.

Many changemakers before us would not be making the tremendous contributions they make in the world today had it not been for the hero's journeys they've walked to get to where they are.

Emmanuel Faber, the former CEO of Danone, found his purpose was kindled when his brother, who had been diagnosed with severe schizophrenia, was hospitalized in a farming village in the Alps. Faber traveled there to spend time with him and found himself in an environment unlike anything he'd ever experienced before. When his brother ran away from the facility—which he did frequently—Faber went looking for him among the gardeners, dairymen, farmers, and other friends his brother had made in his illness. Some of them were homeless, and Faber would sleep among them from time to time. He was forced to adjust some of his assumptions and mindsets about himself and the world.

"I discovered the beauty of otherness," he said movingly in a commencement address at HEC Paris Graduate School of Business. "I had to learn the language of lunatics to discover its intrinsic beauty and to come to terms with the realization that what we call 'normal' is, in fact, a limiting cage." He had surprising insights. "I discovered that one could live with very little and enjoy a very happy life," he said. Immersed in an unfamiliar world, he was forced to see life differently. And one reality that he saw with fresh eyes was that without social justice, an economy has no future. Thus, his purpose was ignited, and he knew what he needed to do.[8]

~ • ~

Where did the passionate advocacy of the co-founders of The Beam Network—Ana Morales, Bertha Morales, and Michelle Yue—come from? Each of them had personally encountered the tumultuous and unhealthy dynamics surrounding wealth within their own families. Even after gaining full agency over their wealth, they were mistreated by financial advisors and were shaken by feelings of disempowerment and confusion.

Their shared experience led them to the profound realization that money is intricately interwoven with one's sense of identity, purpose, and belonging. This revelation galvanized their passions and drove them to initiate a space for women with similar circumstances. Moreover, they envisioned their platform as a catalyst for positive impact on a global scale and aimed to address some of the most pressing challenges women face, including issues related to health and gender parity. Their "road of trials" stirred a shared commitment to empower women and make a meaningful difference in the world.

~ • ~

I first met Raj Sisodia, who wrote the beautiful foreword to this book, when we were both speakers at the World Happiness Summit (WOHASU) in 2021. I distinctly remember the vivid and distressing account he shared about the traumatic experiences of his childhood in India—stories of abuse, heartbreak, and murder—which he also recounts in his 2023 book, *Awaken: The Path to Purpose, Inner Peace and Healing.*

Raj launched the Conscious Capitalism movement with Whole Foods Market founder John Mackey as early as 2007, but he later admits he wasn't fully connected to it with his whole self in the beginning. He wasn't yet connected to his purpose—it was a good concept, a good idea, but it was an idea only. In *Awaken*, he writes, "I remained unconscious for so long because I was stuck in the past and was carrying many unhealed wounds. I did work that was meaningful in a joyless way. I was running on fumes, sourcing the fuel for my work from the praise and gratitude of strangers."[9]

In early 2018, a remarkable synchronicity occurred in Raj's life. He had begun working on a book he would later title *"The Healing Organization: Awakening the Conscience of Business to Help Save the World"* when he received an invitation to participate in a psychedelic plant medicine journey led by a shamanic healer named Laura. He said yes, and the impact of the experience was so profound for him that he returned again a couple of months later. Again and again, he witnessed his fragile ego unraveling layer by layer. Then, Laura pulled him aside to give him a potent message: "You can't write about healing until you work on your own healing," she told him. He knew she was right.[10]

A few months later, Raj embarked on a 10-day personal vision quest through the rainforests of Ecuador, intending to face the harsh reality of the conditions of his upbringing in India along with many of the traumatic experiences he'd suffered as a result of its oppressive caste system. The culmination of his trip happened during a profound ayahuasca experience. Ayahuasca is a powerful psychoactive plant brew used in traditional Amazonian shamanic ceremonies for its hallucinogenic and healing properties. In his altered states of consciousness, with the help of a few visions he received, Raj experienced a conscious awakening. Informed by this new clarity, he was able to integrate his personal suffering and make sense of it, which led to the flowering of his purpose. His mission is to help transform the way business is done around the world—through love.

To begin realizing that purpose, Raj felt that he had to "find consciousness" because he comes from "such an unconscious world." He wrote: "My journey of healing and the reason I helped launch Conscious Capitalism is that through the lens of business, my real work has been to try to heal the patriarchy. Unconscious capitalism was clearly the product of patriarchal traditions. Conscious capitalism has been a stepping stone to my greater purpose, which is to challenge patriarchal mindsets across all sectors of society. I believe I was destined to connect these worlds and do this kind of healing work."[11]

~ • ~

As we expand our conscious awareness, we connect to the soul of our leadership potential. For me, too, it was psychedelic experiences that connected me to my feminine intelligence and sense of purpose. Those profoundly pivotal moments gave me a freedom to exist in a way that unlocks my full potential. I find that I can connect to my real purpose—what's in my heart—and be shown the real cathedrals I want to build.

With these kinds of experiences, a "veil" is lifted so that we can finally see. Yet as we peek into these poignant personal stories of people who are doing great things in the world, we can't help but recognize a pattern: their drive and purpose is borne of evocative, mystical experiences, tragedy, or personal growth, which is followed by processing and integration to get to the truth of what *really* drives them. It wasn't "just" a hero(ine)'s journey; there was work involved.

> *Success, like happiness, cannot be pursued; it must ensue, and it only does so as the unintended side effect of one's personal dedication to a cause greater than oneself.*
> —*Viktor E. Frankl in* Man's Search for Meaning

In other words, purpose doesn't just materialize out of thin air. With a genuine inquisitiveness, we have to plumb the depths within us and reflect on our lives, our experiences, and the people we've known. We have to be honest with ourselves and unpack those catalyzing moments, those influential encounters, and those life-altering events that have contributed to our worldview, our perceptions, and our sense of who we are. We have to bring to light the air in which we've been breathing, the context within which we've been operating, albeit unconsciously. Then, we can unshackle ourselves to express our true power and purpose.

And it takes time. And courage. The truth of our purpose runs deep, and it usually won't allow itself to be unearthed with merely a superficial glance.

You can't just read this chapter or do an exercise and know your purpose. You can't invent a purpose for yourself, either, because it will fall flat and not serve you. Like any good archeological dig, it takes time and respectful attention, and it will require certain tools—in this case, tools like presence, mindfulness, spiritual evolution, and a deep understanding of yourself and your life story—tools we'll discuss in a later chapter.

Questions for Reflection

- Uncovering and accessing your unique purpose requires reflection and self-inquiry, and one excellent tool to help you do both is the Life Map exercise. Creating your own life map will help you answer the question: *What insights about my true purpose can I glean from the pivotal moments and experiences I've had in my life?* The Life Map can also help you make more informed decisions about your future and empower you to be more intentional about living a more purpose-driven life.

- First, write down a list of the key milestones—both the positives (peaks) and the negatives (valleys)—that have shaped your life. For example, list your personal achievements, setbacks, career changes, relationship challenges, emotional growth, or creative inspirations, to name a few. Recall the deeply moving experiences you read about in this chapter and the way those leaders used their challenges to galvanize their purpose. Include the experiences in your own life that resonate in the same way.

- Then, get a separate piece of paper and a pencil ready so you can create a visual representation of your life. Essentially, it will be a version of your own unique hero(ine)'s journey.

- Now, draw a horizontal line across the page to represent your life's timeline, from the year you were born to your current age, left to right. You might want to sketch out your ideas for the future as well.

- Draw a vertical line at a right angle which represents your emotional axis. This vertical line represents your emotional state—or how you feel about each significant event in your life. At the midpoint of this vertical line is a neutral point, indicating a balanced or neutral emotional state. Above this midpoint, you'll place events that represent the peaks. Conversely, below the midpoint, you'll place the valleys.

- Starting from the left end of the timeline (your birth), plot each significant event—each of your peaks and valleys—at the appropriate spot on the timeline. When you've included all of your major life events, draw a line connecting them.

   By combining the horizontal timeline with the emotional axis, you create a two-dimensional representation of your life's journey. This allows you to visualize not only the chronological sequence of events but also how those events have influenced your emotional landscape over time.

- Now, take some time to reflect on your life map. What patterns do you notice? Are there clusters of peaks or valleys during certain periods? How have the valleys contributed to your growth? What can you learn from the peaks? Consider the connections between the events and your personal development. How did you approach the challenges and tests you've experienced in your life? What did you fear, and how did you overcome it? What values emerge as a result? How are you different today as a person and as a leader?

- Hang your life map somewhere in your work or living space where you'll see it regularly.

- Unlocking your purpose doesn't happen overnight, so use your life map as a visual reminder of your journey and your aspirations. Feel free to update it over time as you achieve milestones or face new challenges. You might even find yourself recharacterizing your milestone moments and your relationships with them.

8

Rebels *With* a Cause

Gross National Happiness

Hidden among the mountain peaks and fertile valleys of the Himalayas, sharing borders with China and India, sits the tiny, rugged, and, by Western standards, very poor country of Bhutan. The country had remained isolated for centuries, only recently opening up to Western influence—it wasn't until 1999 that even TV and the internet were introduced there. While Buddhist teachings and philosophy pervade its daily life, it is Bhutan's unique political philosophy that dramatically sets it apart from all other nations. Its highest priority is finding a balance between material progress and the spiritual well-being of its citizens.

In 1972—when paved roads, electricity, and hospitals hadn't yet appeared in the remote country—a journalist traveled there to interview the head of state of the constitutional monarchy. He wanted to speak with their *Druk Gyalpo*—the words translate poetically to "Dragon King." According to folklore, the journalist was intent on humiliating the king, well aware that the country's GDP was about US$50 per capita per year—the second lowest in the world.

After getting a few of his initial questions out of the way, he asked the king, "What is Bhutan's GDP? How is your gross domestic product these days?"

The rest of the story has become legend, as the king didn't hesitate in his response.

"I'm not so interested in gross national *product*," he told the writer. "I'm more interested in gross national *happiness*."

The somewhat strange priorities of the king and his country had never been shared with the rest of the world before. Once the article was published, the news of Bhutan's unique stance traveled around the world and created a lot of buzz. Was this tiny nation actually questioning a fundamental assumption of the West—that GDP alone is the best measurement of a nation's success? Could a person, let alone a whole country, make happiness a priority and still survive in today's world?

When the king's son took the throne in 2006 after the abdication of the *Druk Gyalpo*, he took immediate radical steps to bring his father's vision for the country into reality. While Bhutan had been ruled by a monarchy in isolation for hundreds of years, the rest of the world had modernized profoundly. Now, as Bhutan had arrived on the world stage, the new young king wanted to establish more political allies, and he realized that he couldn't remain an absolute monarch any longer if he wanted to do that. Still, he wanted to ensure that his people's emotional and spiritual well-being remained firmly at the heart of the country's identity.

By 2008, the young ruler oversaw the conversion of the country to a democratic constitutional monarchy and established its first-ever Constitution of the Kingdom of Bhutan. The king's powers were limited to those of a head of state, and a parliament with elected officials and political parties was instituted. And, true to the young king's word, "gross national happiness" was written right into the country's constitution, forever weaving it into its identity and mission.

> *The state shall strive to promote those conditions that will enable the pursuit of gross national happiness.*
> —Article 9, Section 2 of the Bhutanese Constitution

To make the transformation even more real, the country decided to actually *measure* happiness and put forth the world's first Happiness Index. The vast majority of countries around the world measure GDP or have an equivalent measure of economic output. Bhutan decided it wanted to measure the happiness of its people to evaluate its success as a country. The Index includes "both traditional areas of socio-economic concern such as living standards, health, and education, and less traditional aspects of culture and psychological well-being," according to the University of Oxford's Poverty and Human Development Initiative. It was a momentous shift in how a nation might evaluate how it's doing.

In the meantime, the elder *Druk Gyalpo* continued to be active, advocating for environmental conservation and promoting Gross National Happiness principles around the world.

~ • ~

Companies had been measured by the value of their stock price many decades before the writings of Adam Smith. Nations have been measuring their economic performance for just as long, although "GDP" wasn't introduced until the early twentieth century. Such an assessment is unabashedly a one-dimensional one. It doesn't account for other key variables in the rubric of a country's progress, success, or place in the world. It doesn't factor in the prevalence of anxiety and depression of its people, for example, or the multitudes of people unhappy at their jobs, longing for meaning and fulfillment. It fails to consider the levels of trust and social cohesion, physical health, quality of life, or even levels of government corruption. It doesn't calculate the toll that's exacted on the environment in the name of the production of goods and shareholder wealth. Yet, almost without exception, Western countries are considered progressive if they report having a high GDP.

As Bhutan's developmental philosophy placed an intangible aspect of human emotion—happiness—at the heart of its self-assessment, the world took notice. In 2011, the UN General Assembly adopted a resolution, initiated by Bhutan and co-sponsored by 68 countries, that made it a "fundamental human goal" to give happiness as much priority as economic opportunity. In 2012, the UN published its first World Happiness Report. Most of us are familiar with the report because that's how we've become aware that the Nordic countries—specifically, Finland, Denmark, and Iceland—are the happiest in the world. It's important to point out that those countries are *not* the wealthiest ones in the world, but they are rich in social ties and customs that nurture community and belonging. Their citizens also receive significant financial support from their governments.

That same year, Ambassador Hamid al Bayati, the Permanent Representative of Iraq at the time and a leading figure in the overthrow of the Saddam Hussein regime, initiated discussions within the UN to create a day dedicated to celebrating happiness.[1] When I interviewed him in 2020, he described his own haunting experiences as a prisoner of war—his "broken open" moments—and how they shaped his fervent desire to promote genuine happiness—not as a frivolous notion but as a vital aspect of sustainable development.[2] Unanimously, all 193 member states of the UN rallied behind the idea, endorsing the idea of a day that transcends economic measures of progress to embrace a profound pursuit of sustainable happiness. The world's first International Day of Happiness was celebrated on March 20, 2013, and has since been observed annually, coinciding with the release of the World Happiness Report each year.

> *Our main thanks are to the philosophers over the centuries who have clarified the nature of a good life, to subjective well-being researchers over the past half century, to Jigme Thinley, who, as Bhutanese Prime Minister, championed the global study of Gross National Happiness and introduced the 2011 UN Resolution that led to the first World Happiness Report.*
> *—2023 World Happiness Report*

Several other countries were inspired by the UN's actions and began to adopt their own policies to measure and monitor the well-being of their citizens—a demonstration of feminine intelligence in government. Under the visionary leadership of Jacinda Ardern, New Zealand pioneered their Wellbeing Budget in 2019. Similarly, Iceland, guided by Katrín Jakobsdóttir, implemented a Wellbeing Index that same year. Finland's former Prime Minister Sanna Marin, the youngest government leader in the world at that time, championed the implementation of a decision-making approach she called "Economy of Wellbeing." These initiatives, along with Scotland and Wales, culminated in the formation of the Wellbeing Economy Governments partnership (WEGo), with active participation from Canada. Nicola Sturgeon, former First Minister of Scotland, highlighted Scotland's role in creating WEGo to challenge the belief that growth and GDP should take priority over well-being. According to Sturgeon, even Adam Smith, a

Scotsman himself, wouldn't have intended for GDP to become the overall measure of a country's success, given his original intentions when conceptualizing economic indicators.[3]

Karen Guggenheim, the founder of the World Happiness Summit (WOHASU), launched the Como Wellbeing Manifesto at WOHASU 2023 in Lake Como.[4] Drafted by experts in economics and positive psychology, the Manifesto urges all countries and governments to reappraise their goals and put well-being first. These pioneering women have inspired other countries to start re-evaluating how they want to assess their success in the world. How many more will no longer be willing to focus solely on future growth at the expense of the environment and their citizens' happiness?

> *The role of government in transforming how our economies operate cannot be underestimated. So, governments at all levels are natural partners for the Wellbeing Economy movement.*
> —*Katherine Trebeck, founder of Wellbeing Economy Alliance*

Bhutan instigated an innovative and extremely valuable perspective on what constitutes the success of a nation, one that considers the spiritual well-being and happiness of its citizens to be of equal import as its production value. While its priorities are to be applauded, I don't mean to suggest that the West needs to adopt its ways or imply that others should follow in its footsteps. Honestly, Bhutan's unique social and cultural context is not transportable to the West, and, by Western measures, its living standards are abysmal. But Bhutan inspires us to balance and incorporate alternative views of success into the systems we use to measure our achievements as nations. Certainly, its National Happiness Index has its detractors. Still, the discussion it sparks is incredibly valuable as we attempt to refine and adapt the concept for different contexts, explore alternative measures of progress, advocate for the integration of well-being considerations in policy frameworks, and re-assess the role of other non-economic factors in our measures of progress. Certainly, the countries forming the WEGo have found a way.

> *What we choose to measure as a country really matters because it drives political focus, it drives public activity. GDP measures the output of our work, but it says nothing about the nature of that work, about*

whether that work is worthwhile or fulfilling. It values activity in the short term that boosts the economy, even if that activity is hugely damaging to the sustainability of our planet in the longer term.
—*Nicola Sturgeon, former First Minister of Scotland*

Such an exploration requires an intrepid boldness—an integrated, holistic courage that balances both the feminine and the masculine expressions of resolve, determination, and willingness to move forward. It takes bravery and vulnerability to lead a nation based on metrics different from what the rest of the world uses. It takes commitment to acknowledge fears that one's approach might be misguided and to reflect deeply on what the people within one's organization or country really need. That kind of bravery draws on congruence and authenticity, allowing leaders to make decisions and take actions grounded in the deepest of convictions.

Business Reimagined

A myopic focus on maximizing economic gains shouldn't rule our businesses any more than they should rule our governments and social structures. Today's single-minded reliance on economic perspectives and metrics is terribly lopsided to the detriment of all of us. Alone, economic indicators like GDP provide an incomplete picture of societal progress, just as profit alone provides an incomplete picture of success in business.

We need balance. Happiness alone—without economic growth—is a fantastical utopia. But we pay the price if we feed the economic machine at the expense of the other facets of life that are meaningful to us. The pioneering women leading Scotland, Finland, Ireland, and Iceland stood their ground, creating a more conscious worldview that prioritizes the well-being of their people.

We have seen some signs of change in recent years as a small but growing number of business leaders choose to eschew the customs of business-as-usual. Certain rebels in the business world are now reimagining their purpose and creating businesses for good.

Rejecting the shareholder value primacy model, John Mackey and Raj Sisodia developed a model of "conscious capitalism," which emphasizes that companies can pursue profits while also serving and integrating the needs and concerns of customers, employees, vendors, community, and environment. Laura Storm and Giles Hutchins offer a blueprint for leading organizations that are "life-affirming" in *Regenerative Leadership*, proposing a new business model deeply rooted in the "wisdom of nature."[5] In *Reimagining Capitalism in a World on Fire*, Rebecca Henderson lays out a roadmap for how business can help to catalyze the systemic change we need to "save capitalism from itself."[6]

In a similar vein, billionaire entrepreneur Brunello Cuccinelli offers "humanistic capitalism" as the governing force behind his luxury fashion brand. Addressing world leaders at the G20 Summit in 2021, Cuccinelli said, "I decided that the dream of my life would be to live and work for the moral and economic dignity of the human being. I wanted a company that made healthy profits but did so with ethics, dignity, and morals."[7]

Unilever's former CEO, Paul Polman, has written extensively about "net positive" businesses—businesses that take the bold step of delivering on products and services, building profits, *and* helping make the world a better place. "A net positive business serves others," he writes. "It lives within natural boundaries or thresholds to respect the planet and its inhabitants. It observes moral boundaries for how we treat each other, and it tries to repair, restore, reinvigorate, and regenerate. With that framing in mind, our vision of net positive is a business that improves well-being for everyone it impacts and at all scales—every product, every operation, every region, and country, and for every stakeholder, including employees, suppliers, communities, customers, and even future generations and the planet itself. This is a North Star. No company can achieve all these aims at once, but it's where we should be heading if we want a viable economy and planet. To exist as a relevant business today is to enrich the world."[8]

> *Work is love made visible.*
> —*Kahlil Gibran*

To help companies adopt the conscious capitalism model, Mackey and Sisodia enumerate its four tenets: higher purpose, an orientation toward all stakeholders, conscious culture, and conscious leadership. The first, the business's higher purpose, articulates a "why" for the company, one that is beyond the singular intent to maximize profits for shareholders. The higher purpose provides an understanding of what the company is contributing to society outside of products or services. Second, having an orientation toward *all* stakeholders—including customers, employees, communities, vendors, the environment, and investors—as well as shareholders. Third, a conscious culture makes the company's higher purpose and values visible and discernable within its day-to-day operations and practices. Consciously driven companies will care about the wellness of their workforce, encourage engagement, and support individual expression—and their programs and policies will reflect that. Its people will reflect that.[9]

Finally, conscious *leadership* is what makes all of the other tenets possible. It is what inspires and integrates a holistic vision for the entire organization, creating a foundation for everything that happens within it. But conscious leadership is not just a set of skills, natural or learned, to bestow upon a company for the good of its people, its community, and its environment. It's not simply a matter of investing charitably, refashioning policies, eliminating toxic emissions, or crossing things off of a well-meaning checklist. It also requires a personal journey and some self-reflection to discover one's power, one's values, one's strengths, and one's vision as a leader.

After all, companies don't change course by themselves. This kind of transformation will require the flowering of a new kind of leader—one that needs to think differently, feel differently, and lead differently than those we've witnessed for the past 200 years. It will require fairly rebellious leaders who choose to diverge from the societal and economic status quo of the past couple of centuries and the past 50 years in particular.

If that's you, then know that such a leap will require you to envision bigger and wake up from the timeworn approach to business wellness and prosperity. It will require you to lead in a way that brings out the best in those who work with you and for you—a way that encourages creativity and vision while holding respect for all of the players on the playing field. It will require more of you than business leadership has ever asked of you before—attributes that are rare among today's leaders—such as intuition, compassion, empathy, softness, keen listening skills, holistic perspectives, and even humility and patience.

Make no mistake: the commitment to embrace feminine intelligence and lead with wholeness is a risk and takes a certain amount of rebelliousness. Choosing to diverge from the well-worn path of today's business leaders and their self-interested, muscular approach to leadership will not win popularity contests. And while any business venture continually confronts pitfalls and uncertainty, when you choose a conscious path of leadership, the risks multiply. Shareholders might be upset that you started to care about the environment or that you're investing significant time and money in ensuring your employees can build and sustain more satisfaction in their work. You might decide it's time to be responsible for toxic emissions or harmful labor practices around the world, which means you'll need to invest in research and development or some new technology to ameliorate those conditions.

Those kinds of undertakings can take years to accomplish and can be very expensive. As a result, your quarterly shareholder reports won't have the same level of profits to celebrate. In fact, you might decide to do what Unilever decided to do and forgo quarterly reporting to shareholders at all. Said former Unilever CEO Paul Polman, "We needed to remove the temptation to work only toward the next set of numbers … Better decisions are being made. We don't have discussions about whether to postpone the launch of a brand by a month or two or not to invest capital, even if investing is the right thing to do, because of quarterly commitments. We have moved to a more mature dialogue with our investor base."[10]

Short-term perspectives often obscure potential long-term gains. It might be time to take a 20- or 40-year view, discourage your board of directors from making potentially poor decisions for the quarter just to inflate the bottom line, and focus on building real long-term value instead.

Still, the research supports the wisdom and prudence of this choice. A study by *The Accounting Review*, the journal of the American Accounting Association, found that shorter reporting intervals "engender managerial myopia which finds expression in a statistically and economically significant decline in investments along with a subsequent decline in operating efficiency and sales growth."[11] In the long run, they erode managerial effectiveness and reduce profitability.

And if you're going to insist on not polluting the environment, you'll have to take a fresh look at your suppliers. If you're committed to a new vision for your company, but your suppliers are taking egregious actions that aren't aligned with your values, you'll have to invest the time and money to find new suppliers. You'll have to take the risk that you can find one at all.

There's more. You might have to face an onslaught of judgment from people who don't agree with you or understand your bigger vision.

You might have to face people accusing you of not being "hard enough" for leadership as you expose your intentions, purpose, and dreams for a better world and the fact that you care. They might call you an idealist or describe your plans as unrealistic, leaving you more personally vulnerable than the typical hardened, driven corporate leader. Exposing yourself to potential ridicule takes a lot of courage.

That's exactly what happened with Unilever in Q1 2023. It came under attack by activist British fund manager Terry Smith, whose investment fund was Unilever's 15th largest shareholder at the time. Smith pressured the company to improve its performance. Instead of applauding Unilever for its courageous efforts, Smith said the company had "clearly lost the plot" for its purpose-driven marketing and ridiculed Unilever for "defining the purpose of Hellmann's mayonnaise."[12] While recognizing that big multinationals like Unilever have (many) shortcomings, it's important to acknowledge their efforts toward improvement. Yes, there were instances where Unilever's environmental claims were exaggerated and not fully supported by its actions. But, Unilever has also set ambitious goals, such as achieving net-zero emissions across its operations by 2039.[13] Ultimately, when you try to lead with heart and purpose, you are likely to face backlash. This is when you must find the fortitude and persevere.

To be sure, going on your hero(ine)'s journey and carrying the flag of conscious leadership requires courage. Like *Star Wars'* Luke Skywalker, at some point, you'll have to face your demons, unlock your triggers, and make your peace with those who've harmed you—because those challenges weaken you and impede your ability to lead wholeheartedly and with your whole brain. Confronting and making peace with them makes you stronger and can help you discover the purpose of your leadership, inspiring you even more.

> *Take a stand. Be known for your courage and confidence.*
> —*Indra Nooyi former CEO of PepsiCo*

For those of us who want to see a demonstrable change in the world, the times we live in are a call to action. As a business leader, it is an invitation to help turn the tide so that commerce and leadership are no longer synonymous with greed, myopia, and indifference to the well-being of the rest of humanity. The journey will require re-evaluating your approach to problem-solving and leadership itself. It will take exploring and accessing inner resources so you can find and create solutions that benefit more than just a few. Our free market capitalism system's problems are overwhelming; we must generate sufficient personal power to stand for a new paradigm for businesses around the world. Yet it's a deeply personal journey as we learn to be honest about our humanity. It is the trailhead of a leadership quest to discover the heart of courageous leadership.

Questions for Reflection

1. Why does your business exist?
2. What criticism do you anticipate receiving if you were to begin taking the approach of conscious capitalism?
3. Who can help you in your journey?

9 | "B" The Change

It was a radical idea from the start. Could a successful, multinational, publicly traded company measure its success by looking beyond the value of its stock price to the good it could create in the world? Could its intentional efforts to repair its social and environmental footprint be factored in when evaluating the company and its leadership? If so, what metrics would be needed to measure it?

In 2018, world food giant Danone North America (Danone NA), with US$6 billion in sales and a global staff of 10,000 at the time, became the largest corporation in the world to receive B Corporation (or "B Corp") certification for its high ethical standards.

Issued by the nonprofit organization B Lab, the certification measures a company's social and environmental performance, its impact on workers and customers, and its public transparency. As of 2023, there are more than 6,000 certified B Corporations globally.[1] Of course, that is just a tiny fraction of the 334 million or so corporations worldwide, but it's a start.

Now, any company can give lip service to their intentions to do right by social and environmental principles, plaster countless posters on their walls, and be very public about their charitable giving. We've all come across companies that greenwash—loudly publicizing their apparent eco-consciousness while, behind the scenes, they are harming the environment or failing to support their employees. B Corp certification requires companies to be accountable. They can no longer hide.

Setting a New Course

"A company's responsibility doesn't end at the factory gate or office door," Antoine Riboud declared in his now-famous "Speech in Marseilles" in front of 2,000 French business leaders, employees, and journalists at a meeting of the National Council of French Employers (CNPF).[2] The former CEO of Danone, Riboud's vision echoed Allan Gray's commitment to serving the common good with a multistakeholder approach. Despite Danone's original founding in 1919 by Isaac Carasso, Riboud is often credited as its true founder for his role in merging Boussois-Souchon-Neuvesel (BSN) with Évian and Gervais Danone, shaping the company into what it is today.

When Riboud stepped in as CEO in the 1970s, he laid the groundwork for his company's pledge to realize a "dual project" that would embrace both economic success and social progress. It was one of the first times that a large-scale business owner elevated people and the environment right in its business model. It would remain a guiding mission for the company for decades to come.

The global food system is broken. In the hands of faceless conglomerates, it prioritizes making cheap, non-nutritious food, irrespective of any social and environmental consequences. The fact that Danone intentionally avoided the entrenched playbook of its peers deserves credit.

In 2014, Emmanuel Faber was promoted to CEO of Paris-based Danone SA, the global parent company with a market cap of more than US\$40 billion. Since the company's early years, Riboud and, later, his son Franck stressed the importance of developing both the economic and the social impact of Danone's growth. As part of a planned (and controversial) succession process, Faber assumed the role when Franck Riboud stepped down. Having held a variety of executive positions with Danone since 1997, Faber was chosen as the successor in large part because of his strong alignment with the company's commitment to sustainable and socially responsible practices. While not a "product man," and while some thought of him as a "lost intellectual," Faber's commitment was deep—almost evangelical—rooted in his strong Catholic views.[3] So much so that Riboud is rumored to have said he chose "the monk" over "the player" as his successor.[4]

In one of his boldest moves as CEO, in 2015, Faber decided that Danone's US dairy business would acquire WhiteWave Foods and the new company would be named Danone North America. But it wouldn't simply be a classic merger. It was an intentional and strategic creation of a new entity that would more easily meet B Corp requirements. Thus, the move was grounded in a much bigger and more ambitious vision—to create a new subsidiary "with a point of view on the world."[5]

~ • ~

To help him accomplish such a large-scale project, he tapped Lorna Davis. Lorna had worked at Danone from 1997 to 2006, leading several country business units, eventually ending up at their China-based biscuit business. In 2006, Kraft bought that business, and Lorna became president of Kraft's Food business in China. In 2011, she left Kraft to lead the North American Biscuit business for Mondelez International, a producer of well-known food brands, such as Oreos and Chips Ahoy. And in 2014, she returned to Danone as the Chief Manifesto Catalyst, reporting directly to Faber.

To Lorna, the timing was perfect. Despite the fact that she was running a US$6 billion business unit at Mondelez and had lots of money, power, status, and an apartment overlooking Central Park in Manhattan, she was feeling a lot of personal unrest. "I did it day in and day out and day in and day out, and then I couldn't do it anymore," she told me. That's when Faber went to New York to see her.

"He asked me if I'd come back to Danone and help him move the company into the next phase of its purpose journey. And I thought maybe there is a place where I can take all the skills I've learned over the years, and I can find a way to really help transform business to be a force for good." She paused. "Besides, who wants to sell another fucking Oreo!? This would be my way of bringing love back to corporate America."[6]

Then, Faber wanted Lorna to spearhead the acquisition and B Corp project. He knew it would take strong leadership and an authentic drive to create positive change and to lead the multinational company through the massive assessment, evaluation, problem-solving, and re-adjustment stages required for B Corp certification.

As Chief Manifesto Catalyst, Davis's agenda largely consisted of helping Danone forge a new relationship between people, profit, and the planet. So when she first became aware of B Lab, she quickly recognized the natural correlation between Danone's mission and the principles of B Corps.

She later said that she and Faber chose B Corp certification for Danone specifically because it had three critical elements. "First, it has a legal framework, and the transformation of the legal system is really important, and big corporations need to play a role in that. Secondly, the certification is hard, and it's competitive, but there's a real benefit both from a strategic point of view and from an achievement point of view. And, thirdly, because it's a movement. It's very young. It's kind of hip."[7]

Lorna felt that when a company commits to certification, it can ultimately transform the company from within. "Once you make a statement like, 'Our goal is to bring health through food to as many people as possible', it carries implications for your pricing, your products, the categories you choose to work in, and the way you treat people on the planet," she told me. "The more you bring in the context in which you choose to operate, the more the implications become obvious. Over time, navigating those implications becomes embedded in your strategy, and ultimately, it makes its way into your behaviors in a virtuous cycle."[8]

In 2015, Faber unveiled his Manifesto, which memorialized Danone's mission to bring "health through food" to as many people as possible. Then, in 2016, he launched Danone Manifesto Ventures, the company's VC arm, that would invest in brands and entrepreneurs that proved to be aligned with the company's ethos of health and wellness. By doing so, Faber aimed to foster innovation and contribute to the evolution of the food industry; he wanted the world to see food as "precious" and "as a human right, not a commodity."[9] Soon after, Faber oversaw the adoption of a new slogan for the company—"One Planet. One Health."—and adjusted the company's earnings per share metrics for its carbon emissions (carbon-adjusted EPS) so that the multinational corporation's success would be directly linked to its environmental performance.

> *Economy without social progress is barbarity. Social progress without economy is utopia. This is why the ultimate goal of the free-market economy needs to be social justice. And the right to food is a fundamental of social justice.*
> —*Emmanuel Faber, former CEO of Danone*

Faber could have made very different choices. Given that, historically, the investment community had considered Danone an underperformer, a new strategy more focused on the bottom line could have garnered widespread applause and positioned Faber as the admirable "turnaround guy." But Faber was intent on accomplishing more than just turning the company around; he was on a mission to realize its "dual project" goal and turn it into a force for good.

Bringing Love Back to Corporate America

It was a courageous step for both Danone and B Lab, the nonprofit that established B Corp certification, because no multinational corporation the size of Danone NA had ever even attempted to achieve B Corp certification before. B Lab had been focusing on small- to medium-sized companies in its first eight years because its founders felt that real innovation was happening at the level of small businesses, and they felt that smaller companies would have fewer barriers to the certification process.

Even before Danone came knocking on B Lab's door seeking certification for its North American subsidiary, B Lab had been working for several years on evolving its assessment metrics to be accessible to large multinationals. But when Danone NA, a large global company, expressed interest in certification, B Lab's process accelerated. Still, Faber didn't want to wait for B Lab to finish working on the modifications, so he signed up to be part of the process.

By December 2015, Danone had made three commitments to B Lab: it would pilot B Lab's B Impact Assessment (BIA) tool with some of its subsidiaries; it would help B Lab introduce the BIA to larger companies; and, ultimately, it would test the expanded and refined BIA when it became available. (While a typical BIA consists of roughly 250 questions, as a multinational, Danone NA had to answer more than 1,500 assessment questions.) The singular goal of their efforts was to smooth out the certification experience for larger companies without sacrificing B Corp standards.

Faber pointed out the risks both organizations took in this quasi-partnership. "[B Lab took] a huge risk of demonetizing their currency, basically, by lending their equity to a large company. Any large company has class actions, tax rulings, legal issues, and all kinds of skeletons that the nice little startups do not have yet. They need to determine how to live with that, basically. On our side, we run the risk of going for essentially the wrong overall metrics if their system doesn't work or if it is not more broadly adopted or recognized as a game changer."[10]

Meanwhile, Danone's undertaking didn't go unnoticed by the world banking system. Just before certification was approved, 12 of the world's largest banks executed a €2 billion bank loan to Danone SA that would lower its interest rates as its B Corp certification expanded.[11]

The banks' actions represented a profound paradigm shift to Faber. It's a shift that might serve to encourage our current global business community to reflect on its values of ruthless capitalism, competition, individualism, and endless economic growth. It challenges conventional notions of who gets access to capital—usually, leaders willing to "win" at all costs—and prompts us to question whether our financial systems adequately account for the positive impact and ethical practices of B Corps, public benefit corporations, nonprofits, or any company that's not set up to maximize profits at the expense of society's well-being.

In practical terms, a commitment to certification demonstrates a long-term perspective and a holistic approach to business, which can be interpreted as reduced risks and increased stability. Thus, lenders might perceive B Corps as being less likely to face reputational damage, legal issues, or negative environmental impacts, all of which can affect financial performance. As Faber said, "These banks have identified B Corp [certification] as lowering the beta risk of our credit status." It's thus possible to infer that a B Corp has a better credit rating than a company without B Corp credentials.

Then, Danone wanted more. Just when Danone NA was celebrating its new B Corp status, Faber announced that Danone SA would boldly promise to achieve full certification for its entire US$23 billion global enterprise by 2030 as well. As of 2023, an impressive 75% of Danone SA's global business is B Corp-certified. And the company has set an even more ambitious goal: to accomplish that mammoth task by 2025 instead of 2030.

Movement Builders

In the meantime, a veritable movement had begun. "This is how movements and revolutions start," Ben Anderson, a.k.a. "B Keeper," and former CEO and Co-Chairman of the Board of B Lab US, told me. "It's not so much that we're creating certification as we're creating a movement. The more people you get on board, the more power in numbers is happening, the conversation is happening, and the energy around it is happening. When we put people down, that's not going to move us in the right direction."

In fact, more than 200,000 companies around the world have used B Lab's BIA, its free assessment tool, as a benchmark for their performance in fulfilling their social, environmental, and transparency goals. "The [BIA] assessment makes the unconscious conscious," Ben told me, "because the companies are using it as a framework, as a way to have language around measuring their progress. They are looking and learning and developing pathways to grow."[12] In effect, B Lab has opened the door for hundreds of thousands of companies to fine-tune their policies that implement accountability to their employees, customers, and their environment. Whether they get full-fledged certification or not, innumerable micro-improvements are happening all around us every day.

> *We are really community builders first, looking to galvanize a*
> *movement, but we do it through certification . . .*
> *People will go further through their connection to each other*
> *than just based on a cause.*
> —*Ben Anderson, former B Lab CEO*
> *and board of directors co-chair*

On a larger scale, more developments were emerging. Inspired by the B Corp global community's progress and committed to the principles of the B Corp movement, several billion-dollar multinational corporations decided to join forces to form B Movement Builders (BMB), a "collaborative and cooperative coalition" that is committed to "catalyzing the global movement of business as a force for good."[13] BMB's initial pioneering group—including Danone, Natura & Co., Bonduelle, Gerdau, and Magalu—have a combined revenue topping US$60 billion and their employees numbering 250,000 in more than 120 companies. Just to join BMB, a corporation must have over US$1 billion in revenues. Other large organizations have since joined the movement as well.

Through their collective action, BMB is working to share the narrative of a new vision for successful business, promote the adoption of new standards, catalyze policy changes, develop networks of communities working toward change, and change business leaders' perspectives about what's possible for business. Together, these corporate giants are driven to cultivate transparency and accountability, affect capital markets, and ultimately have a substantive positive impact across the global business community.

Even as the vast majority of corporations worldwide stay stuck in the profit-maximization paradigm of the past couple of centuries, the organizations that make up the BMB bring tremendous potential to the movement to transform how business is defined and operated—from self-interest and the prioritizing of shareholder value above all else to business as a force for good. They dare to aim for something higher, recognizing that even incremental changes can ultimately add up to a dramatic pivot toward honoring and supporting even those "outside the factory gate."

Of course, any time progress is made, there will be naysayers downplaying accomplishments, questioning motives, and doubting efficacy. Across the global media landscape—digital, audio, and print alike—countless voices complained about B Lab's choice to expand its certification to fit large multinationals. They pointed out that the designation was designed for smaller companies and questioned whether B Lab could successfully attenuate the system to accommodate larger organizations without watering down the results.

Some cried foul, saying that, with such a change in charter, perhaps neither the nonprofit nor the certification could be trusted. Some early adopters of B Corp standards expressed fears that the designation would become meaningless and accused B Lab of enlisting multinationals to help them be "less bad" rather than transforming them into authentic forces for good. Others who worked in the sustainability industry said they worried that allowing subsidiaries of large corporations to attain the status, even if the parent is not certified, would allow the large companies to benefit from B Corp status without having to fully do the work. It was greenwashing, they claimed, and it would reduce the credibility of their own hard-fought certification across the board.

That fervor got especially loud in the spring of 2022 when B Lab Global certified Nespresso, an operating unit of the Nestlé Group based in Switzerland. Competing coffee brands wrote letters citing reported human rights violations on the farms that grow the company's coffee and questioning the environmental impact of the single-use nature of its products. After all, is that what "business as a force for good" ultimately looks like?[14]

But the naysayers aren't doing the math. Simply put, multinationals interact with human and natural resources at such a great scale that if you get a multibillion-dollar company, like Danone, to move 10% in the right direction, then you've had a greater impact on a global scale than a thousand startups combined. Why would we want to discourage large organizations from trying to become better—even incrementally? Large companies taking these bold steps are more visible, leave a bigger footprint, and make a bigger splash. And they can be tremendously inspiring to help the "movement" grow even further. Do we really want to discourage large organizations from trying to improve, even incrementally, if it means evolving the broader business ecosystem for the better?

It's true that when we observe multinationals from a distance—and midstream—it can seem as if they are taking a long time to get the job done. So, are they dragging their feet? Are they working hard enough to get 100% certified? Or are they just putting on a good show? But it's also true that a journey of a thousand miles takes a single step, one at a time, to get to the destination. It's an incremental process, and it simply takes time to turn a big ship around.

B Lab argues that larger companies have more at stake, not less. The greater a company's scale, influence, and impact, the greater its obligations to stakeholders. B Lab has also built in a required recertification process that demands further improvements every three years. As a result, accreditation has greater meaning over time.

> *Don't let perfect be the enemy of good.*
> *—Voltaire*

Perhaps the greatest risk to this "movement" of ours is that companies get so concerned about getting accused of greenwashing or so fearful of backlash for not "doing enough"—even as they're in the process of improving their engagement with their employees, customers, and the environment—that they keep their cards close to the vest and don't publicize their efforts at all. Or worse yet, they become disheartened, paralyzed by fear, or discouraged from even attempting to change. That's when the wheels of progress will decidedly slow down. Ben Anderson told me he knows many companies trying to do really good things, but they're scared to talk about it because they don't want to be accused of greenwashing.[15] While we understand their fears, the choice to do nothing limits the momentum of the movement. If people aren't talking about what good is being done simply because nothing's ever good enough to please the crowd, then many others could conclude that nobody's doing anything, and they might just give up.

We have to have the courage to take the steps forward. Our willingness to stick our necks out and make a statement—by virtue of our very presence on the world stage as players in the movement for change—provides encouragement and inspiration for other companies, both small and large, to follow. We become role models and leaders, giving the nod to those who follow that the road ahead has been tried, tested, and proven valuable. "Come on in," our presence assures them. "The water's fine."

> *Lighthouses don't go running all over an island*
> *looking for boats to save;*
> *They just stand there, shining.*
> *—Annie Lamont*

And Then He's Gone

Faber invested significant resources to fulfill the B Corp requirements and ensure compliance along every part of Danone's production chain—from farmers to suppliers, from relationships to raw materials. And as a result, Danone's earnings slumped, and shareholders weren't happy. In spite of Faber's efforts to improve profitability while making Danone more accountable to all stakeholders—shareholders, employees, vendors, and the environment alike—in 2021, Danone's third-largest shareholder, Artisan Partners, and activist investor Bluebell Capital challenged the company's management structure and strategy, criticized the organization's performance. And Faber was forced out.

There are differing accounts of what happened. The battle was described in a 2022 article in *Vanity Fair France Magazine* as a "tumultuous saga" with "last-minute betrayals, suspicions and slanders, unexpected alliances, deep throats, fatigue, and tears too."[16]

For some, Faber's complex personality was the problem. It comes across in his book, *Chemins de Traverse*, in which he laments that the world of finance induced in him "a mixture of fascination for its power and instinctive defiance." He "[did] not like the powerful" and remained defiant, finding nothing more pleasurable than "breaking their rules."[17]

A sort of "Steve Jobs of France," Faber had his critics, as most visionaries do. In a candid and emotional interview with me, Flemming Morgan, a former member of the executive committee, bemoaned Faber's "lack of emotional intelligence," his "unilateral decision making," and his "control-freak" tendencies, all of which stemmed from his "highly introverted nature" and prevented him from executing on the company vision.[18] Flemming even memorialized his concerns in a letter to the Board, saying, "The endless reorganizations, the byzantine complexity, and sheer number of projects coupled with the incomprehensible decision-making process have ended up suffocating and exhausting the organization, leading to ever poorer performance."[19] Faber even unceremoniously fired Lorna. She later admitted he was the only boss who ever made her cry.[20]

Still, Faber was deeply committed to Riboud's dual commitment to advance social progress while building economic success for the company. Yet, Danone's activist shareholders prioritized the share price above all else—true to the typical self-interested, impatient, and short-sighted approach of many of today's business leaders. Even though Danone was a food products company with a mission to feed the world and do good for the planet, shareholders could not wait to see how Faber's bold efforts would flower—and pay them back—in the future. It's the capitalist story we have seen play out time and time again, fueled by the misaligned incentives of money managers we explored in Chapter 1.

An article in *Forbes* at the time summed it up this way: "Emmanuel Faber will enter history as one of the leading executives promoting stakeholder capitalism and centering core business units around ESG objectives. Yet his footprint and departure reveal a pervasive rift between staunch supporters of sustainable capitalism and hard-rugged corporate activists."[21]

It left a bad taste in many people's mouths. People once again started to question and even doubt if purpose and profit are compatible, if anyone can trust that businesses can thrive and succeed if they seek to fulfill both a vision for social good and a vision for growth and enrichment. That's the real tragedy—that, subconsciously or consciously, people still believe that we can't have both.

While Danone's new CEO, Antoine de Saint-Affrique, does not have Faber's charismatic celebrity and is more focused on economic performance, Danone's "dual-project" ethos seems to live on there. I witnessed their commitment first-hand during my visit to Danone's Paris offices in 2023. I was there to facilitate my workshop, "The Heart of Courageous Leadership," which aimed to help participants align their strengths with a business purpose they cared deeply about.

The passion of the participants was palpable. When we delved into the discussions, it was evident how much the company mission was not just a corporate mantra but something people felt connected to. Their eyes lit up with shared ambition and a collective purpose. The current and former Danone employees I spoke with unequivocally expressed that the "dual project" ethos continues to be in Danone's "DNA."

While neither Lorna nor Faber are at Danone anymore, their impact on the global business leadership community is undeniable. They started a trend, and that's the legacy that matters most. Their advancement of Antoine Riboud's leap of faith years ago inspired others to explore what's possible and helped to open minds and start conversations about transforming the business paradigm to one that embraces environmental and social objectives.

Both of them continue to live their purpose and work hard to keep the mission alive. In December 2021, Faber was appointed the inaugural chair of the newly established International Sustainability Standards Board (ISSB). Through his political involvement and impact investing ventures, he is more focused on climate activism and sustainability than ever. The break from Danone actually strengthened his resolve, emboldened him to face the challenges that lay ahead, and inspired him to redefine his purpose and himself. In December 2021, he told *Time Magazine*, "I suddenly discovered that I was totally free to reinvent myself, in terms of where do I want to spend time and with whom and how. Which is a privilege, really." And: "I've defined myself as a business activist. I'm an activist of business being part of the solution, being the fundamental solution, *the* solution."[22]

Having served as a global ambassador for B Lab and a member of its board of directors, Lorna continued to make a profound impact long after her time at Danone by helping organizations transform the way they interact with their resources and their stakeholders. Now, she's mentoring and coaching business leaders, extending her reach to help organizations driven by purpose to achieve their goals. Having shunned the "power over" paradigm of the masculine mentality that proliferates in the corporate environments she'd been working in, Lorna shifted to embody the feminine leadership model—wielding "power with" others and encouraging collaboration, listening, and support skills—with an unwavering passion and authenticity.

"It's never going to be down to individuals," she says. "It's going to be down to some notion of interdependence, some notion of sequence, some notion of generations, some notion of being part of the whole for the greater good."[23] Her commitment to fostering businesses as catalysts for positive change is heartfelt and—in my opinion—undeniably cool.

From its inception, Danone did the unexpected. Before it became fashionable, Antoine and Frank Riboud embraced both social and environmental accountability as well as responsibility to shareholders. Under Faber and Lorna's leadership, Danone went even further and accomplished what no multinational had done before, and other corporate giants followed suit. The results of their risk-taking might not have materialized in the exact ways they imagined, but they catalyzed change in a greater way than they could have dreamed. They have catalyzed change for a long time to come.

> *Advice number one: You have the right to want things and to want things to change. Advice number two: Wanting is not enough. To change things, you have to take over. And advice number three: You have to stop being afraid. Together with others, you can do anything, and you must.*
> *Because there is no one else to do it but you.*
> *—Sanna Marin, former Finland Prime Minister*
> *New York University commencement address, May 2023*

The movement has begun. The time is now to be the change you wish to see in the world. Now's the time to gather courage, be contrarian if necessary, and forge ahead toward greater goals. Even if what you do isn't perfect, even if you risk the disfavor of others, even if others whine about your progress or question your authenticity, even if you don't fulfill 100% of your goals and vision—the actions you take will ultimately spark a flame in others to explore the possibility that they, too, can be instruments of change and help light the way to a better world.

As Antione Riboud reminded the crowd in his speech in Marseilles, "We should lead our companies with our hearts as much as with our heads, and we should not forget that while the energy resources of the earth are limited, those of humankind are infinite as long as we feel motivated."

Questions for Reflection

1. Do you believe in the compatibility of purpose and profits? What new possibilities can you explore for integrating purpose and profits in your own endeavors?

2. How do you differentiate between greenwashing and genuine environmental commitment?

3. As B Lab embarked on a quest to certify multinationals, they encountered their fair share of challenges. However, both B Lab and Danone refused to be hindered by the elusive pursuit of perfection. Instead, they recognized that progress, no matter how incremental, holds its own merit. Multinationals might *never* be able to demonstrate the same level of dedication to environmental responsibility as startups—but given their influence, shouldn't they try?

4. What is your own relationship with perfection? Have you ever hesitated to act because it didn't meet your standards of perfection? Have there been situations when incremental progress or imperfect actions could have yielded positive outcomes? What can you do now to cultivate the "courage to be imperfect" so that you can move more decidedly toward your goals?

10

Tools of the Masters

Honing Your Leadership

Leadership is always somewhat autobiographical; like a mirror, it reflects the depth or superficiality of a leader's personal evolution. The personal journeys of those who lead are inevitably reflected in their choices, practices, and styles of leadership, which, in turn, can either propel their organizations to the promised land or be responsible for their demise.

Now, it can be tempting to look at some of the highly acclaimed leaders today and conclude that they were born with their unique talents, their extraordinary brilliance, their drive, and their vision—and maybe some were. But regardless of how it appears, most noteworthy leadership comes as the result of passion, drive, and intentional work. To upgrade to an evolved and aware leader, you have to desire it and pursue a path to becoming one. So, where do you start?

> *More than once in the history of Whole Foods Market, the company was unable to collectively evolve until I myself was able to evolve. In other words, I was holding the company back. My personal growth enabled the company also to evolve.*
> *—John Mackey, co-founder of Whole Foods*

129

Having worked closely with leaders over the years, I've noticed that there are four spheres of our work we need to master deeply in order to elevate our consciousness and truly succeed at leadership. We need to master *time* since we abdicate our power and forfeit control whenever we let ourselves be run by the relentless tick of the clock. We need to master *relationships* because true leadership thrives on collaboration and interconnection. We also need to embrace uncertainty with grace, for the more ambitious our vision, the more uncertainty we will inevitably encounter. Getting comfortable with uncertainty creates the space for us to connect to our spiritual intelligence, freeing us from the confines of the analytical mind. And we need to master our *emotions*, as they are an inextricable part of the human fabric, and volatile ones—ours or those of others we work with—can derail even otherwise effective leaders.

These four building blocks comprise what I call the TRUE model, referring to the mastery of four significant dimensions of life: time (T), our relationships (R), the inevitability of uncertainty (U), and our human emotions (E). Proficiency and skill in these areas are absolutely essential to success. I call it the TRUE model as a reminder that to be true leaders, we need to be true to ourselves, our authentic selves. That's where our power is, along with our genius and our inspired vision.

> *Be not afraid of greatness. Some are born great,*
> *some achieve greatness, and others*
> *have greatness thrust upon them.*
> *—William Shakespeare*

Importantly, it is access to our feminine intelligence that will truly open us up to mastery of time, relationships, uncertainty, and our emotions. True leadership is rooted in grace and mindful awareness, which liberates our wisdom, our energy, and our creative potential to serve our purpose. It starts with exploring our *being* and the transformative power of presence. We'll never reach our full potential as leaders if we only draw on half of our inner resources—our masculine side. While our masculine mentality, with its analytic, logical, and assertive characteristics, is essential to our success, we must strive to embody our duality of intelligences—masculine and feminine—to step into true mastery of leadership.

Wholeness isn't just a sentimental or abstract concept. It allows leaders to navigate the complexities of the modern world, build stronger relationships, make wiser decisions, and drive positive change. It's a reminder that leadership is not one-dimensional; true mastery comes from embracing the full spectrum of our human intelligence.

Time Mastery

In 1970, at Princeton University Seminary School, a pair of inquisitive researchers, John Darley and Daniel Batson, designed an experiment to investigate the influence of time pressure on human behavior. Picture, if you will, a group of seminary students asked to give a talk on the Biblical parable of the Good Samaritan. The researchers divided the students into three groups. Those in the first group were led to believe they were running late and needed to hurry to deliver their talk; a second group was given a bit more time; and a third group was told they had "plenty" of time. The area around the school was somewhat staged so that when the students made their way to the designated location to deliver their speeches, they'd walk by an actor slumped in a doorway, in obvious pain and discomfort, moaning and coughing in distress.

The results of the study were shocking and disturbing—if not a little ironic, considering the students' chosen field. While 63% of those given the most time to prepare their talk offered to help the distressed man, only 10% of those in the rushed group offered any kind of kindness. (A few seminary students even admitted to stepping over the man as they rushed to their destination building!) "Ironically," wrote the researchers, "a person in a hurry is less likely to help people, even if he is going to speak on the parable of the Good Samaritan."[1]

Thus, the Good Samaritan Study—which continues to echo in the corridors of universities even today—emphasizes questions about ethics, the interplay between intention and the pressures of time, and our susceptibility to external influences when we're making choices.

But what stands out to me is what it says about our blind spots. In the study's post-experiment interviews, many of the rushed seminary students confessed that they didn't even *see* the man in the alley crying out in pain. (Of course, those who stepped over him did see him; his condition was simply irrelevant to them.)

If feeling hurried can get even seminary students to throw their ethics and empathy out the window, what does it mean for the rest of us? As Daniel Kahneman writes in *Thinking Fast and Slow*, "We can be blind to the obvious, and we are also blind to our blindness." Literally, we fail to *see* the challenges and opportunities in our path. As leaders, what might this blindness cost us?

In our highly competitive culture, we tend to see busyness as a badge of honor—but it shouldn't be. If haste obscures valuable data, it robs us of our effectiveness and impairs our vision. Said Darley and Batson: "Maybe people's cognition was narrowed by the hurriedness ..." In *your* hurriedness, what might you be missing?

As a leader, you must have a wider vision. Like a chess player, you need to see all the possible plays in front of you so you can consider the interplay of probabilities and choose what will bring the best result. Unless you are relaxed and open, present, and unhurried, you won't be able to do that.

> *I insist on a lot of time being spent, almost every day, to just sit and think. That is very uncommon in American business. I read and think. So I do more reading and thinking and make less impulse decisions than most people in business.*
> *—Warren Buffett*

When I was working as a corporate lawyer, time was uppermost in our minds. Inside law firms, hurry is revered; success is measured by billable hours. I fell into the trap along with everyone else. Hyper-focused on getting things done in six-minute billable increments, my field of awareness remained tight and constricted, and details about the bigger picture could be missed and come back to haunt me. Most of us were exhausted, deflated, and defeated, trying to accomplish a ridiculous amount in a limited time-frame. Yet, such a culture doesn't only happen in law firms. Throughout the Western world, you'll find people frenetically trying to beat the clock, fit things in, and accomplish more than time allows.

A perpetually stretched schedule is the enemy of progress. Time-starved decision-making erodes the very foundation of visionary leadership since creativity and inspiration require presence in time and space. Time poverty also perpetuates the status quo as it shrinks the mental space and reduces the opportunity to question established norms, explore new ideas, or think deeply about complex issues. We fail to actually *see* the undiscovered universe of possibilities for creating positive change in our businesses and social structures.

Being in action is an expression of the masculine energy within us— and most of us have become nonstop "doers." Yet, if we let ourselves get swallowed up in unconscious, nonstop doing, we'll end up trying to do everything without doing anything well. To chart new courses and conquer summits, we need to free ourselves from the dominant cultural narrative and spend time in our internal landscape. We need to allow our leadership to flow from our inner character by tapping into the wisdom that lies in the gaps between our actions and in the spaces between our thoughts.

I often explain that my role as a leadership advisor is to offer leaders the gift of time. I give my clients the space to pause and step back from the whirlwind of their obligations. In that space, they could be in stillness; they could reflect and let go of preconceived notions and expectations. In that state, not knowing and confusion were encouraged while the need to control and get a quick "fix" was weakened. They found that their saboteurs loosened their overwhelming grip.

With compassion and curiosity, resistance can be examined, awareness can expand, and imagination can awaken. Only within such a setting, from a place of grounding, could my clients regain agency over their decisions and become more capable of discerning if they were being driven by their compulsion for urgency or if they were hearing the call of their vision.

> *You should sit in meditation for 20 minutes a day unless you're too busy. Then you should sit for an hour.*
> —*Jon Kabat-Zinn, founder of Center for Mindfulness at UMass Memorial Health*

How can you get grounded, cultivate thoughtfulness, and connect to your inner resources? Only by resisting the trap of busyness and allowing yourself to spend time being. If you want to access your inner power and sow the seeds of your feminine intelligence, you need to carve out more time for being intentional, mindful, and introspective. I don't just mean that you should take breaks; you need to set up intentional practices of cultivating inner alignment within yourself. By doing that, your time will slow.

Think about how you fill your calendar. Whether it's business, personal, health, or entertainment, we are flooded with an endless parade of opportunities to take up our valuable time. As author Yuval Noah Harari points out, we are "deluded by irrelevant information," and it is our choice whether we consume it or not.

To master time, be intentional and strategic about how you spend it—and to do that, you need the self-awareness to know what gives you energy, what drains you, and what generates the greatest impact. Figure out what's truly essential to your purpose and well-being. Decide what are the things you're good at, what you're passionate about, and what makes you come alive—and then prioritize those. Consider *when* you work best, whether it's in the morning or at night, and schedule your most important tasks during your optimal times; it's a simple yet crucial strategy. You'll make a bigger difference while enjoying a much deeper level of satisfaction in your work.

> *The difference between misery and happiness depends on what we do*
> *with our attention.*
> —*Sharon Salzberg, author and mindfulness teacher*

This is what all great leaders do. Every outstanding leader I've ever coached has been extremely selfish about their calendar. They know their options are (1) to go to a million meetings, try to put out a million fires, and run around complaining that they're too busy, or (2) to say no to whatever isn't essential. They carve out time to dedicate to thinking, reflecting, and/or being. Become a great leader: Do less and do it well.

Relationship Mastery

Birthing your vision and infusing vitality into your boldest aspirations will require you to master the art of persuasion. Power and influence, when wielded with finesse and feminine intelligence, are inspiring invitations for others to join you on the journey of creating a business that is a force for good.

The way we manage power and influence in our relationships colors every aspect of what we try to accomplish. If we've taken an ego-centric, adversarial, masculine approach, it can be extremely difficult to create mutually beneficial, aligned relationships. If we're misusing power, we might find ourselves struggling with stakeholders and negotiations. We cannot order, control, or force others; those "strategies" emanate from fear and produce uninspiring results. By weaving the feminine principles of connection, empathy, and collaboration into our approach to relationships with the people we seek to lead and inspire, we will achieve genuinely satisfying results and embody our authentic leadership.

> *There is no doubt that the quality of our relationships determines the quality of our lives.*
> *—Neha Sangwan, MD, founder of Intuitive Intelligence*

Renowned for her work in the field of human relationships, Belgian-born author and psychotherapist Esther Perel offers a framework to help us recognize that we all land somewhere along a continuum between the two extremes of intense independence and cooperative interdependence. On one end, there are the independent types who like to maintain their individual identity and be self-directed and self-reliant. On the other end, there are those who thrive in an environment of interdependence, where cooperation, teamwork, and support are natural and necessary for the outcomes they seek.

Of course, our independent nature can easily map to a masculine approach to relating with others, while interdependence is clearly an expression of our feminine intelligence since it exudes compassion and connection to the group. But we are not seeking dominance of one part over another; we are seeking the balance between the two, that sweet spot that let us leverage the values of both. That provides a wholeness and a power that neither "part" can offer on its own.

Where are you on that spectrum? Do you tend to be independent, generally focusing on your own needs and goals without thinking about how to empower and inspire the group? Or do you lean towards interdependence, obsessing about group dynamics and interplay at the expense of your own congruence, internal power, or well-being? Neither extreme of the continuum is right or wrong or good or bad; neither independence nor interdependence is "better" than the other. But interestingly, leaders typically tend to fall on the independent end of the spectrum—and there lies the risk.

If you find yourself an independent sort—as I am—you'll find that there will always be a time and place for you to wield your leadership, take ownership, be the decider, and move things forward powerfully. Your self-referencing is powerful and esteemed. But if you are blocked off from others and see yourself as the hero(ine) who's there to save the day (or the world), it will be a challenge for you to get others on board. You might overidentify with position and status, and your ego may undermine you. Isolation will be your downfall.

Ideally, you learn to be flexible. Learning that you're an independent type, you make the extra effort to move further along the continuum. Perel calls it "relational intelligence"—adapting yourself to recognize the value of the group dynamic and having a deeper awareness of the humanity in the people you work with. In return, you get the language and the fluidity to work with people along the entire spectrum. For a leader, it's invaluable.

~ • ~

Empathy is the ability to understand and share the feelings, perspectives, and experiences of another person. It enables individuals to connect with others on a deeper level, to be attuned to their needs and emotions, and to demonstrate understanding and support in times of joy, sorrow, or distress. Think about the leaders you look up to—and the leader you want to become. They are trusted, they communicate with clarity, they listen well, they inspire, they create alignment and cohesiveness in their teams, and they elevate the vibration and energy of the collective. Each one of these capacities is empathy in action, an expression of feminine consciousness. And while it might seem counterintuitive to a masculine-dominant culture, leaders who exhibit empathy and compassion are able to unlock intrinsic motivation and energy and unlock greater performance out of the people around them. Studies also demonstrate that the ability to connect emotionally to another and see their perspective makes leaders better at the art of negotiating, which, of course, is central to any leadership role.[2] On the other hand, research reveals that leaders who display a lack of empathy trigger responses in the parts of the brains of their team members that are associated with avoidance, reduced focus, and a surge in negative emotions.[3]

> *Although it is now clear to me that human connections are essential to engagement, they're still not something that business schools and*

> *boardrooms think about or talk about much. This must change, as*
> *human magic, in the context of an effective strategy, leads to exceptional*
> *performance.*
> —Hubert Joly, former Chairman and CEO of Best Buy

Unfortunately, power can create the illusion of exceptionalism; it also harbors a shadow side that is capable of corrupting even the best of intentions. When we find ourselves in positions of influence, our capacity for empathy can wane—sometimes even accompanied by discernible changes in brain function.[4] That is why effective relationship mastery is a dynamic dance between the internal and external focus of attention. On the one hand, we turn our attention inward to assess our own alignment, intentions, and drivers. On the other hand, in a state of grounded congruence, we turn our attention outward toward those we seek to influence with empathy and compassion.

While this might not be a popular assessment, I believe it comes down to love. Now, most of us in the business world are somewhat phobic about using the word "love" in the context of leadership and organizations. But truly, that is exactly what we should talk about if we want to evolve our own consciousness and use our elevated state to cultivate real relationships. One of the greatest gifts we can give another person is to be fully present, compassionate, curious, genuinely listening, and energetically available for connection. We want to move away from the conventional, masculine "power over" paradigm of the past millennium and lean more into our feminine intelligence—being sensitive to the whole, to our connection with others, and to what inspires us within that connection.

> *Power without love is reckless and abusive, and . . . love without power*
> *is sentimental and anemic. Power at its best is love implementing the*
> *demands of justice, and justice at its best is power correcting everything*
> *that*
> *stands against love.*
> —Dr. Martin Luther King, Jr.

Barbara Fredrickson, known for her work on positive emotions and author of *Love 2.0*, defines love as "micro-moments of positive connection."

In other words, love isn't just about grand gestures or deep emotional experiences; it's also about the brief, often unnoticed moments of connection and positivity that occur in our daily lives. That might be all that's being asked of you—micro-moments. Over time, these brief instances of positivity accumulate and contribute to the overall quality of our relationships. They create a reservoir of positive emotions that can help us weather inevitable challenges and conflicts. As one of the world's most prominent thought leaders, Deepak Chopra, writes in *The Soul of Leadership*, "What is common to every encounter is that one self makes contact with another self. Make sure that when you part, the other feels nurtured, enhanced, validated, encouraged, or appreciated." When you commit yourself to building relationships with love, your small habits and interactions will naturally evolve.

This is especially relevant if you're finding it difficult to bring others on board with your vision. If you frequently find yourself aggravated and stressed, and you blame others for their faults and shortcomings, you're already on poor footing to lead. From such a position, it will be difficult to create alignment and lead with conviction and effect. You need to invest in upgrading your mastery of relationships and, most likely, your self-awareness. Recognizing everyone's humanity and fallibility brings in the bigger picture and opens you up to innovation and ingenuity.

Finally, it has to be said that making a practice of listening to others—listening deeply and listening well—is indispensable for elevating your relationships. Do you listen actively, with curiosity, without interruption, and without partitioning off half of your attention to prepare how you're going to respond? You must listen with energetic authority, focusing your attention on the other person. Quiet your internal dialogue and self-consciousness. Listen—not just with your intellectual mind—but with your body and heart. Listen for what is not being said. By actively listening, you create a safe space for open communication and vulnerability. You'll be amazed at how much more can be accomplished when you listen fully.

> *Leadership is about empathy. It is about having the ability to relate to and connect with people for the purpose of inspiring and empowering their lives.*
> —*Oprah Winfrey*

Then, be intentional. Take time to understand people's life stories, filters, and worldviews. What really drives them? Use your focused attention to identify their gifts and deepest desires. Delve into their past experiences, values, and beliefs. The knowledge you glean will allow you to appreciate why people think and act the way they do and will give you a deeper understanding of the opportunities and obstacles being presented. Such insights open up more effective decision-making and creative problem-solving for you and increase the trust other people have in you, their ability to have courageous conversations with you, and even their desire to move forward in step with you.

Find the practices that work for you to center, build empathy, and genuinely connect with those around you. When you do, your words will inspire more deeply, your agreements will come along more quickly, and your teams will follow more cooperatively to help you manifest your vision.

> *Leadership is hard to define, and good leadership even harder. But if you can get people to follow you to the ends of the Earth, you are a great leader.*
> —Indra Nooyi, former CEO of PepsiCo

Mastery of Uncertainty

As leaders forging our own hero(ine)'s journey, we are constantly treading new paths into the unknown. We boldly take risks, attempt to open new doors to opportunity, and go about putting in place new processes and structures that will grow the business, improve our products, compete in the marketplace, and more. And in the midst of all that action, we face constant, unrelenting uncertainty. So, how do we master it? Just as importantly, how do we get it to work for us rather than against us? And how can we tap into the inherent power of uncertainty to transform us into leaders who can sustain a bold vision with strength, tenacity, and resilience?

Conscious leadership is not a whisper; it's a clarion call to global leaders who are ready to brave the storm and command the helm in these uncertain, tumultuous times. Mastering the uncertainty integral to all of our endeavors calls forth in us a willingness to embrace and grapple with the unknown rather than fear it.

The only thing that makes life possible is permanent, intolerable uncertainty, not knowing what comes next.
—Ursula K. Le Guin, author

Very often, it's a fear of uncertainty and the inability to know how to dance with it that causes leadership to fail. Always in a hurry for answers and wanting to stay "in control," leaders don't take the opportunity to slow down, feel, and connect with themselves and their intuition in the moment. Instead, they attempt to deal with their challenges while they're dissociated from themselves and not whole. Shut down emotionally and not having time to "be," they can't receive the messages from their own higher intelligence to guide them through the rough seas of uncertainty they naturally encounter.

Unfortunately, our social and cultural conditioning creates dysfunction within us, engendering disconnection from our spiritual selves. We then default to a reductionist approach, which typically uses structure and analysis to problem-solve and thrives on certainty, linear thinking, and a focus on being correct. All of these are expressions of a masculine mindset, which can be invaluable when logical thinking and assertiveness are called for, such as when we want to work efficiently and pragmatically and when we need to establish order and control. But, as Albert Einstein famously observed, "No problem can be solved from the same level of consciousness that created it." In our age, a new level of thinking is needed to solve the world's biggest problems.

Let's take a look at how we typically go about solving problems. Reductionism involves reducing complex systems or processes into their constituent parts in order to study them—and assuming that understanding the individual parts will lead to the understanding of the whole. The problem with this worldview is that it can lead to an incomplete and/or distorted picture of what we unquestionably deem "reality." Complex systems can get oversimplified, emergent properties can be neglected, and the crucial bigger picture can get lost. Any complex system—whether it be an economic system, the human brain, or a social network—can exhibit behaviors that can't be fully understood through reductionist methods alone. While science and rationality have propelled humanity forward in countless ways, they often fall short in providing answers to life's most profound questions and challenges. Leaders who recognize this limitation are open to exploring the vast realm beyond the measurable and quantifiable. They understand that there are aspects of human existence, consciousness, and the universe that defy reductionist explanations.

Here, the distinction between complicated problems and complex ones—often attributed to two influential theorists, Herbert Simon and Warren Weaver—is helpful. *Complicated* problems, as Simon proposed, are those with many interconnected parts, but they follow discernible rules. While they may be intricate, they are ultimately solvable through systematic analysis and expert knowledge. Reductionism is especially useful when dealing with complicated problems that have clear cause-and-effect relationships. Fixing your car is complicated, and so is doing your taxes; they can be solved with rational, predictable, and logical methods.

On the other hand, *complex* problems, as Weaver articulated, aren't governed by fixed rules, and that makes them inherently unpredictable. Everything from multistakeholder management to the climate crisis are complex problems that don't have clear solutions, and their outcomes emerge from dynamic, often chaotic, interactions. Complex problems require feminine intelligence—they call for adaptive, holistic approaches that acknowledge the inherent uncertainty in their dynamics. They cry out for the ability to embrace the chaos.

> *Learning to tolerate the 'don't know' mind or just being still, holding the whole of awareness, not having to know anything. This is the true inner work of redirection – and almost the opposite of the conditioning of most managers.*
> —*Otto Scharmer and Katrin Kaufer, creators of the Theory U Model of Change Management*

We must be wary of just how much the prevailing masculine mindset glorifies the practices of testing and verifying—through measurement—as the only ways to comprehend and unlock the secrets of existence. On the one hand, it's understandable why it has occurred. Numbers and metrics are concrete, definable, and seemingly simple to understand. They give us ways to perceive what might otherwise be obscure, vague, unpredictable, and ambiguous. Unfortunately, this fixation leads us to overcommit to our reductionist viewpoints, shutting ourselves off from considering alternative perspectives and perceptions. Arrogance and rigidity to other ways of seeing, knowing, and experiencing the world prevent us from personal development and confine us within a limited understanding of our world.

And what do we sacrifice as we uphold the rigidity of our mental constructs? Creative thinking, innovation, and, ultimately, progress beyond what we can envision with our current imagination. Making matters worse, we prioritize the things we can measure, and we typically devalue what we consider immeasurable—often setting aside what just might have held profound meaning for us if we had dared to look at them another way.

Ancient philosophical and spiritual traditions have long shared wisdom and contemplative practices that enrich and broaden worldviews and provide insights into higher states of being and living. To truly master uncertainty demands that we transcend our limiting cultural and social beliefs, seek other perceptions, and cultivate a deep connection to what lies beyond culture and society—the mystical and the Divine. I spent the majority of my life devoid of any spiritual dimension, a realization that didn't dawn on me until after my first psychedelic-assisted therapy encounter. When I later sought to articulate the indescribable nature of those experiences, I grappled with the challenge of reconciling my insights with objective scientific data that I'd previously relied on to govern my understanding of the world. It wasn't until I recognized that I have more than one avenue to perception, understanding, and awareness to serve me and my role as a leader that I felt truly invigorated. Yes, I can utilize my masculine skills when they are called for, and I can also invoke my more holistic intelligence—a sort of spiritual intelligence—to see the bigger picture and come up with more complete and satisfying solutions.

> *I'm consciously shedding the assumption that a skeptical point of view is the most intellectually credible. Intellect does not function in opposition to mystery; tolerance is not more pragmatic than love.*
> —*Krista Tippett, journalist and author*

Accessing our spiritual intelligence helps us master uncertainty by enabling us to transcend egoic, fear-based reactions and instead approach uncertainty with a sense of interconnectedness, inner peace, and a heightened capacity for creativity and empathy.

Leaders who cultivate a connection to something greater than themselves are also better equipped to inspire others with a sense of wonder and awe, inviting them to explore uncharted territories and push the boundaries of what is known. Spiritual intelligence also breeds humility in us, a quality often overlooked in leadership. Instead of reacting to uncertainty with fear, resistance, or the need to control, spiritual insight allows us to shift our focus from self-centered concerns to a broader, more interconnected perspective—and we experience uncertainty as a natural part of life's flow and enjoy its unexpected gifts in the process.

It is a spiritual intelligence that fuels our willingness to go beyond the confines of analytical thinking to explore new perspectives and experiences that are only available at higher levels of personal consciousness.

Thankfully, feminine energy thrives in the seas of chaos. When we're in our feminine energy—intuitive, feeling-oriented, and unstructured as it is—we can feel safe in the midst of uncertainty and not knowing. When we are embodying our feminine intelligence, we are more open to ambiguity and more receptive to the flow of life's unpredictable march of events. That receptivity gifts us with a broader and deeper perception of what we're concerned with, informing and guiding us to more holistic and sustainable outcomes. Again, embracing our feminine intelligence serves us both as people and as powerful leaders.

As we learn to be comfortable with uncertainty—and ultimately embrace it—we discover new resources of adaptability and resilience. In a world where change is constant, we are better prepared to weather storms and navigate uncharted waters. We can draw from inner reservoirs of strength and wisdom, guiding our teams with a steadiness that comes from a deeper understanding of the interconnectedness of all things.

> *I would never die for my beliefs because I might be wrong. The world is*
> *full of magical things patiently*
> *waiting for our wits to grow sharper.*
> —*Bertrand Russell, philosopher*

Learning to navigate uncertainty with strength and grace requires breaking away from some of the limiting beliefs, ideologies, and paradigms we've absorbed from our culture. It requires being open to new ideas and might involve challenging societal norms, questioning traditional wisdom, and exploring unconventional ideas and solutions. It can only come about within an atmosphere of openness to new possibilities and acceptance of innovative perspectives. For that reason, braving the unknown with openness can be much less comfortable than hiding behind cultural assumptions and perceptions, but it is ultimately that much more exciting, fulfilling, and transformative.

Many modalities are available to help you untether from conventional expectations and belief structures. Somatic awareness and grounding techniques can help to re-ignite body awareness, intuition, and the right brain. Psychospiritual work can help to release limiting socio-cultural beliefs, and emotional-psychological healing works to safely explore and dislodge deeply held traumas and allow intellectual and emotional openness to flourish more naturally.

> *One key to success is knowing the difference between knowledge and wisdom. One is information from the past, while the other is the key to the future.*
> —*Bill Crawford, psychologist*

As we remain steadfastly open to the unknown, we are given more opportunities for growth and discovery. As we become more open to new and different ideas, we find ourselves navigating the ever-changing landscape of life with greater ease and wisdom. Mastering uncertainty is not a rejection of science or reason but an expansion of our cognitive and spiritual horizons. It empowers leaders to see beyond the surface and tap into a wellspring of creativity and inspiration. As the world grows increasingly complex, leaders who embrace uncertainty are poised to powerfully usher in new possibilities and shape a future that transcends our reductionist past.

So, can we accept the invitation to become more comfortable with the unknown and allow ourselves to become more receptive, more intuitive, and more creative? Can we allow ourselves to be in our feminine energy? When we're in that space, we are brave and wise enough to let go of the need to look at reality only through numbers and measurements. We can let go of the need for certainty and embrace possibility even if we don't have our answers right away. Many great leaders, innovators, futurists, and technologists have found comfort in the mystical and unconventional. Maybe it's time for you to do the same and discover the deeper insights, broader strategies, and perhaps the genius that lies within you.

Emotional Mastery

Emotional mastery unfolds as a profound journey of self-discovery, a path that elevates your emotional intelligence and gracefully aligns it with your leadership aspirations. The first step involves the act of shedding protective layers, emotional blocks, and barriers—a courageous act that allows your emotions to be genuinely and deeply felt.

The next step involves understanding your own emotions—knowing what you feel, acknowledging those feelings, and giving them a name. It necessitates a deep understanding of your own emotional landscape—a skill in recognizing, articulating, and embracing the full range of your feelings. Once this intimate familiarity takes root, the bedrock of leadership is laid as you learn to adeptly navigate and regulate your emotions while judiciously shaping their expression within your relationships.

When we master our emotions, our world opens up before us. The emotions we may have deemed unsuitable or unwelcome, such as anger, fear, or shame, are no longer shackles; they cease to bind our energy and confine us to a state of contraction. Further, when we tap into feminine intelligence, we can access and alchemize these emotions. We can explore and release our resistance, ultimately manifesting a state of expansion. When we look inward, we can finally understand and explore what we truly desire. We can be honest about our longing and our dissatisfaction. We can harness our inner power and energy.

If you are dissociated from your own emotional life, there could be enormous repercussions. If you're emotionally unavailable, reactive, and controlled by unresolved trauma, then you are not leading; instead, you're unwittingly allowing your emotions to lead you. In this state, you unconsciously allow your emotions to dictate your actions and reactions, eroding the very essence of leadership.

In our attempts to shield ourselves from the discomfort of negative emotions, we inadvertently create barriers that block the experience of positive ones as well. It's akin to building a fortress around our hearts to fend off pain, only to discover that it also barricades us from the profound pleasures of genuine emotional connection and fulfillment. A wealth of research in the field of positive psychology attests to the transformative impact of positive emotions on leaders. It reveals that experiencing positive emotions not only enhances creativity, productivity, and resilience but also fortifies the very essence of effective leadership.

Are you tired of being blocked from experiencing true love, joy, and awe? Are you exhausted from being pulled into downward spirals of anxiety, which subvert your confidence, your negotiations, and your relationships? How many times have you made a bad decision because you were incongruent, not centered, or battling overwhelm or emotion? If you're emotionally fragmented, you might be able to be effective in the short term, but it will collapse at some point. You'll hit a wall, emotionally and spiritually exhausted, and need to take time out.

How much more successful could you be if you could shed decades of emotional baggage or if you were no longer needing to be numb just to survive? Having worked with hundreds of clients, both in one-on-one settings and within group contexts, I consistently saw that once people learned to stop fighting or trying to suppress their negative emotions and allowed themselves to *be* and *feel*, integration and empowerment began. With emotional blocks cleared away, with masks put away, people are more open to creativity and innovation, and they experience more clarity and vibrant, dynamic insights and breakthroughs. Real wisdom, maturity, and growth are the result.

> *It takes courage ... to endure the sharp pains of self-discovery rather than choose to take the dull pain of unconsciousness that would last the rest of our lives.*
> —Marianne Williamson, US presidential candidate and spiritual teacher

Unfortunately, our culture comes with a full set of baggage around emotionalism. In work settings especially, we are indoctrinated that emotions are a weakness, and we're encouraged not to experience or show them at all. For the sake of efficiency and productivity, we're encouraged to disconnect from ourselves—there is no time to waste on feelings. So we cut parts of ourselves off, compartmentalize, shrug things off, and elegantly don the facade of socially acceptable leadership behavior. In the meantime, any suppressed negative patterns take up space and block us from accessing the treasures of our feminine intelligence—our creative potential, authentic expression, and integrity within.

Powerful leadership—with integrity and courage at its heart—demands that we explore and integrate the wounded parts of ourselves to achieve a higher level of consciousness and experience a greater sense of wholeness.

Tools to Get Started

There are different ways to do your inner work and begin releasing the emotions, traumas, and belief systems that block you from your creative potential and your connection to your most authentic self. If you've not already begun such a journey, I urge you to find the methods that you resonate with. Here are a few I recommend for leaders:

Meditation. All the areas of mastery discussed in this chapter have to do with reconnecting with your inner self, slowing down, and cultivating mindfulness so you can engage more fully with your feminine energy. Through meditation, you become an observer of your thoughts and emotions, gaining insight into their transient nature. The practice empowers you to disentangle from the grip of relentless mental chatter, creating space for a more profound understanding of yourself. Within this mental clarity, you might just uncover priceless hidden facets of your being, such as wisdom, creativity, and intuition. For some, meditation becomes a portal to unveiling the profound essence of ourselves that is concealed beneath the ceaseless internal dialogue of the mind.

Beyond self-awareness, meditation is a potent tool for emotional regulation. It teaches you to witness your emotions without judgment, allowing you to respond to life's challenges with greater equanimity. By disarming the emotional chatter that often exacerbates stress and anxiety, meditation helps you regain control over your emotional responses, fostering resilience in the face of adversity.

Meditation has probably been the single most important reason for
whatever success I've had.
—Ray Dalio, founder of Bridgewater,
the world's largest hedge fund

Three Breaths. Some people tell me they can't meditate well or they don't have time for it, so I suggest they start with a simple practice of taking three breaths. I call it a "micro-practice" because it just takes a moment, and you can do it almost anywhere, anytime—in a meeting, in a difficult conversation, or any time you feel triggered. It simply helps you be present in those volatile, uncertain moments so you can feel your emotions instead of defaulting to suppressing and dissociating.

To do the technique, simply breathe in through the nose and out through the mouth very slowly three times. As you do so, you're pressing "pause" on your reactivity and cultivating present-moment awareness. The practice engages your sympathetic nervous system, which calms you down, allowing you to operate from a place of choice once again so you can respond better in the moment.

Body Work. Somatic (body-centered) therapies, such as yoga, tai chi, ecstatic dance, biofeedback, and Eye Movement Desensitization and Reprocessing (EMDR)—even prayer—serve as conduits for re-establishing a profound connection with our emotions through the body. This integration of body-centered approaches is rooted in embodiment theory, a framework that challenges the conventional, masculine notion of the mind as a separate entity from the body. Instead, embodiment theory emphasizes and draws on the intricate interplay between physical experiences, sensations, and movements with our cognitive processes, emotions, and perceptions. It is a deeply feminine approach.

Physical Exercise and Nutrition. Physical health is critical to our overall well-being and influences every aspect of our lives. Exercising regularly has been shown to improve many aspects of life beyond muscle strength, including mood, cognitive function, and quality of sleep. Good nutrition helps our bodies function at their best overall. Simply put, our physical health is the foundation upon which we build a vibrant and fulfilling life; it makes it possible for us to pursue our goals and passions with vigor and vitality. Leaders who solely prioritize cognitive intelligence over physical well-being (a masculine approach) *will* find themselves ill-equipped to engage in the holistic modalities necessary for effective leadership. Discovering what physical activities bring joy and fulfillment is one key to success, whether it's cardio work, weight lifting, Pilates, or even a soulful Saturday morning SoulCycle class. Find what moves your body and spirit.

Altered States of Consciousness. Psychospiritual experiences, including those achieved with the use of professionally supervised psychedelics and practices like holotropic breathwork, offer a unique avenue for individuals to embark on a profound journey of self-mastery. Altered states of consciousness have been shown to facilitate deep introspection and emotional processing, providing an opportunity to confront and heal past traumas. They can also serve to expand one's perception of time and cultivate a deep sense of presence and openness. Chapters 11 and 12 delve even deeper into this fascinating realm.

Know What You're Feeling. Be sure to develop your emotional vocabulary. Do you have words for what you feel? Practice just naming your emotions. When I asked my clients how they felt, some responded by telling me what they thought instead. Yet, feelings and thoughts are very different from each other. Notice how your feelings show up in your body. A certain amount of emotional awareness is absolutely essential to your aliveness as well as your leadership. Of course, it takes practice to get good at it, so be patient as you learn about yourself in this way.

Be Open to Change. It takes a willingness to allow yourself to be transformed in the process of learning. If you value innovation, for example, you must become friendly with patience as you allow your brain to go into flow states and be creative. If you want to express yourself confidently and authentically as you lead, you have to explore and diffuse many of the emotional blocks and triggers that keep you unfree. If you want to unleash your vulnerability, you'll have to connect with deeper parts of yourself than you've perhaps ever connected to. If you want to slay the dragons of adversity, you have to access your inner resources that allow you to navigate through uncertainty. If you want to fortify your leadership, you can allow yourself to discover the wisdom, energy, and humanity of those you are leading.

Questions for Reflection

1. To master time, what are you willing to surrender? What will you say no to?
2. Which relationships in your life would benefit from a renewed infusion of love and attention?
3. How can you cultivate a deeper connection to your spiritual intelligence to navigate uncertainty with grace and resilience?
4. Do you allow yourself to *feel*? Can you name the emotions you're feeling right now?

11

Psychedelic Leadership

Beyond the Taboo

In 1965, Stuart Brand was sitting on the roof of his house in North Beach, San Francisco, tripping on LSD, looking up at the sky, feeling a deep, visceral connection to the Earth and all of life. He had the thought that if we humans could simply see an image of the whole Earth, it could profoundly change our perspectives about ourselves and our relationship with our planet. He soon launched a vigorous campaign to get NASA to release photos of the Earth. A year later, his efforts seemed to pay off—for the first time, NASA released a photo of the Earth taken from a satellite in space. Three years later, a second photo of the Earth, dubbed "Earthrise," was released; Brand called the subject of the image "a little blue, white, green and brown jewel-like icon." No one on our planet had seen anything like it before. It was the Earth, seen through the lens of an astronaut aboard Apollo 8 as it was orbiting the Moon.[1]

Nature photographer Galen Rowell described the photo as "the most influential environmental photograph ever taken,"[2] as it depicted the Earth, floating alone in the vastness of space, exuding beauty, fragility, wonder, and magnificence—all at once. The image seemed to wake something up in people's hearts, somehow revealing how vulnerable yet interdependent we all are in our tiny world.

And it was a psychedelic experience that set these events in motion, ultimately launching an environmental movement in the United States and around the world.

Steve Jobs regarded his experiences on LSD as profound, shaping his visionary thinking. Sergey Brin, the co-founder of Google, is said to have explored magic mushrooms.[3] Billionaire philanthropist and entrepreneur Elizabeth Kotch has attributed her ability to overcome deep childhood trauma to the therapeutic effects of MDMA-assisted therapy.[4] Nobel-prize winner Francis Crick, credited for uncovering the structure of DNA with James Watson, publicly recognized how his LSD experiences influenced his scientific insights.

Psychedelics have offered many business leaders a lifeline, aiding in overcoming mental health challenges and fostering personal breakthroughs with ripple effects on their leadership values.[5] Notably, both co-founders of the Conscious Capitalism movement, Raj Sisodia and Whole Foods founder John Mackey, openly share how psychedelics shaped their vision of bringing love and healing into the business world.[6]

Further, interest in the potential applications of psychedelics has been expanding in the business world. Gwyneth Paltrow, creator of the US$250 million lifestyle brand Goop, hosted her employees on a team-building retreat centered around psilocybin, the "magic" ingredient in psychoactive mushrooms.[7] Echoing this trend, *The Economist* reports a notable uptick in corporate leaders who are integrating psychedelics into their companies' wellness programs.[8] Among them is David Bronner, CEO of Dr. Bronner's Magic Soap, who champions the inclusion of ketamine-assisted therapy in employee mental health benefits.[9] Meanwhile, media outlets like *Time Magazine, Business Insider, The Wall Street Journal, The New York Times,* and many more report on leaders who utilize psychedelics to enhance their lives, deepen the human experience, and generate business breakthroughs with positive global impact.

> *Taking LSD was a profound experience, one of the most important things in my life . . . it reinforced my sense of what was important—*

> *creating great things instead of making money, putting things back into the stream of history and of human consciousness as much as I could.*
> —*Steve Jobs*

In 2022, the World Economic Forum (WEF) in Davos, where power players gather to more or less decide the fate of the world, hosted a Medical Psychedelics House. The program was designed to facilitate a dialogue among scientists, scholars, and global leaders about the future of psychedelics. Leading academic institutions are delving into psychedelics' transformative potential as well, underscoring their emerging significance in business leadership. "There's a need for new and innovative solutions to increasingly complex systemic problems, and organizations are calling for leaders with more connectedness, self-awareness, compassion, and empathy, and psychedelics may indeed have an increasing role to play," notes the *MIT Sloan Management Review.*[10]

These narratives are more than compelling; they're a testament to the profound power of psychedelics, which have been recognized for millennia by diverse cultures and ancient civilizations around the world.[11] Yet it's only in recent decades that the Western world has begun to appreciate the capacity of these substances to challenge outdated concepts and assumptions and introduce new perspectives on business, politics, and social structures. When engaged with safely and intentionally, psychedelics can catalyze life-altering insights, enhance our connection with the natural world and one another, and rekindle our sense of the Divine. They can deepen our understanding of feminine intelligence, as feminine consciousness is embodied in these altered states. As we navigate the psychedelic landscape with wisdom, respect, and inclusivity, we stand poised to harness the transformative insights from psychedelic experiences to catalyze a new era of enlightened leadership.

A Brief History

Long before modern leaders discovered their transformative powers, psychedelics had been charting the course of human consciousness. The very word "psychedelic" harkens back to ancient Greece, when the word loosely meant "mind-manifesting," and it's there that we find the echoes of these substances' storied history. Greek luminaries once sought clarity and connection through the Eleusinian Mysteries, an ornate nine-day ritual in which the potion "kykeon," which was believed to be made from ergot, a key ingredient in LSD, was consumed in rites that promised divine inspiration.[12] The ceremonies sparked pivotal experiences that influenced many great thinkers of the era, including Plato and Cicero, perhaps even molding the bedrock of Western thought.

Psychedelic substances have been woven into rituals and traditions across myriad cultures and continents worldwide. In the Americas, shamans from Indigenous communities communed with the Divine through sacred plant medicines, including hallucinogenic mushrooms and ayahuasca, while in the ancient Vedic practices of India, soma was imbibed to transcend the mundane. Every practice across the globe, whether it was in the rituals of African tribes or among the shamans of Siberia, was a testament to the human desire to explore the depths of the psyche and connect with a greater reality.

> *For among the many excellent and indeed divine institutions which your Athens has brought forth and contributed to human life, none, in my opinion, is better than those mysteries . . . In [them], we perceive the real principles of life.*
> *—Marcus Tullius Cicero*

But as our modern, masculine-dominant Western culture took root over the past millennia, these native rituals were largely considered foreign and uncivilized—merely meaningless remnants of inferior cultures. As the focus on the separation between church and state, religious dogmas, and scientific materialism proliferated, they were misunderstood, criminalized, and shunted to the sidelines. Ignorant of—and, more likely, threatened by—their power, Western cultures judged and ultimately suppressed them.

Despite its ignorance, the West inadvertently synthesized the potent substances central to these ancient practices, initially through serendipity, not intent. While researching stimulants for circulation at Sandoz Laboratories in 1938, Albert Hoffmann synthesized LSD for the first time. In 1948, he accidentally ingested some of the substance and had the first known LSD trip.

In 1955 Maria Sabina, a Mexican "*curandera*" or traditional healer, played a pivotal role in facilitating the Western world's awareness of psilocybin mushrooms through her healing work on ethnomycologists Valentina and Gordon Wasson. The Wassons' mystical experiences with Sabina were later published in *Life Magazine* in 1957, detailing their experiences with her in Mexico.[13] In the 1960s, LSD and psilocybin mushrooms burst into the mainstream, igniting a cultural and scientific revolution. Harvard University's Psilocybin Project was at the forefront of research into their therapeutic applications. Harvard's team, among other leading academic institutions, explored the therapeutic potential of psychedelics in treating mental health issues, contributing to a promising but short-lived wave of research. Concurrently, therapists outside university settings were also starting to use psychedelics in their work and witnessing profound breakthroughs in patient outcomes, further inspiring scientific inquiry into their efficacy.

As awareness of psychedelics blossomed in the psyche of the United States and the United Kingdom, backlash followed. Shocked by the widespread popularity of the substances and the anti-war and anti-establishment sentiments and social unrest that were associated with them, those in power pushed back. Timothy Leary, a Harvard psychologist, emerged as a prominent advocate for psychedelics and consciousness expansion. He was famously tagged "the most dangerous man in America" by President Nixon for his advocacy and his rallying cry that caught the United States' attention: "Turn on. Tune in. Drop out."

Leary's outspoken, nonconformist views led to fear and retaliation from authorities. At that time, scientific research into psychedelics was still in its infancy, and facts to help shed light on the subject were few and far between. In the meantime, the media was pumping out negative portrayals of psychedelic experiences, exacerbating the public's fear and misunderstanding.

> *Part of what psychedelics do is they decondition you from cultural values. This is what makes it such a political hot potato. Since all culture is a kind of con game, the most dangerous candy you can hand out is one which causes people to start questioning the rules of the game.*
> —*Terence McKenna, ethnobotanist and mystic*

As a result, government authorities stepped in. Under the Controlled Substances Act (CSA) of 1970, the Drug Enforcement Administration (DEA) classified LSD, psilocybin, and other psychedelics as Schedule I substances, characterizing them as having "no currently accepted medical use" and a "high potential for abuse and the potential to create severe psychological and/or physical dependence."

In the wake of the DEA's actions, other governments followed suit. The US' diplomatic and economic influence and its vigorous "War on Drugs" campaign fueled a widespread international consensus that rendered the manufacture, distribution, and use of psychedelics illegal around the world. Subsequently, scientific research into psychedelics was effectively halted as stringent regulations and the stigma associated with Schedule I classification created insurmountable barriers to the study of their substances and their potential benefits.

It's noteworthy that MDMA, commonly known as "ecstasy" or "molly," didn't enter the public consciousness until the 1980s, and it did so largely through underground psychotherapy circles. Initially synthesized in 1912 by Merck, a German pharmaceutical company, for use in a medication to control bleeding, it wasn't until the 1970s that MDMA's psychoactive effects began to get attention as a focus of research. Alexander Shulgin, the US chemist and pharmacologist, synthesized the compound again, self-administered it, and documented its effects, earning him the moniker "Dr. Ecstasy" by the *New York Times*. But the DEA soon stepped in. In 1985, recognizing its growing popularity and potential for abuse, the DEA swiftly classified MDMA as a Schedule I substance, mirroring the earlier restrictions placed on other psychedelics.[14]

This is a tremendous and deeply regrettable loss.

Here's the truth of the matter. Contrary to the widespread misinformation and alarmist propaganda, a substantial body of scientific research has now demonstrated that, with appropriate protocols and practices in place, psychedelics are generally safe, and instances of harm are extremely rare.[15] In fact, research shows that alcohol[16] (and horseback riding!)[17] far surpasses all psychoactive drugs in terms of its potential for harm.

But psychedelics do open people's minds to new and higher perceptions, prompting them to rethink their conditioned paradigms and assumptions—and that can be tremendously threatening to those who maintain the social/political order.

At the same time, this awakening can uncover the feminine intelligence within us, an untapped capacity to see beyond conventional boundaries. This kind of intelligence is uniquely valuable when it comes to forging new paths for leadership. To have a means to open our minds and re-evaluate our cultural values and principles of capitalism in the spirit of wholeness and solution can empower and embolden our leadership like never before.

> *Psychedelics are upstream from every other issue. It's how you get people to really heal on a deep level, connect to nature, to their authentic self, to each other, and to start grappling with the huge environmental and social crises we're confronting.*
> —David Bronner, CEO of Bronner Soaps

The Psychedelic Renaissance

In the 1990s and early 2000s, scientists began to revisit psychedelics research from the 1950s and 1960s. In 2000, a research group at Johns Hopkins University led by Roland Griffiths, PhD, obtained regulatory approval in the United States to resume research with psychedelics. In 2006, Griffiths released a landmark study on the safety and enduring positive effects of a single dose of psilocybin, which soon inspired a renewal of psychedelic research worldwide.[18] The research team reported that 67% of participants rated their experience as either the most meaningful experience in their lives or among their top five.

Today, we're experiencing what many are calling a "psychedelic renaissance"—a new medicalized and science-driven wave of thinking about psychedelics' use, primarily for mental health. Clinical studies have shown promising results in the treatment of mental health conditions such as depression, anxiety, and post-traumatic stress disorder (PTSD). The promising results led the Food and Drug Administration (FDA) to designate "breakthrough therapy" status for MDMA to address PTSD in 2017 and, in 2018, for psilocybin to target depression. And, the 2018 publication of *How to Change Your Mind: What the New Science of Psychedelics Teaches Us About Consciousness, Dying, Addiction, Depression, and Transcendence* by influential journalist, Michael Pollan, and the subsequent Netflix documentary, led to a huge rise in social, cultural, and even recreational interest in the main-stream West.

The resurgence of psychedelic research owes much to Dr. Robin Carhart-Harris, who has shown the neurological effects of psychedelics through brain imaging studies. Trial participants would get a CT scan while they were tripping on LSD or psilocybin. Equally influential is Rick Doblin, PhD, founder and president of the Multidisciplinary Association for Psychedelic Studies (MAPS). In the 1960s, well before MDMA was sched-uled, Doblin recognized the therapeutic potential of MDMA, and his work has been instrumental in steering clinical trials that ultimately demonstrated the substance's efficacy in treating PTSD. Thanks to his groundbreaking efforts, MDMA-assisted therapy was considered for FDA approval for PTSD therapy in 2024, a historic step that would have prompted a reconsideration of its Schedule I status. Unfortunately, the FDA rejected approval in the summer of 2024 citing concerns about research methods and data integrity, and requesting an additional clinical trial to support the therapy's efficacy and safety.

Despite these setbacks, MAPS continues to lead in research and devel-opment, having crafted supportive and structured guidelines to harness the full potential of these powerful substances. Having been trained in the MAPS protocols, I have witnessed the imperative of effective preparation for a psychedelic session, often undertaken weeks or months in advance to ensure a positive and constructive experience. I've also seen the potential disasters that can occur without them.

Ideally, preparation is done ethically, respectfully, and with conscious intention. It includes a discussion of any potential risks, helps to establish an alliance and rapport between therapist and client, highlights unresolved emotional problems that may arise while under the medicine, and cultivates a mindset conducive to introspection. Establishing supportive conditions, known as "set and setting," is of paramount importance. "Set" encompasses the client's mindset, intentions for, and attitude about the impending medi-cine experience, while "setting" involves the physical and social environ-ment. Lastly, a thoughtful integration plan is critical for safely and meaningfully incorporating psychedelic insights into one's life.[19] The importance of this cannot be understated.

As research into psychedelics expands, they have been gaining accept-ance in legal arenas around the world as well. In 2023, Australia approved

MDMA and psilocybin to treat PTSD and treatment-resistant depression, respectively. Numerous other jurisdictions, including Switzerland, Austria, and Portugal, are legalizing and/or decriminalizing psychedelic substances to treat certain medical conditions. Canada has provided exceptions for legal use of psychedelics in particular religious contexts. Oregon is the first state in the United States to create a regulatory framework for psilocybin services, with Colorado, Washington DC, and parts of California following suit in various ways—some even decriminalizing possession for personal use altogether. And ketamine is legally available in medical settings (and "off-label" for some mental health treatments) in the United States, Canada, Australia, and parts of Europe.

In the Netherlands, psilocybin-containing truffles have been legal for some time, but the mushrooms have not, and are used recreationally, ceremonially, and in various contexts—including solo experiences, one-on-one facilitation, and increasingly popular group "psychedelic retreats." This growing acceptance not only bolsters the legitimacy of psychedelics; it also acts as a catalyst, dismantling barriers to access. Such changes have the potential to shape the trajectory of our future leaders.

Every "renaissance" has a dark underbelly that comes with risks of its own. If psychedelics were to be used erratically and irresponsibly, they could inadvertently give rise to what Chögyam Trungpa Rinpoche coined as "spiritual materialism" and what others might call "spiritual bypassing." In this context, wannabe "psychonauts"—explorers of altered states—might misuse sacred experiences for self-aggrandizement or personal gain of power or money, leading to a distorted form of spirituality. We see this manifesting as self-declared shamans or spiritual gurus exploit the mystical for their personal narratives, taking practices to absurd extremes. This pursuit of "enlightenment" can devolve into narcissism, where the focus shifts from genuine spiritual and personal growth to the external validation of one's perceived spiritual prowess. Such behavior perpetuates a superficial and distorted understanding of the transformative power of psychedelics, ultimately undermining the potential for authentic growth and collective transformation.

But there is a way to embrace psychedelics with respect, thoughtfulness, and elegance. There is a potential with these medicines for big shifts in short periods of time. While access to powerful states of consciousness can also be achieved through meditation, breathwork, movement, and even silence, these alternatives demand a lot of time, commitment, and resources—factors often challenging to ask for from the broader population. So, let's explore how we can use pharmacology for personal and collective progress.

Psychedelics to Transform Leadership

Through a temporary doorway into a fantastical dreamscape, we can become more open, curious, and comfortable with uncertainty. At the fringes of ordinary perception and conventional understanding, we can gain access to profound truths within ourselves about our very existence and reason for being. These priceless insights can supercharge our capacity for leadership by unlocking our feminine intelligence. Furthermore, we don't even need to completely detach from the external world to incorporate the wisdom from these experiences into our everyday consciousness. Their very nature is to open the doors of our perception, shift our worldviews, and discard old filters for us, allowing us to reclaim our inherent connection with ourselves, our planet, and our future. They allow us to see more clearly and take action more consciously and more powerfully, so that we may amplify impact.

The potential of psychedelics to reshape personal paradigms, uproot assumptions, and transform leadership values and behaviors represents a bold frontier for societal change. By prompting us to question our conventional understanding of our relationship to all of our ecosystems—natural, economic, business, and social—these catalyzing substances offer us a viable path to a more empathetic, inclusive, and purpose-driven world.

> *What if, through responsible exploration with psychedelics, we free our minds? Free-thinkers are more difficult to manipulate and control, which begs the question: Why are psychedelics illegal?*
> *—Zoe Helene, originator of "psychedelic feminism"*

While psychedelics offer great potential for personal enlightenment, they also promise a feast of invaluable skills that can guide and empower leadership mastery. A critical review of 77 studies by the MIND Foundation suggests that experiences with psychedelics can lead to increases in empathy, cognitive flexibility, creativity, openness, nature-relatedness, spirituality, and self-transcendence, among others—all critical to leadership mastery.[20] From the ability to disrupt mental patterns and spark novel perspectives to embodying an expanded sense of empathy and a more intimate connection to nature—the gifts of psychedelics become superpowers for leaders who want to make a lasting impact in the world through their organizations.

Leaders who engage with psychedelics might begin to view their organizations less and less as profit-generating machines and more as living, evolving entities contributing to the betterment of society. They might aspire to foster a culture that values shared purpose and collective thriving over competition and individual gain and build a better, more sustainable future.

There's no doubt that business and cultural leaders using psychedelics might be an unconventional, eyebrow-raising proposition for some, particularly within more traditional circles. However, as the business landscape and world economies become increasingly complex, variable, and volatile, there's never been a more urgent need for leaders to unlock the profound resources within us to help us address and command the challenges and opportunities before us.

Essentially, if more leaders of our communities and organizations were to safely and intentionally engage in psychedelics, they could pave the way for a more conscious and sustainable economic model—a model that prioritizes mutual growth and societal well-being over unchecked competition and exploitation, fostering a healthier and more balanced relationship with our planet, our communities, and our future.

New research studies of enterprise leadership are beginning to emerge. Dillfuzi "Daphne" Wusiman, in collaboration with the Evolute Institute, spearheaded a groundbreaking initiative in 2023 involving a retreat for nine business leaders. Her aim was to rigorously test a three-month developmental program featuring a psychedelic experience with psilocybin-containing truffles.[21] Once she began delving into her research findings, she found that results demonstrated the program's capacity to profoundly impact one's leadership mindset, giving participants heightened empathy, increased self-awareness, and a more holistic approach to decision-making.[22]

Dr. Rachelle Sampson and Dr. Bennet Zelner, faculty at the University of Maryland's Smith School of Business, initiated the Connectedness Leadership Study, a novel research investigation of the impact of psychedelic-assisted, consciousness-expanding experiences on leadership practices and decision-making. With this work, Sampson and Zelner hoped to observe the translation of transformative personal experiences into tangible shifts in business practices and systemic change.[23]

Comprehensive studies of the impact of psychedelics on leadership are absolutely critical in our perilous and volatile times, times that are calling out for bold, creative leadership born from wholeness.

> *[Psychedelics] could decondition us from the cultural values that are making us so sick by reconnecting us not just to ourselves and one another, but to that which we have distorted in our hyper-individualistic, blindly consuming culture: the sacred.*
> —*Alexander Beiner in* The Bigger Picture: How Psychedelics Can Help Us Make Sense of the World

PowerTripp

Even as psychedelics gain more acceptance and applications in arenas beyond the medical model, we have to be honest with ourselves about the risk we face—that their unique gifts will be commodified and commercialized in the context of the relentless hunger of our current capitalist paradigm. What can happen when transformative experiences meet capitalist market forces? What can happen if feminine intelligence values are not integrated into our commercial, profit-prioritized culture? If these sacred plants and psychoactive compounds are adopted by the corporate culture in an extractive way and promoted only as mental health drugs and optimization-wielding tools, we will lose the narrative around psychedelics being agents of a new social order. Mental health is a valuable application for the healing qualities of psychedelics. Opening minds to greater creativity, empathy, and focus can help people function better. Yet, we can't shut ourselves off from the mystical, the sacred, and the flowering of the feminine that these psychoactive substances so generously offer. As Indigenous peoples have demonstrated for centuries, we need to respect the medicine, or we lose the heart of the gift we're being given.

Let's not strip the sacred practices of their profound teachings by relegating them to serve as tools that perpetuate the current paradigm. We don't just want to be more creative and optimized—we want to reap the wisdom, deepen our connection to our inner superpowers, absorb the higher awareness offered, and integrate these shifts to help us transform our business and our world. The opportunity is clear. With the help of psychedelics, we can dramatically shift our culture, values, and principles away from shareholder primacy capitalism, domination of resources, and self-centered interests toward a prosperous, sustainable, and healthy global landscape.

Yet capitalism has a way of taking the things that threaten the existing power structure and disassembling, recontextualizing, and repackaging them into forms that don't upset the status quo. It has repeatedly taken innovative solutions and reshaped them to fit into the existing capitalistic machine in order to keep money flowing into the usual pockets—and keep those in power in power. By cheapening and commodifying what has been sacred or transformative, opportunities for change and awakening are decimated. If the media and corporate powers control the narrative around the use of psychedelics, how long will it be before Big Pharma extracts the active molecular structures in these substances and packages them for their own incentive structures—turning us into Prozac Nation 2.0? It becomes one more prescription; it becomes integrated into our existing dysfunctional system. As soon as it's one more cog in the wheel of capitalism, we simply fall back into our same routines, and we don't have the kind of awakenings that allow us to shift to a different way of life.

> *We need to act with caution as the gold rush blows over from cannabis to the psychedelics.*
> —*Amanda Feilding, founder of the Beckley Foundation*

To be clear, I love optimizing my skills and pushing the envelope of my mental, emotional, and spiritual wellness in the world. But there's a difference between optimizing ourselves so we can reconnect to love and be of service in the world and hacking our psychophysiology to be able to work more hours, be more efficient, and boost our creativity so we can beat the competition. The latter is right in line with the medical model—treating isolated symptoms piecemeal and ignoring our wholeness. Such an approach overlooks the pervasive sense of alienation induced by living in an extractive capitalist system, wherein our mental health crisis is fundamentally rooted in disconnection from self and spirit. There is a dissonance between reaching nirvana and navigating the structures that govern our everyday lives.

Profit-hungry drug companies impose restrictive contracts and patents to prevent their discoveries from entering the public domain. To maximize gains, costs are minimized, usually meaning that expensive and time-consuming therapeutic support and integration mechanisms are dismantled, less-qualified, less-costly workers are employed, corners are cut wherever possible, and best practices disintegrate. As business executives bring psychedelics into the meta context of capitalism, they're missing what's really of value. In order to make a meaningful impact on the world's economic ecosystem and solve some of the world's biggest problems, we need to not just fix some of our parts and be new-and-improved cogs in the great unconscious wheel of capitalism; we need to fortify the best version of ourselves so we can truly be of service and in harmony with our world.

As leaders of enterprises, our decisions have profound effects on the world. When we choose to elevate our consciousness, open our doors of perception, and reconnect with that vital, essential part of our humanity— our feminine intelligence—we will naturally create a more conscious, empathetic, beneficent world around us.

There's no question that safe and intentional experiences with psychedelics can help us shift the existing centuries-old paradigm and that a conscious business model is possible to ensure innovation, attract new participants, and create standards of safety. These substances, if treated appropriately, can help us remove obstacles that have long held us back from upgrading ourselves and becoming the conscious leaders we want to be. The opportunity is to innovate technologies that move the world forward, to have creative insights that can inspire new questions, and to create new paradigms for what is possible. Psychedelics may just be the "medicines" we need to heal our broken capitalistic models—and in the process, we may just heal ourselves.

Questions for Reflection

1. How might a safe, legal, and intentional psychedelic experience change your life?
2. Research shows that with appropriate preparation and safeguards, psychedelics can enhance creativity, empathy, and overall well-being in

the workplace. How do you think such practices might influence conventional ideas of corporate culture?

3. How can we safeguard the integrity of the practice of using psychedelics, preventing them from succumbing to commercialization and capitalist market pressures?

12 | Seeds of Conscious Leadership

The Earth Spoke, and I Listened

I sat with my guide on the bare ground. She had brought a jar of dried "Hawaiians" with her—beautiful mushrooms that look a lot like the young portobello mushrooms you find in the grocery store. She encouraged me to pick out a few, so I slowly and carefully selected the ones that spoke to me, ones that somehow seemed to have a wise and enchanting vibe. While they didn't taste great, they were chewy, earthy, and surprisingly pleasing to eat.

I sat and waited, quietly staring at the soft blue sky above. After about 30 minutes, I turned my eyes to the Earth and watched in awe as I saw her moving. She was alive—and she was breathing. Wanting to get closer, I laid my whole body down and soon found myself sobbing. In that one singular yet infinite moment, I was deeply aware of the Earth's nurturing spirit and felt wrapped in her limitless love. At the same time, I began to feel what *she* was feeling. I felt her strength, her vitality, and, paradoxically, her vulnerability. I felt her disappointment about the way she was treated. Then, unexpectedly, I felt the full weight of her grief and her simmering rage.

A torrent of emotion overwhelmed me, and I dissolved into more tears. I felt in tune with Earth's breath; it was an ethereal connection that transcends conventional understanding. I felt the palpitations of the ground; I resonated with her rhythms; her gentle ebb and flow echoed within me. Her powerful pulsation, akin to a silent whisper of the planet, was a testament to her living essence. Each inhalation was a manifestation of life's vibrancy; each exhalation was an affirmation of relentless resilience.

The experience was both heartbreaking and enlightening. It shook me to my core yet filled me with a profound awareness of the bond we share with our planet. It was a poignant reminder of the interconnectedness of all life forms, of our collective responsibility to safeguard our celestial home, and of the urgency with which we need to act to mend our strained relationship with her. (And she really is our Mother.)

Then, a strange and unbidden thought came into my mind. As a rule, I rarely think about my formal legal education and the years I spent working as a corporate lawyer. But as I sat with the Earth in timeless time, I had a thought that seemed to be whispered into my mind by some external force.

It struck me that real change won't be realized until we dismantle some of our deeply ingrained assumptions around property laws. Our legal framework needs to be systemically realigned so that it honors and upholds the premise that the Earth has a life, a spirit, and a life force. She, too, must be granted a voice on the legal world stage.

> *You think you own whatever land you land on. The Earth is just a dead thing you can claim. But I know every rock and tree and creature has a life, has a spirit, has a name.*
> —*Pocahontas in* Colors of the Wind

That is precisely the work being carried out by the Earth Law Center (ELC), the nonprofit I mentioned in Chapter 3, which works on a global scale to give more robust legal protections to natural bodies, such as rivers, forests, and species around the world. Its work isn't just about passive appreciation for nature's beauty or utility; it's about active stewardship and a legal acknowledgment that the Earth has its own voice and agency.

Upon hearing her whisper, it was as if a door opened, beckoning me forward, inviting me to make a powerful difference, to serve authentically, and to bring my expertise and my open heart to a greater purpose. It wasn't enough to just take care of the recycling bin anymore. This was a calling to be personally involved in the cause in the most authentic way and to connect ever more deeply with my own roots.

Working with, and advocating for, ELC is the practical integration of my spiritual expansion. The real message of psychedelic leadership is that everyone has the potential to contribute authentically should they dare to open their heart to their unique calling.

Nature Mother

Since the advent of civilization, our relationship with the natural world has been a ragged one, chiefly consisting of a struggle for survival and/or dominion. Over the centuries, we have developed technologies and systems that make us less vulnerable, hoping to shield ourselves from the uncertainties of the natural world. Thus, the narrative of dominance, control, and extraction took hold, and we allowed ourselves to view nature simply as an adversary to be conquered and a resource to be exploited.

Today, our legal and economic systems reflect this perspective. Land ownership, for instance, reinforces the idea of nature as an object owned and controlled by humans. Similarly, our economic models often treat nature as an externality—something outside the system that can be freely used or impacted without cost. But, to our surprise, with the compelling emergence of environmental crises such as climate change and biodiversity loss, we are beginning to realize the costs of objectifying nature and relating to it only as a resource to be exploited.

Yet, psychedelics can help us fall back in love with nature. For many, the perception of separation temporarily dissolves, revealing nature's vibrant aliveness, and we feel unshakably and inextricably intertwined with it. We're not separate; what's outside us isn't just one more "other" in our life experience. There is a brotherhood, a sisterhood, a kinship of aliveness.

Psychedelics can transform our relationship with the land. It is no longer based on ownership. It's no longer informed by the media's distant threats, nor is it buried within complex scientific analyses. Instead, our relationship with nature becomes a palpable, personal, pulsating experience that infuses us with an undeniable sense of responsibility and care. What was abstract is now intimate; our cerebral understanding of the necessity to care for our planet blossoms into a visceral, resonant, and abiding personal call to stewardship.

> *What happens when we forget the smell of the sea, the feel of the grass, the bite of the wind on our cheeks? When we fall out of love with nature, we can bear its destruction. When we destroy our own home, on some level, do we fall out of love with ourselves?*
> —*Dr. Sam Gandy in* From Egoism to Ecoism: Psychedelics and Nature Connection, TEDxOxford

With the shift in consciousness that often accompanies psychedelic experiences, we can discover that the sense of dominion that we've capitalized on for millennia has simply stemmed from an age-old reductionist, masculine mentality; it is a human construct that obscures a genuine, restorative, and even joyful interconnectedness we have with the entire natural world.

Research backs this up, showing that those who use psychedelics tend to have increased concern for the environment.[1] A survey conducted among 150 psychedelic users indicated a universal increase in their feelings of connection with nature following their psychedelic experiences.[2] Notably, 16% even pivoted careers toward more environmentally focused roles. Psilocybin mushrooms, especially, were most commonly linked with an increased affinity for nature and environmental concerns.[3] In a consolidated analysis of eight studies, 38% of participants reported lasting positive changes in their relationship to the environment months after their psilocybin experiences.[4]

Think about the value of this. When you recognize that you are but a small part of a vast and interconnected cosmos, you are more likely to approach your role with a sense of reverence and respect for all forms of life. Such humility can lead to sustainable and regenerative leadership practices that prioritize the well-being of not just the organization but also the broader ecosystem.

Imagine seeking ways to honor your responsibility as a leader. Imagine awakening to your desire to leave the world better than how you found it. Being the change with clarity, passion, and creative thinking. Having the courage to reinvent the way you approach choices that bear on the natural world. Witnessing your vision become more animated, focused, and resolute as it gets sourced from a deeper and more authentic place in you.

Until we have these kinds of breakthroughs in consciousness, those of us who are aligned with the values of and aware of the necessity for corporate environmental, social, and governance (ESG) and corporate social responsibility (CSR) initiatives have to rely on our get-it-done, masculine intelligence to check the checkboxes. Unfortunately, that's a dreary and frustrating process that often overshadows how imperative the effort is. Worse, the practice can turn robotic and generate disconnection and resentment in those tasked with its care. This is because when the spirit of these efforts is reduced to mere formalities, they lose their meaning, leaving many disillusioned and disempowered.

> *And into the forest I go. To lose my mind and find my soul.*
> —*John Muir, founder and first president of The Sierra Club*

Genuine transformation can occur when we experience a direct and existential connection with the natural world, which is an awakening of our feminine intelligence. Such a connection transcends bureaucratic drudgery, and the sacrifices we make—whether they be time, resources, convenience, or immediate profits—feel not only meaningful but imperative. It's then that we move beyond mere compliance to embrace actions that genuinely honor and rejuvenate the natural world.

The Creative Spark

The creative force in us is what makes us uniquely human. It's an essential cognitive ability that has allowed us to express ourselves, innovate, and birth civilizations. Today, more than ever before, leaders must be able to think creatively, generate creative vision, lead creative teams, and embark upon creative solutions. In today's world of lightning-fast change and impending crises, bold imagination and innovative vision are urgently needed to solve complex problems.

> *The billionaires I know, almost without exception, use hallucinogens on a regular basis. [They're] trying to be very disruptive and look at the problems in the world . . . and ask completely new questions.*
> —*Tim Ferris, psychedelics investor, author*

In fact, certain forms of psychedelics can provide a huge, qualitative boost to creative potential. Researchers from Imperial College London found that these mind-altering substances create a "more unified brain" through new neural connections[5] and can induce a "flexible brain state" or a state of "unconstrained cognition."[6] This means that under the influence of psychedelics, rigid thought patterns take a backseat and pave the way for unguided, spontaneous thoughts to come to the surface. That, in turn, frequently leads to novel insights, perspectives, and solutions to problems that have not yet been explored.[7]

A fascinating 2021 study revealed that psilocybin increases spontaneous creative insights and sparks novel ideas.[8] And, researchers at Johns Hopkins University discovered that psychedelic-assisted psychotherapy can enhance cognitive flexibility, helping patients with anxiety and depression—conditions often linked to rigid thinking—experience significant improvements in their symptoms.

> *A lot of people have been pointing out that the modern world is in crisis . . . and . . . it takes significant cognitive flexibility to solve complex problems. So, I think all this research is timely. It's making us a little less afraid of a powerful problem-solving tool. Going forward, I have a hunch that's going to matter.*
> *—Robin Carhart-Harris, PhD, former head of Imperial Psychedelic Research Group and Director of Psychedelics Division, Neuroscape, UCSF*

Psychedelics help promote "lateral thinking," a term coined in the 1960s by Edward de Bono to describe a creative thinking and problem-solving technique that approaches problems and quandaries from unconventional angles and perspectives. It stands in contrast to "vertical thinking," the traditional, logical tactic for problem-solving. Instead, lateral thinking can artfully engage unrelated ideas with a great tolerance for ambiguity and paradox. As an intuitive and collaborative approach to problem-solving, it reflects the essence of feminine intelligence in creativity.

Psychedelics also help us tap into the enigmatic "flow" state, that exhilarating feeling when you're fully immersed and focused, losing track of time as everything else disappears. Flow is experienced as a state of optimal functioning, heightened concentration, complete absorption in the task at hand, and a super-human connection to one's surroundings. Flow often sparks creative insights and innovative thinking, making it a priceless state for solving the world's biggest problems. Yet, while pro athletes, musicians, and artists effortlessly access this state, many business leaders grapple with finding it.

The mystery of "flow" has been under the scientific microscope for over half a century, dating back to the 1970s when Mihaly Csikszentmihalyi, a pioneer in positive psychology, first investigated it. Steven Kotler and Jamie Wheal not only elevated Csikszentmihalyi's work in their book, *Stealing Fire: How Silicon Valley, the Navy SEALs, and Maverick Scientists Are Revolutionizing the Way We Live and Work,* but also spearheaded the Flow Genome Project. This initiative studies the relationship between peak performance and altered states. The conclusion of their research was clear: Visionary leaders regularly access flow states. This heightened state of awareness, perception, and cognitive functioning directly influences tangible and measurable outcomes, particularly in the realm of innovation.

Many complex brain functions are involved in the facilitation of flow states by psychedelics, particularly through the induction of "hypofrontality"—a temporary reduction in activity in the prefrontal cortex, the brain's hub for high-level cognitive functions. As revealed by research from Imperial College London's Robin Carhart-Harris, psychedelics appear to facilitate this process by disintegrating entire neural networks, especially the default mode network (DMN).[9]

The DMN is active during unfocused states and is linked to self-referential thinking, mind-wandering, and introspection. An overactive DMN results in what some call the "monkey mind," a restless and uncontrollable stream of thoughts that hinder presence and focus. Psychedelics, along with other consciousness-altering practices like breathwork and meditation, have the ability to disintegrate the DMN network temporarily, allowing us to focus and tap into our creative potential.

What if I had not taken LSD ever; would I have still invented PCR? I don't know. I seriously doubt it.
—Kary Mullis, Nobel Prize-winning inventor of the polymerase chain reaction (PCR) process

Importantly, research into the effects of psychedelics on creativity within the leadership arena is shifting to "microdosing." The term refers to taking a very small, "sub-perceptual" amount of a psychedelic substance, typically about one-tenth to one-twentieth of an active full dose. These small doses typically won't produce the full psychedelic effects—the raindrops won't shimmer, and the flowers won't dance. But anecdotal evidence suggests they can result in subtle enhancements of creativity, mood, focus, and productivity—one could say a "psychovitamin."

> *My aim was to hit that 'sweet spot', where vitality and creativity are enhanced, while leaving me in control of my concentration. It was, in a way, comparable to what people are doing today with microdosing.*
> —*Amanda Feilding, founder of the Beckley Foundation*

Microdosing has gained popularity in corporate and startup cultures since around 2015, especially among those looking to boost mental performance and reduce day-to-day anxiety without experiencing the intense effects typically associated with a full psychedelic experience.[10]

Many entrepreneurs claim to have birthed ideas for new companies while microdosing, affirming its potential as a catalyst for creative innovation. And several candid business leaders now speak publicly about the role microdosing plays in their professional lives, undeterred by the legal restrictions prevalent in most areas. These accounts can be found across many platforms, including notable features like *The Wall Street Journal*'s article "Magic Mushrooms, LSD, Ketamine: The Drugs That Power Silicon Valley," which illustrates the intertwining of psychedelics and entrepreneurship in today's landscape.

Peer-reviewed research on psychedelic microdosing is still scarce; however, countless blogs, online forums, and slack channels are overflowing with discussions about the practice.[11] These platforms offer detailed guides and share personal stories about the effects and experiences of microdosing. Despite the limited scientific consensus, some research suggests that microdosing plays a crucial role in neuroplasticity, the brain's ability to reorganize itself by forming new neural connections, which, in turn, supports creativity by enabling the brain to make diverse connections between different regions and ideas.[12] Thus, further research into the benefits, potentials for abuse, and applications for leadership is timelier than ever. As the concept gains traction, psychedelics could very likely be the new coffee.

Connection with Others

In 2021, a group of Palestinians and Israelis came together for a novel purpose—to participate in an ayahuasca ceremony together. "Suddenly, you hear the language you most hated, and suddenly it is sending you into love and light," said an Israeli participant after listening to his Arab counterpart. Astonishingly, the things that would have historically triggered intense hatred and anger sowed love and access to universal truth. One Palestinian soldier experienced himself as a Jewish soldier and felt his pain. One of the Jewish soldiers re-experienced an event he'd endured from the perspective of a Palestinian. The medicine shifted their rigid narratives and created a sustainable, personal web of empathetic connections, laying the groundwork for profound sympathy and even capacities for peace-building.[13]

Research demonstrates that psychedelic substances increase empathy, an essential component of the mastery of relationships—part of the TRUE model—and one of the superpowers of conscious leadership.[14]

> *Feminine consciousness, when intermingled with psychedelic knowledge, carries and reveals the essence of inclusivity, interconnectedness, and balance.*
> —*Maria Papaspyrou, Chiara Baldini, and David Luke in* Psychedelic Mysteries of the Feminine

In particular, empathy is often talked about, but in practice, it is undervalued as a quality of conscious leadership. Empathetic leaders are able to unlock a genuine sense of motivation, drive, and passion in those they lead. It helps them elevate performance in others and cultivates a culture of belonging—two priceless qualities for those in leadership positions. Yet, in our day and age, the leaders who truly exhibit empathy are few and far between. Empathy is a rich expression of feminine consciousness and emotional intelligence and is often overlooked and undervalued in our capitalistic culture of competition, domination, and zero-sum gaming. So, how can we increase empathy in our leaders?

When it comes to empathy training in leadership development settings in organizations, the focus is predominantly on cognitive empathy—that is, being at least intellectually aware of another's plight. However, with cognitive empathy, we can still cut ourselves off from feeling another person's humanity. It is not a qualitative shift. On the other hand, it is emotional empathy that is truly transformative. That is when we have the felt experience of knowing the dignity of another, of understanding that we're all human, and of having a true love for them, regardless of any conflict we've had in the past.

Psychedelics can be of use here, too. MDMA, in particular—referred to by many as the "love drug"—is recognized for quieting people's fear and defensiveness and instilling a sense of emotional closeness, empathy, and understanding toward others.[15] When we're under the influence of MDMA, we typically display greater "prosocial behavior" and have a greater desire and ability to bond with others. Due to this profoundly prosocial nature, MDMA has been used in conflict-resolution settings and has made a beautiful contribution to couples therapy.[16] Just imagine the reach of peace if the fear, disconnection, and alienation we hold toward those in our homes, workplaces, cities, states, and the world over were to dissolve and be replaced with love. Are we really going to say no to that?

Connection to Self

But before we can empathize with and—dare I say—love other people, we must first empathize with and love ourselves. And that often requires emotional healing. The current medical discourse on psychedelics deals with exactly these issues—helping with depression, post-traumatic stress disorder (PTSD) trauma, existential distress in terminal patients, and a host of other mental health problems.

Fortunately or unfortunately, many of us haven't been diagnosed with a mental health diagnosis, yet most of us have faced deeply traumatic life events that have shaped us profoundly. Parents arguing, divorcing, moving to another place, being bullied—all of these "little" traumas can result in devastating wounds that we carry with us as adults. So, how do hyperachieving leaders deal with them in the context of the existing energetically masculine and emotionless leadership paradigm? No matter what their gender, most shove the lifetime of indignities and traumas they've experienced deep into their subconscious minds. Those buried traumas nevertheless continue to affect us, eroding self-love, confidence, and self-esteem and causing the buildup of defensive patterns that serve no one—personally or professionally. Such injuries to the emotional body, although perhaps not severe enough to warrant a medical diagnosis, can have profound repercussions on our ability to connect with ourselves and others.

When we suppress our traumatic childhood experiences in the name of rationalization and achievement, we disassociate from ourselves. We harden. We avoid the brutal hurt that we encountered when we were vulnerable and impressionable children. So we lock our hearts, trying desperately to keep it safe. As C.S. Lewis poignantly writes in *The Four Loves*, we "wrap it carefully round with hobbies and little luxuries; avoid all entanglements." To avoid a broken heart, "lock it up safe in the casket or coffin of your selfishness," he says. As children, before the indignities of trauma, our hearts are alive, open, and brimming with love. But know that in "that casket, safe, dark, motionless, airless, it will change. It will not be broken; it will become unbreakable, impenetrable, irredeemable."

This is the dark place where the feminine is hidden away. As a result, we lead companies, communities, and countries the same way we lead ourselves—disassociated from our feminine aspects, from our emotions, from our compassion, and stuck in our traumas. These feelings and thought patterns lead to behaviors that burden us and limit our leadership potential.

We might look at situations through the distortion created by personal biases, blaming and projecting our broken internal landscape onto others. Our stories block us from being more present, open to possibilities, and interpreting information objectively in the here and now. The cost of being unconsciously controlled by these filters and dark emotions is high.

Conscious leadership won't be sustainable in this form. We need to unlock and befriend our resentment, our anger, and our sadness. We need to liberate our emotions so we can heal and be whole. It is in this act of brave confrontation and release that we find liberation, turning what once controlled us into a source of strength, awareness, and self-empowerment.

Here's one high-profile example. When Tim Ferris was two years old, he was sexually abused by his babysitter's 12-year-old son. The abuse continued for two years, and it happened at such a young age that Ferris completely forgot the whole experience by the time he came into adulthood. However, even though he believed he had forgotten, there was an underlying sense that something was wrong buried deep within his subconscious.

It took a journey with psychedelics within the introspective environment of a silent retreat and the heightened awareness induced by fasting to release and bring up the flashbacks of the childhood assault.[17] Ferris was personally transformed by the healing of the trauma, as was his leadership.

While not all of us have childhood abuse in our history, we all have had childhood experiences that are traumatic and disturbing in their own way and contribute to the formation of our identities and inform our leadership style.

Psychedelic experiences don't create our intense emotions out of thin air; rather, they dredge them up from the depths of our psyches. Psychiatrist Stanislav Grof, who originated the use of LSD in psychotherapy, called psychedelics "non-specific amplifiers"—they can amplify what's in our hearts and minds and bring up memories, emotions, and thought patterns that have long been buried within. With the necessary support and skills to acknowledge, heal, and integrate those wounds, we can benefit ourselves greatly and unlock our aliveness, purpose, and positive impact on the world.

In the altered states of consciousness induced by psychedelics, emotions come up, and people often drop into direct contact with what they have never allowed themselves to feel before. Sometimes, what comes up is beautiful and awe-inspiring, but just as important are the feelings of anger, sadness, or fear that arise, providing a means for people to interact with them consciously and with awareness. As these darker elements bubble up, we can look at them from a place of wholeness and finally allow them to be released. I, for one, saw and let go of a lot of raw, primal, and animalistic anger I'd been holding, and I gained deep insights into my relational intelligence as a result.

Cleaning up these pain points creates new depth and space and new opportunities to adventure into the higher consciousness of our relationship with nature, creativity, and perhaps even our higher purpose. Disentangling from rigid negative patterns and reactivity to fear becomes possible when we integrate these experiences into our daily lives. That space-making is absolutely essential to our healing and transformation, and, in turn, has positive repercussions in the world around us. This is why our quest to mend our business and societal structures must begin with our own self-healing and why psychedelics can play a powerful role in building our congruence and heightened self-awareness as leaders.

Your vision will become clear only when you can look into your own heart. Who looks outside, dreams; Who looks inside, awakes.
—*Carl Jung*

As a leadership coach, I work with clients on issues within their conscious awareness; addressing thoughts and emotions that are more or less readily accessible and articulable. Today, most coaching—and, in fact, many therapies—continue to function in this way. The approach is crucial to laying the groundwork for self-awareness. However, these methods don't usually reach the deeper layers of the psyche where painful experiences are so often buried and out of reach of the conscious mind. To complement my work with them, some of my clients seek additional support from psychedelic-assisted therapy specialists to help them accelerate their healing and personal development. This approach serves them well. Nothing else I've witnessed helps people deepen their connection to themselves and enhance their self-understanding as much as the safe, intentional, and guided use of psychedelics. These leaders found that the experiences removed many of the barriers to their inner wisdom and their insights from lessons learned that they could put into play both personally and professionally.

A Higher Connection

Psychedelic experiences are sometimes wrapped in a spiritual dimension of sorts, typically characterized by a sense of unity or oneness with the universe, a feeling of transcending time and space, and a deep sense of peace and joy. They often involve a sense of encountering ultimate reality—the Divine. They are marked by ineffability—being frustratingly difficult to find words to describe them to others—because they go beyond the realm of ordinary experiences. They can give rise to a deepened sense of purpose and meaning. Yet spiritual intelligence—the feeling of connection to something greater than ourselves—also informs personal, social, and emotional intelligence.

It turns out that leaders who cultivate spiritual intelligence are better equipped to inspire others with a sense of wonder and awe and have more ease in the face of uncertainty. Humility often blossoms, too, a quality that is rare and often overlooked in leadership. According to *Rolling Stone* magazine, David Bronner, CEO of Dr. Bronner's Magic Soaps, believes that "psychedelics can be 'boundary dissolving,' providing people with a deeper 'understanding of their relationships to others, themselves, and the planet.'" With this "boundary-free world view," Bronner said, "people could embrace both social justice and multistakeholder capitalism."[18]

> *The sacred, however we may personally experience it, gives us a higher value than profit or status. It can, if we orient ourselves toward it, help us overcome the intense incentive structures that so often capture our values.*
> —*Alexander Beiner in* The Big Picture: How Psychedelics Can Help Us Make Sense of the World

Many people think science and spirituality don't mix, but it's not true. Einstein said that the most beautiful thing we can experience is the mysterious—it is the source of all true art and science. Under the right conditions, "entheogens"—a term given to psychedelics when used with a sacramental intent—can occasion true mystical experiences that wrap us in reverence and enchantment and expand our awareness and consciousness. And we are better leaders for it.

While introspection and discourse offer us valuable tools to explore and understand ourselves, transformation often requires a more profound, experiential shift. Psychedelic experiences, with their potential to immerse us in alternative realities, serve as powerful catalysts for such a change. They allow us to feel and embody higher perspectives, not just as intellectual concepts but as lived experiences. This felt understanding can solidify and energize our commitment to change, turning abstract thoughts into tangible shifts in perception and behavior and fostering a truly embodied transformation.

Since they can cause us to fundamentally challenge our traditional frames of reality and long-held beliefs and assumptions, psychedelics can help open us up to new worlds of possibility. We become imbued with a deepened sense of mutual respect, understanding, and cooperation. Such shifts do more than merely transform our internal perceptions; they can radically reshape our societal values and, consequently, our collective behaviors. As we grapple with increasingly dire and complex challenges in our world, the insights and transformations brought to the doorsteps of leadership by the use of psychedelic experiences might be key to building a brighter and more sustainable future for all of us.

> *Why are we wired to have these salient, felt-to-be-sacred experiences of encountering ultimate reality of the interconnectedness of all people and all things—experiences that arguably provide the very basis of our ethical and moral codes common to all the world's religions?*
> *—Roland Griffiths, PhD, Director of the Center for Psychedelic and Consciousness Research and Professor of Psychiatry and Behavioral Sciences at Johns Hopkins Medicine*

Some legal authorities have recognized the potential for psychoactive sacraments to facilitate spiritual exploration, leading to their legalization in certain contexts. For instance, several churches in Canada have received legal approval for the use of ayahuasca. In the United States, legal exemptions to use entheogens in religious practices exist for the Santo Daime and the Native American Church that incorporate the use of ayahuasca and peyote, respectively, in their rituals. They are repeatedly under attack and in need of defense. As Comanche Chief Quanah Parker explained while testifying in front of the Oklahoma legislature regarding the legality of the use of peyote as a religious sacrament, "The White Man goes into his church house and talks *about* Jesus, but the Indian goes into his tipi and talks *to* Jesus."[19]

The potential gifts that psychedelic substances offer might be profoundly useful for our survival as a species, and by making them available in a safe and intentional environment to healthy populations, we might begin to calm the flames of our burning world and find the solutions that are currently evading us so strikingly.

> *An indisputable and profound inner knowing arises that we can all access individually and perhaps collectively . . . which can give rise to profound worldview shifts of an uplifting kind, an awakening to a sense of freedom, peace, joy, and gratitude that most people simply find*

unimaginable. Further research may ultimately prove to be crucial to the very survival of our species.
—*Roland Griffiths, PhD*

Questions for Reflection

1. What do you see as the connection between feminine intelligence and certain expanded states of consciousness brought on by psychedelics?
2. How would your approach to leadership be transformed if you could effectively unlock and release past traumas, subconscious filters, and/or deep-seated assumptions that hold you back? Have methods you've already used been effective?
3. What aspects of your life or career would benefit from a heightened sense of creative expression? What new paths or solutions might emerge for you?
4. In what ways might psychedelics expand your perspective on creating a greater impact for the world, the planet, and the people around you?

13

Awake Not "Woke" Capitalism

Leading with Wholeness

It is no small task to be a catalyst of the transformation of the prevailing paradigm of business leadership, a model that is steeped in centuries of presumptions about society, economics, the hierarchies of men over women and nature, and the limited amount of good a business can (or should) contribute to the world.

It's been around 250 years since Adam Smith, often hailed as the "father of capitalism," laid the intellectual groundwork of our current economic philosophy. And it's been 60 years since Milton Friedman built upon these ideals to popularize "shareholder primacy," contributing to the broken systems we know today. The most dangerous creation of our society is the belief that there is no other way.

Perhaps now at its evolutionary apex, our economic model sure has many advantages as well as innumerable flaws—many of them disastrous. On top of that, the leadership of the past several decades has failed to find sustainable, let alone regenerative, solutions for the issues that threaten our comfortable lifestyles, our global commercial interplay and engagement, our natural ecosystems, our health, and our very existence. Instead, our problems keep growing exponentially.

These calamities are forcing us to question and re-examine our existing conventions, practices, and financial models so we don't allow the gains we've made over the past few hundred years to slip through our fingers.

After all, our free enterprise system has been one of the pillars of our prosperity. Through social cooperation, we exchange goods and services with each other, collectively creating and producing far more value than we could individually. In this economic system, the sum is greater than each of the individual parts alone. Our living standards have lifted us into realms of comfort, convenience, opportunity, education, and medical solutions our ancestors couldn't have dared imagine. Freedom, leisure, and luxury are realities for many people.

So, as we rally around a shared intention to upgrade and retool our commercial systems for the sake of our very survival, we need to remember and appreciate that the way we live and work in the Western world now is vastly better than ever before.

But the past 60 years have trapped our leaders into beliefs and practices fueled by a hyper-masculine consciousness—driven by the need to produce faster, compete harder, build higher, profit more, expand without limit, and accumulate more and more stuff. But at what cost? If we take the time to look, we see that masses of people have lost themselves and have severed from the essence of their being in the process. We have collectively untethered from our vitality, our joy, our sense of wonder. We are so blinded that we risk turning our home planet into a desolate wasteland.

The problem: Winners of the rat race, fundamentally, are still rats. Mesmerized by elusive rewards at the finish line, many of us are sleepwalking, carrying the weight of fear, anxiety, and existential dread. Lacking a genuine clarity of purpose, we are exhausted, burned out, and disconnected. We are robots masquerading as humans.

> *We buy things we don't need with money we don't have to impress*
> *people we don't like.*
> —*Tyler Durden, in* Fight Club

How did we get here? We have too often rejected feminine consciousness. For us to pull ourselves out of the declining systems and move forward, creating a world where we feel the joy of aliveness and set up our organizations to be regenerative, symbiotic, and collaborative forces within the global financial landscape, we must reject outdated assumptions around "success" in business—and life. We must question the cost of rational self-interest, short-term profits, and winner-take-all attitudes. We must rebuff our insatiable appetite for profits, growth, self-centeredness, and domination. Instead, we must fully activate our feminine intelligence in order to restore our lives, our aliveness, our organizational, cultural, and humanistic wellness, and our planet.

To be clear, to help usher in a transformed collective economic landscape into a force for good, we don't want to ignore the extraordinary benefits and advantages the capitalist free market system has brought us. It has elevated living standards and taken millions of people out of poverty. Since 1990, the number of people living on less than US$1.25 a day has been reduced by half, and approximately 700 million more people have entered the global middle class.[1] On average, we are 4.4 times richer than we were in 1950.[2] Scientific advances have fueled medical and technological breakthroughs. Tossing it out—burning down the very house we live in—clearly isn't the answer. But it's imperative that we overhaul our business ethos. It's not just about shareholder wealth; it's about enriching communities, regenerating the health of the planet, and reconnecting to joy, awe, and love.

> *Don't aim at success. The more you aim at it and make it a target, the*
> *more you are going to miss it. For success, like happiness, cannot be*
> *pursued; it must ensue, and it only does so as the unintended side effect*
> *of one's personal dedication*
> *to a cause greater than oneself.*
> —*Viktor E. Frankl, in* Man's Search for Meaning

We need not trade healthy profits for a healthy planet. But we must acknowledge the futility and shortsightedness of seeking infinite growth on a planet with finite resources. For an elegantly refined capitalism to thrive, we don't have to abandon our humanistic values—health, happiness, balance, sanity, family, community, and even self-actualization. Lisa Jackson, who oversees Apple's environment, policy, and social initiatives, nails it: "The choice between a healthy planet and good business strategy has always been a false one."[3] The World Economic Forum (WEF) estimates that we can unlock roughly US$10 trillion of business opportunities by transforming the economic systems that are responsible for 80% of nature loss.[4] We can thrive economically without sacrificing our well-being or that of our planet. By tapping into our infinite imagination and by integrating feminine intelligence, businesses can wield a net-positive and nature-positive impact on our communities, our countries, and our planet.

When John Mackey co-founded Whole Foods Market in 1980, he embraced that wider, bolder vision, seeking to benefit not just shareholders (and customers) but all the other stakeholders with which it was engaged as well. And, in a bold move, he took on Milton Friedman himself in what turned out to be Friedman's last public debate before his passing in 2006. An "enlightened" company, Mackey emphasized, must serve "all six of our most important stakeholders: customers, team members, investors, vendors, communities, and the environment."[5] In that way, Whole Foods roused and galvanized the latent global consumer desire for responsible access to healthy foods and grew the company beyond everyone's expectations. In 2017, Amazon purchased Whole Foods for the tidy sum of US$13 billion. Mackey's commitment made the company the wellness behemoth it is today.

The Inner Power of the Feminine

Economic growth is a good thing, but we need for it not to be heartless. Profits are desirable, but not at the cost of life, love, and the well-being of future generations. Expansion is good, but not at the expense of the thriving, dynamic, interdependent ecosystems in which it resides. When the masculine aspect operates unchecked, devoid of the balancing influence of the feminine, its sole focus tends to be on power, rigor, and financial growth. Anything else is a pleasant happenstance.

Feminine intelligence is characterized by a deep connection to oneself—to one's inner world—and to an intuitive sense of interconnectivity with all other living things. It is our intuition, empathy, and creativity; it seeks to foster growth and healing in ourselves and others. The feminine values the place of emotions and relationships in shaping our experiences and places a strong emphasis on communication and collaboration. It prioritizes the needs of the community over individual gain and seeks to contribute to the creation of a more equitable and compassionate world. It recognizes the inherent connection to the natural world, understanding that our well-being is intricately linked to the health and balance of the environment that sustains us.

Masculine intelligence is characterized by a focus on the outer world and a desire to achieve individual success and recognition. It leans on rationality, logic, and material success; It values productivity and efficiency and seeks to create a system that rewards those who excel. Thus, it can view the natural world as a resource to be exploited for human gain and usually values competition, independence, and individualism over community and interconnectedness.

There's an easy temptation to assume that masculine and feminine qualities are inherently contradictory, caught in a perceived polarity. We're often taught that such qualities can't co-exist—we can be empathetic, or we can be pragmatic, but we can never be both. The dispute is often echoed in the corridors of power, where one side wants profits and growth but tends to be heartless in its quest, and the other side wants to be a force for good in the world but is naive in the face of hardened business people. This perceived duality is simply false. In *Built to Last: Successful Habits of Visionary Companies*, authors Jim Collins and Jerry Porras prove that builders of great companies can choose to reject the tyranny of the "or" and embrace the genius of the "and." We can hold a number of seemingly contradictory ideas simultaneously. (It's left-brained thinking that has a way of creating distinctions, contrast, and conflict where co-existence is actually possible.) Rigor, practicality, profits, and financial success are not incompatible with love and imagination, empathy, and creativity. We have all of these qualities available to us—regardless of our gender—and we are not limited to choosing one over the other. Integration, not division, makes us whole. Allowing ourselves to access and express all of our internal resources—masculine and feminine—galvanizes our leadership, coupling an open heart with the power to make positive change in the world.

> *For hundreds of years, the Bird of Humanity has been flying primarily with one wing, the masculine wing, causing it to become overly muscular, overdeveloped. In fact, the wing has become violent*

causing the Bird of Humanity to fly in circles and keep repeating
the same path of flight . . . The 21st century is when the female
wing of the Bird of Humanity will fully extend and allow the male wing
to relax, and instead of flying in circles, the Bird of Humanity will
finally begin to soar.
—*Mary Portas, founder of Portas and Co-Chair of the Better Business Act*

To evolve our world toward a more radiant, courageous, and noble one, the dynamic interplay and balance between these two potent forces is absolutely essential. And while our masculine character has been pervasive and imperious for centuries, we must now reclaim our feminine intelligence fully, promote it to full partnership, and engage it abundantly in the huge task before us. Then, once we've cultivated the inner wisdom and expansive insights of our inner feminine intelligence, we can tap into our masculine determination to get things done. We can go out into the world and create a business that not only thrives financially, it becomes a transformative force for good. Our efficiency, productivity, and rationality become unstoppable when we are fueled by the inner values, inner alignment, and inner genius that is sourced from within.

This has become the biggest existential question of our time. How do we elevate our own consciousness in the midst of a combative, careless, win-or-lose culture and have our actions resonate and multiply enough to create substantive, systemic change? When our emerging and existing leaders upgrade their consciousness, that's when we can effect enduring positive change. It's when we shift our capacity to draw from our innate feminine intelligence that we lead our businesses and the world into a more prosperous, wholly functional, and inclusive future.

I alone cannot change the world, but I can cast a stone across the
waters to create many ripples.
—*Mother Teresa*

Wholeness opens the door to this transformation. It takes wholeness— that is, equal access to the genius of both our feminine and masculine energies—to empower us to uplevel our businesses and alter the trajectory of today's global financial systems. It takes courage, authenticity, and personal power, all of which are spawned by the revelations of our feminine intelligence. It takes feeling and owning our emotions, allowing our hearts to blossom in fullness, and embracing compassion and empathy for others. It takes mental and emotional purging so that we can make room for higher insights, imagination, and creative thinking to elevate our work and bring viable, solution-oriented values, behaviors, and competencies to our organizations and the global business and leadership stage.

Do you really want to see change happen in the world? If you do, this shift becomes a personal imperative forged in a personal journey. By awakening your own consciousness individually and unlocking your feminine intelligence, you can tap into your genuine desire to effect change. It's not a spectator sport—caring alone is not enough. It's time to stand tall and be of service.

> *I want you to panic. I want you to feel the fear I feel every day. I want you to act. I want you to act like you would in a crisis. I want you to act like your house is on fire. Because it is.*
> —*Greta Thunberg*

Voices in Crescendo

Look around and you'll see the growing desire for businesses to participate far beyond their own profit motive—and business leaders are beginning to respond and act. In 2018, Larry Fink, CEO of BlackRock, one of the world's largest investment managers and one of the most influential voices in the industry, wrote a now-famous annual letter to the CEOs of companies in which BlackRock invests. "Society is demanding that companies, both public and private, serve a social purpose," he wrote. "To prosper over time, every company must not only deliver financial performance but also show how it makes a positive contribution to society. Companies must benefit all their stakeholders, including shareholders, employees, customers, and the communities in which they operate."[6] Businesses will not succeed if society fails. Business cannot exist on a dead planet. It is time to disrupt outdated beliefs and old-boy habits grounded in self-interest and profit primacy.

It's not just altruism, either; it actually pays to do so. Companies that embrace a wider scope of values and demonstrate concern for more than just profits are getting more respect in addition to more business. As Sangeeta Waldron writes in *Corporate Social Responsibility is Not Public Relations: How to Put CSR at the Heart of Your Company and Maximize the Business Benefits,* "People want all businesses to do better! There is going to be growth in people wanting and buying brands that reflect their values."[7]

Patagonia is one such company at the forefront of the debate on the purpose of business. It has legally structured itself to fight climate change and make Earth its only shareholder, eliminating the need to answer to unaligned interests. It is consistently applauded for its trust, citizenship, and ethics—and has one of the most loyal customer bases in the industry.[8] "'Business as usual' is not good enough anymore, and we want to lead by example," said former Patagonia CEO Rose Marcario. "The plain truth is that capitalism needs to evolve if humanity is going to survive. More than ever, business needs to step up for democracy and a civil society."[9]

In fact, companies prioritizing sustainable strategies can be *more* profitable than their counterparts. In *Firms of Endearment: How World Class Companies Profit from Passion and Purpose,* the authors, after extensive financial analysis, reveal that these companies outperformed the S&P 500 businesses by a staggering 14 times over a 15-year period.[10] While some cynical investors might scrutinize these claims and the research methodology, it's undeniable that profitable and socially conscious businesses can and do thrive.

Companies that don't believe this and fail to stay ahead expose themselves to the risk of being overtaken by innovative newcomers. In response to disturbing allegations of child slavery within the global chocolate supply chain, Tony's Chocolonely, a Dutch confectionery company, boldly emerged in 2003, providing a 100% slave-free alternative. Henk Jan Beltman, who once donned the notable title of Chief Chocolate Officer, said Tony's "exists to prove it's possible to turn a profit and do good at the same time." They've executed that mission admirably, and today's consumers agree. "Businesses that just focus on profit are anti-social enterprises," the company asserts.[11] As consumers wield their purchasing power and the workforce—especially millennials and Gen Zers—gravitate toward socially responsible employers, those businesses prioritizing sustainability and ethical practices are expected to come out on top in the long run. Responsible value creation is the biggest business opportunity for the twenty-first century.

Investors, too, are transforming the rules of the game and publicly supporting sustainable and regenerative goals and principles. Their actions remind us that "success" is not necessarily defined by short-term profit. This shift in mindset is not only a moral imperative; it's a smart business move. PwC, one of the Big Four accounting firms, estimates that sustainable investing will make up more than half of global assets by 2025.[12]

More employers are apparently responding to the demands of the times, placing workplace culture and well-being priorities among their stated company objectives.[13] The work pays off in more ways than one. Fulfilled employees prove to be more motivated, translating their positive mindset into superior performance and better overall results for their organizations. A study by the London Business School tracked the 100 best places to work in the United States over 25 years and revealed that they had enjoyed a 50% greater increase in share value compared to their counterparts.[14] It's not merely about profits; it's about the abundant dividends reaped from cultivating a workplace where people thrive.

> *We believe that business is good because it creates value. It is ethical because it is based on voluntary exchange; it is noble because it can elevate our existence, and it is heroic because it lifts people out of poverty and creates prosperity.*
> —*Raj Sisodia and John Mackey, in* Conscious Capitalism

There are more clear signs that the tide is turning. In 2015, the UN member states adopted the Sustainable Development Goals (SDGs), a set of interconnected goals aimed at ending poverty, protecting the planet, and ensuring peace and prosperity by 2030. While achieving this ambitious agenda seems daunting, the UN's initiative has sparked a global conversation and catalyzed a seismic shift away from business as usual.

In 2019, the Business Roundtable (BRT), an association of 181 CEOs from some of the United States' largest companies, redefined the very *purpose* of a corporation. According to the BRT, a corporation's objective isn't, in fact, just to maximize shareholder profit but to deliver long-term value to all of its stakeholders—including customers, employees, suppliers, and the communities in which it operates.[15] That same year, the WEF created the Davos Manifesto for a "better kind of capitalism." (Davos, Switzerland, is where business and political titans gather every January for the annual meeting.) "The purpose of a company," they wrote, "is to engage *all* its stakeholders in shared and sustained value creation."[16]

More and more consumers in the West are demanding that the roles and responsibilities of businesses within their economic and social ecosystems be upgraded to enhance life rather than degrade it. The calls of the many—people who won't tolerate or support companies whose values don't align with their own humanity—are coming to a crescendo. They will not be ignored.

Disregarding the cultural and climate zeitgeist is no longer a viable strategy for businesses. Soon enough, thriving will be elusive for those not perceived as championing interests beyond their own bottom line through tangible practices. Even global diamond mining companies, traditionally perceived as distant from such concerns, are attuned. Bruce Cleaver, Chairman of De Beers Group, highlighted this shift, stating, "The time will come when there will be a threshold question that consumers will ask, which is, 'Can I trust this brand?'" he said. "And if the answer is 'No,' they won't buy anything. It will become a binary question."[17]

With attitudes and behaviors markedly different from previous generations, younger people are demanding to be heard, and their actions and voices are helping us evolve our capitalist model to a more sustainable one. Having grown up in a time when the climate crisis has dominated headlines, they care enough to explore the mission and purpose of the companies they do business with and to demand more from the businesses they support. Seeking authenticity and alignment, they're taking the time to ensure their spending aligns with their values, and they're becoming more politically involved.

> *A leader's legacy is not determined by the accolades they receive, but by the values they instill in the next generation of leaders.*
> —*Malala Yousafzai, the youngest Nobel Prize winner in history*

In 2021, Forbes surveyed millennials and Gen Zs and reported that, before engaging with companies, they evaluate how they treat the environment, protect personal data, and position themselves on social and political issues. Almost 50% of those surveyed said they'd made choices in the past two years about what organizations they'd be willing to work for based on their personal values.[18]

"The recent embrace of stakeholder capitalism is, at least in part, an illustration of the influence millennials and Gen Zs have already had. Businesses are increasingly being held accountable for their impact on society," said Michele Parmelee, Deloitte Global Deputy CEO and Chief People and Purpose Officer.

In the midst of all these encouraging signs, it's understandable that many of us get cynical and doubt whether the change we're seeking will be great enough and go far enough to make a substantive difference equal to the task at hand. If too many are only making superficial changes and we don't make considerable shifts as a whole, we won't move humanity forward toward a truly flourishing world. We don't want to be naive to the realities. We recognize that there are many forces at play. Too many companies put on a public display of doing the "right things" and making eco-friendly promises and practices while disguising a hornet's nest of harmful practices. But it's also, to some extent, the point. Greenwashing and other practices lacking integrity can only be carried out by those who are out of touch with their feminine intelligence. As conscious leaders, then, we demonstrate that leading with wholeness works—for our organizations, for our shareholders, for our employees, for our planet, and for the collective. Letting ourselves get sucked into a cynical paradigm will only prevent us from gaining traction and will make it harder to catalyze a true movement of transformation.

A New Era of Leadership

What should be at the center of our economic universe? A focus on life and love and building a world together that we all want to live in. The degradation of the feminine principle within our cultures and societies and the neglect of our feminine consciousness within us must be stopped if we are to seed a business environment that elevates humanity. A pivot is required, one that embraces feminine intelligence and leads with wholeness.

Imagine our collective consciousness transforming the global business enterprise into a passionate pursuit of higher value and innovation. Imagine a revolution of leadership that consistently includes the well-being of humanity among our priorities when we shape short-term and long-term business objectives and strategies. Imagine a global network of leaders who feel driven to safeguard our beautiful planet even as we pursue greater productivity and sustainable profits for shareholders. Imagine harmonizing the forces of capitalism with the universal ideals of human rights, peace, and preservation of the planet.

To reverse the damage wrought over the past few centuries, critical re-evaluation of our current businesses and institutional practices is imperative. The status quo is no longer tenable. A new era of leadership is undeniably and urgently required to propagate fundamental system change, fostering a global landscape that is not only prosperous but also regenerative and robustly healthy.

It will take imaginative leaders like you to forge new paradigms of thought and establish a deeper connectedness to both the internal and external worlds if we are to survive, let alone thrive.

It will take purposeful leaders like you to redefine the purpose of your businesses so they are life-affirming and generate hope for future generations.

It will take courageous leaders like you to step out of the existing paradigm and choose a different path, leaders who are willing to cast a new model of what "leadership" can mean in today's world.

This is your time. It is your opportunity to dig into yourself and your purpose, unlock your authenticity, and engage your courage and passion. Know that it's doable to lead a business that thrives financially, grows as a force for good, and allows you to keep your heart and soul intact.

The beauty of our journeys of conscious leadership is that we make a difference in countless lives—starting with our own. Yes, we personally benefit. You don't need to sacrifice what's important to you. You don't need to relinquish your joy, trade in gratification, or forfeit great achievement. It is a precious time to be alive and lead.

In this new paradigm, any business can be a conscious business. You don't have to plunge into nonprofit territory or rush to secure B Corp status. The beauty lies in the simplicity of infusing conscious values into the DNA of any business, whether it's a newly established startup or a well-established corporate division. The point is that whether you're creating a new body wash, like Faith In Nature, or innovating with a regenerative chocolate snack, do it with conscious values.

To do so, envision your business as a dynamic part of an interdependent system, not confined by industry norms. Look upstream and downstream; understand the ripple effects of your decisions. Seek out regenerative practices that not only benefit your bottom line but also contribute positively to jobs, the environment, and a spectrum of conscious initiatives. This approach is not just an alternative; it's a nuanced, strategic way to navigate the business landscape, ensuring sustained success with a positive impact.

Look around and see where changes can be made to align your company's values with those of your feminine intelligence. Do your inner work. Dedicate yourself to mastering the intricate dance of time, nurturing relationships, navigating uncertainty, and understanding the complex landscape of your emotions. Awaken your inner wisdom through purposeful and deliberate contemplation.

True happiness eludes those who relentlessly chase profits and greater wealth alone; to truly experience awe, joy, and peace, we need to be whole and fulfilled. When we fail to transcend the superficial, spiritless values we're socialized with, we are tethered to the status quo, a treadmill of unfulfilling pursuits.

Mounting data consistently reveals a prevailing sense of depression and dissatisfaction in our world. It's an existential and spiritual crisis. Why? Because so many of us find ourselves adrift, disconnected from our authentic inner purpose, detached from the vibrant aliveness that life has to offer. The yearning to break free from this disconnect and tap into the power within to envision, rally, and create for the good of the whole is the key to unlocking genuine happiness.

The journey of conscious leadership is not only about making a difference in the world; it's about giving yourself a meaningful, fulfilling, vital, and joyful life. It's about living with purpose and authenticity and wholeness through the embrace of your feminine intelligence. Isn't that who you want to be?

This is a time for boldness, action, and intentional leadership. This is your time to realize your vision of contribution and change-making. It cannot wait, so start now. What will you do tomorrow to begin?

> *This is the true joy in life, the being used for a purpose recognized as a mighty one . . . being a force of nature instead of a feverish, selfish little clod of ailments and grievances complaining that the world will not devote itself into making you happy.*
> —*George Bernard Shaw*

Questions for Reflection

1. Is the world better or worse off because your business is in it?
2. How can your leadership support a business strategy focused on planetary health and societal well-being?
3. How will your evolved leadership contribute to your personal sense of fulfillment and joy?

Notes

Chapter 1

1. "*Homo economicus*," a term originating from classical economics, represents a theoretical and often simplified model of human behavior in economic contexts. This concept assumes that individuals are rational, self-interested actors who make decisions based on maximizing their own utility or well-being, typically in a monetary or material sense. The term is commonly associated with John Stuart Mill and finds its roots in Max Weber's work, particularly in his essay, "Objectivity in Social Science and Social Policy" (1904).
2. Mishel, L. and Kandra, J. (2021). CEO pay has skyrocketed 1,322% since 1978. *Economic Policy Institute* (10 August). https://www.epi.org/publication/ceo-pay-in-2020 (accessed 29 October 2024).
3. "The point is, ladies and gentleman, that greed—for lack of a better word—is good. Greed is right. Greed works. Greed clarifies, cuts through, and captures the essence of the evolutionary spirit. Greed, in all of its forms—greed for life, for money, for love, knowledge—has marked the upward surge of mankind." Gordon, G. (1987) *Wall Street*; Stone, O. (Director) (1987). *Wall Street*, 20th Century Fox.
4. Gelles, D. (2022). *The Man Who Broke Capitalism: How Jack Welch Gutted the Heartland and Crushed the Soul of Corporate America—and How to Undo His Legacy*, 3. Simon & Schuster.
5. Gelles, *The Man Who Broke Capitalism*, p. 7.
6. Gelles, *The Man Who Broke Capitalism*, pp. 4–5.

7. Grow, B. (2007). Out at home depot. *Business Week* (4 January). https://www.nbcnews.com/id/wbna16469224 (accessed 29 October 2024).

8. Many commentators at the time were skeptical that Welch really saw the light, wondering if he was just out for publicity.

9. Guerrera, F. (2009). Welch condemns share price focus. *Financial Times* (12 March). https://www.ft.com/content/294ff1f2-0f27-11de-ba10-0000779fd2ac (accessed 29 October 2024).

Chapter 2

1. Taylor, J.B. (2020). *Whole Brain Living*, 5. New York: Hay House.

2. Koenig, A.M., Eagly, A.H., Mitchell, A.A., and Ristikari, T. (2011). Are leader stereotypes masculine? A meta-analysis of three research paradigms. *Psychological Bulletin* 137 (4):616–642. https://doi.org/10.1037/a0023557.

3. Gerzema, J. and D'Antonio, M. (2013). *The Athena Doctrine: How Women (and the Men Who Think Like Them) Will Rule the Future*. San Francisco: Jossey-Bass.

4. Eagly, A.H. and Johnson, B.T. (1990). Gender and leadership style: a meta-analysis. *CHIP Documents 11*. https://opencommons.uconn.edu/chip_docs/11 (accessed 18 March 2024).

5. Eagly, A.H. and Johnson, B.T. (1990). Gender and leadership style.

6. Teboul, E. (2022). Interview with Scilla Elworthy, 2 November.

7. Bigio, J. and Vogelstein, R.B. (2016). How women's participation in conflict prevention and resolution advances US interests. *Council on Foreign Relations Press* (October). https://www.cfr.org/report/how-womens-participation-conflict-prevention-and-resolution-advances-us-interests (accessed 18 March 2024).

8. Helliwell, J.F., Layard, R., Sachs, J.D. et al. (eds.) (2022). World Happiness Report 2022. New York: Sustainable Development Solutions Network.

9. Helliwell, J.F., Layrad, R., Sachs, J.D. et al. (eds.). World Happiness Report 2024. University of Oxford: Wellbeing Research Centre.

Chapter 3

1. Mackey, J. and Sisodia, R. 2014. *Conscious Capitalism: Liberating the Heroic Spirit of Business*. Boston: Harvard Business Review Press.

2. Pink, D.H. (2009). *Drive: The Surprising Truth About What Motivates Us.* New York: Riverhead Books.
3. Kaminski, I. (2022). Eco beauty company "appoints nature" to its board of directors. *The Guardian* (22 September). https://www.theguardian .com/environment/2022/sep/22/eco-beauty-company-faith-in-nature-board-directors (accessed 29 October 2024).
4. Cullinan, C. (2003). *Wild Law: A Manifesto for Earth Justice.* Green Books. (Recommended for readers interested in exploring concepts of earth governance and jurisprudence.)
5. Apple (2023). *2030 Status | Mother Nature | Apple.* YouTube video, 2:14 (12 September). https://www.youtube.com/watch?v=QNv9PRDIhes (accessed 18 March 2024).

Chapter 4

1. Teboul, E. (2023). Interviews with Melvyn Lubega, 24 April and 23 November.
2. Lubega, Teboul, 23 November 2023.
3. Lubega, Teboul, 23 November 2023.
4. Lubega, Teboul, 23 November 2023.
5. Lubega, Teboul, 23 November 2023.

Chapter 5

1. Teboul, E. (2023). Interview with Lindsay Kaplan, 27 July.
2. Kaplan, Teboul, 27 July 2023.
3. Brown, B. (2010). *The Gifts of Imperfection.* Hazelden Publishing.
4. Kaplan, Teboul, 27 July 2023.

Chapter 6

1. Teboul, E. (2023). Interviews with Anthony Farr, 8 February, 8 March, and 2 June.
2. Farr, Teboul, 8 February 2023, 8 March 2023, and 2 June 2023.
3. Farr, Teboul, 2 June 2023.
4. Gray, A. (2015). A letter from our founder. *AllanGray* (31 December). https://www.allangray.co.za/globalassets/about-us/our-ownership/a-letter-from-our-founder.pdf (accessed 16 October 2024).

Chapter 7

1. Malnight, T.W., Buche, I., and Dhanaraj, C. (2019). Put purpose at the core of your strategy: it's how successful companies redefine their businesses. *Harvard Business Review Magazine*, September–October.

2. O'Brien, D., Main, A., Kounkel, S. et al. (2019). Purpose is everything: how brands that authentically lead with purpose are changing the nature of business today. *Deloitte Insights* (15 October).

3. Wrzesniewski, A. and Dutton, J.E. (2001). Crafting a job: revisioning employees as active crafters of their work. *The Academy of Management Review* 26 (2): 179–201. https://doi.org/10.2307/259118.

4. George, W.W., Palepu, K.G., Knoop, C.-I. et al. (2013). Unilever's Paul Polman: developing global leaders. *Harvard Business School Case Study*, 413-097. 23 May.

5. Polman, P. and Winston, A. (2022). *Net Positive: How Courageous Companies Thrive by Giving More Than They Take*, 85–86. Harvard Business Review Press. UK Edition.

6. Polman, P. and Winston, A. (2022). *Net Positive*, 85–86. HBR Press.

7. Polman, P. and Winston, A. (2022). *Net Positive*, 223. HBR Press.

8. Bel, D. (2016). Without social justice, there is no future for the economy. *Medium*, 30 June. https://medium.com/@dominiquebel/without-social-justice-there-is-no-future-for-the-economy-b87537166e89 (accessed 16 October 2024).

9. Sisodia, R. (2023). *Awaken: The Path to Purpose, Inner Peace and Healing.* Wiley. Prologue.

10. Sisodia, *Awaken*, Ch. 12.

11. Sisodia, *Awaken*, Ch. 12.

Chapter 8

1. Hugh O'Brian Youth Leadership (2017). *ASLA Honoree: His Excellency Ambassador T. Hamid Al-Bayati – Day of Happiness.* YouTube video, 5 June. https://www.youtube.com/watch?v=CcbhqTZdLYA (accessed 18 March 2024).

2. Al-Bayati, T.H., Teboul, E., Ben-Shahar, T. et al. (2020). *Our Post Pandemic Future: The Importance of Cultivating Resilience and Identifying the Key Factors that Impact Global and Personal Perceptions of Happiness.* Webinar, 11 May.

3. Sturgeon, N. (2019). Why governments should prioritize well-being. TEDx Summit, July.

4. Layard, R., Lord (2023). Como wellbeing manifesto: let's put wellbeing first. WOHASU – World Happiness Summit, 29 November. https:// worldhappinesssummit.com/como-wellbeing-manifesto/ (accessed 29 October 2024).

5. Hutchins, G. and Storm, L. (2023). *Regenerative Leadership: The DNA of Life-Affirming Twenty-first Century Organizations.* Tunbridge Wells: Wordzworth.

6. Henderson, R. (2020). *Reimagining Capitalism in a World on Fire.* New York: Penguin Random House.

7. Binkley, C. (2021). Brunello Cucinelli calls for "dignity and morals" at G20. *Vogue Business*, 3 November.

8. Polman, P. and Winston, A. (2022). *Net Positive*, 7. HBR Press.

9. Mackey, J. and Sisodia, R. (2014). *Conscious Capitalism: Liberating the Heroic Spirit of Business.* Boston, MA: Harvard Business Review Press.

10. James, G. (2018). Why Unilever stopped issuing quarterly reports. Inc. com, 23 January.

11. Kraft, A., Vashishtha, R. and Venkatachalam, M. (2018). Frequent financial reporting and managerial myopia. *Accounting Review* 93 (2), 249–275. https://doi.org/10.2308/accr-51838

12. Naidu, R. (2023). Investor Fundsmith accuses Unilever of "virtue signaling" and prioritising Peltz. *Reuters*, 10 January.

13. Unilever PLC (2024). Our climate transition action plan. Unilever, 22 March. https://www.unilever.com/planet-and-society/climate-action/our-climate-transition-action-plan/ (accessed 29 October 2024).

Chapter 9

1. How many Certified B Corps are there around the world? https:// www.bcorporation.net/en-us/faqs/how-many-certified-b-corps-are-there-around-world/ (accessed 9 April 2024).

2. Riboud, A. C.N.P.F. National Conference Marseilles - 25 October 1972 (Marseilles). https://www.danone.com/content/dam/corp/global/danonecom/about-us-impact/history/antoine-riboud-speech-marseille-en.pdf (accessed 9 April 2024).

3. Bommel, S. (2022). Stronger than "Succession", the tumultuous saga of the transfer of power at Danone. *French Vanity Fair* (3 January). https://www.vanityfair.fr/pouvoir/article/plus-fort-que-succession-la-tumultueuse-saga-de-la-passation-de-pouvoir-chez-danone (accessed 1 November 2024).

4. Teboul, E. (2023). Interview with Lorna Davis, 2 August.

5. Marquis, C. and Sapuridis, E. (2018). Danone North America: the world's largest B Corporation. *Harvard Business Review* (6 December). https://case.hks.harvard.edu/danone-north-america-the-worlds-largest-b-corporation/ (accessed 29 October 2024).

6. Davis, Teboul, 19 May 2020 and 26 January 2023.

7. Marquis, C. and Sapuridis, E. Danone North America: The World's Largest B Corporation, HKS Case Program. https://case.hks.harvard.edu/danone-north-america-the-worlds-largest-b-corporation/ (accessed 9 April 2024).

8. Davis, Teboul, 19 May 2020.

9. Faber, E. (2017). Food is a human right, not a commodity. LinkedIn, Article, 22 June. https://www.linkedin.com/pulse/food-human-right-commodity-emmanuel-faber/ (accessed 29 October 2024).

10. Marquis, C. and Sapuridis, E. The world's largest B Corporation.

11. Faber, E. (2018). To B or not to B Corp: that is no longer a question. LinkedIn, Article, 12 April. https://www.linkedin.com/pulse/b-corp-longer-question-emmanuel-faber-1/ (accessed 1 November 2024).

12. Baoul, E. (2023). Interview with Ben Anderson, 23 February.

13. B Corp. B Movement Builders: Multinational companies recognizing the leadership of Certified B Corps and committed to the principles of the B Corp movement. https://bcorporation.net/b-movement-builders (page no longer available).

14. Raval, A. (2024). The struggle for the soul of the B Corp movement. *Financial Times* (19 February). https://www.ft.com/content/0b632709-afda-4bdc-a6f3-bb0b02eb5a62 (accessed 28 March 2024).

15. Anderson, 23 February 2023.

16. Bommel, "Stronger than 'Succession'."

17. Faber, E., Imrie, M., and Schwartz, R. (Trans.) (2013). *All That Glitters: Business on a (Social) Mission*, 15 Chemins de traverse, January.

18. Teboul, E. (2023). Interview with Flemming Morgan. 1 August.

19. Letter sent to the Board by Flemming Morgan, dated February 27, 2021.
20. Davis, Teboul, 2 August 2023.
21. Van Gansbeke, F. (2021). Sustainability and the downfall of Danone CEO Faber (1/2). *Forbes* (20 March). https://www.forbes.com/sites/frankvangansbeke/2021/03/20/sustainability-and-the-downfall-of-danone-ceo-faber-12/?sh=437c02985b16 (accessed 17 October 2024).
22. Walt, V. (2021). A top CEO was ousted after making his company more environmentally conscious. Now he's speaking out. *Time* (21 November). https://time.com/6121684/emmanuel-faber-danone-interview/ (accessed 17 October 2024).
23. Davis, Teboul, 2 August 2023.

Chapter 10

1. Darley, J.M. and Batson, C.D. (1973). From Jerusalem to Jericho: a study of situational and dispositional variables in helping behavior. *Journal of Personality and Social Psychology* 27: 100–108.
2. Galinsky, A.D., Maddux, W.W., Gilin, D. et al. (2008). Why it pays to get inside the head of your opponent: the differential effects of perspective taking and empathy in negotiations. *Psychological Science* 19 (4): 378–384. https://doi.org/10.1111/j.1467-9280.2008.02096.x
3. Boyatzis, R.E., Passarelli, A.M., Koenig, K. et al. (2012). Examination of the neural substrates activated in memories of experiences with resonant and dissonant leaders. *The Leadership Quarterly* 23 (2): 259–272. ISSN 1048-9843. https://doi.org/10.1016/j.leaqua.2011.08.003.
4. Solomon, L. (2015). Becoming powerful makes you less empathetic. *Harvard Business Review*, 21 April. https://hbr.org/2015/04/becoming-powerful-makes-you-less-empathetic?utm_medium=paidsearch&utm_source=google&utm_campaign=domcontent&utm_term=Non-Brand&tpcc=paidsearch.google.dsacontent&gad_source=1&gclid=Cj0KCQjwztOwBhD7ARIsAPDKnkBtzuoTGu8wNOTnEhggOq3iRdVnyneZzxl3eEYZ5L70aJ2qc4wdHogaAtTBEALw_wcB (accessed 16 October 2024).

Chapter 11

1. Gandy, S. (2019). From egoism to ecoism: psychedelics and nature connection. TEDx TED Conferences, 4 April. https://www.youtube.com/watch?v=zuzPaVEuUiM (accessed 9 April 2024); Pollan, M. (2022). *How to Change Your Mind*. Directed by Alison Ellwood and Lucy Walker. Netflix. https://www.netflix.com/gb/title/80229847 (accessed 29 October 2024).

2. Earthrise (n.d.) Wikipedia. https://en.wikipedia.org/wiki/Earthrise (accessed 17 October 2024).

3. Grind, K. and Bindley, K. (2023). Magic mushrooms. LSD. Ketamine. The drugs that power Silicon Valley. *The Wall Street Journal* (27 June). https://www.wsj.com/articles/silicon-valley-microdosing-ketamine-lsd-magic-mushrooms-d381e214 (accessed 17 October 2024).

4. Newer, R. (2023). *I Feel Love: MDMA and the Quest for Connection in a Fractured World*, 206 New York: Bloomsbury Publishing.

5. 1heart and PsyX (n.d.). The altered state of business: the potential for psychedelics & sacred plant medicines to elevate our leaders and institutions. https://www.1heart.com/the-altered-state-of-business/ (accessed 17 October 2024).

6. Mackey, J. (2023). The Whole story: The Whole Foods market way to higher profits, better people, and a healthier planet. https://johnpmackey.com/the-whole-story/ (accessed 29 October 2024). Portfolio, 2023; Sisodia, R. (2023). *Awaken: The Path to Purpose, Inner Peace and Healing*. Wiley.

7. The Goop Lab with Gwyneth Paltrow (2020). The healing trip. Netflix. https://www.netflix.com/gb/title/80244690 (accessed 17 October 2024).

8. Business, *The Economist* (2022). Bosses want to feed psychedelics to their staff. *The Economist* (8 June). https://www.economist.com/business/2022/06/08/bosses-want-to-feed-psychedelics-to-their-staff (accessed 17 October 2024).

9. Callahan, C. (2022). How Dr. Bronner's came to offer psychedelic therapy as a mental health benefit for employees. *WorkLife* (28 July). https://www.worklife.news/culture/ketamine-assisted-therapy/ (accessed 17 October 2024).

10. Oppegaard, K. and Meister, A. (2022). Could psychedelics open new doors for science and business? *MIT Sloan Management Review* (3 November). https://sloanreview.mit.edu/article/could-psychedelics-open-new-doors-for-science-and-business/ (accessed 17 October 2024).

11. George, D.R., Hanson, R., Wilkinson, D. et al. (2022). Ancient roots of today's emerging renaissance in psychedelic medicine. *Culture, Medicine and Psychiatry* 46 (4): 890–903. https://doi.org/10.1007/s11013-021-09749-y. Epub 2021 Sep 2. PMID: 34476719; PMCID: PMC8412860.

12. Kotler, S. and Wheal, J. (2017). *Stealing Fire: How Silicon Valley, the Navy SEALs, and Maverick Scientists are Revolutionizing the Way we Live and Work.* Harper Collins. Silver, L.S. (2020). Psychedelics, creativity and entrepreneurship. *American Journal of Management* 20 (3): 27–36.

13. Wasson, G. (1957). Seeking the magic mushroom. *Life* (13 May). https://www.cuttersguide.com/pdf/Periodical-Publications/life-by-time-inc-published-may-13-1957.pdf (accessed 29 October 2024)

14. For a detailed history of MDMA read: Newer, R. (2023). *I Feel Love: MDMA and the Quest for Connection in a Fractured World.* New York: Bloomsbury Publishing.

15. Schlag, A.K., Aday, J., Salam, I. et al. (2022). Adverse effects of psychedelics: from anecdotes and misinformation to systematic science. *Journal of Psychopharmacology* 36 (3): 258–272. https://doi.org/10.1177/02698811211069100. Epub 2022 Feb 2. PMID: 35107059; PMCID: PMC8905125; Johansen, P.Ø. and Krebs, T.S. (2015). Psychedelics not linked to mental health problems or suicidal behavior: a population study. *Journal of Psychopharmacology* 29 (3): 270–279.

16. Nutt, D.J., King, L.A., and Phillips, L.D. (2010). Drug harms in the UK: a multicriteria decision analysis. *The Lancet* 376 (9752), 1558–1565. https://doi.org/10.1016/S0140-6736(10)61462-6.

17. Nutt D. (2009). Equasy—an overlooked addiction with implications for the current debate on drug harms. *Journal of Psychopharmacology* 23 (1): 3–5. https://doi.org/10.1177/0269881108099672.

18. Griffiths, R.R., Richards, W.A., McCann, U. et al. (2006). Psilocybin can occasion mystical-type experiences having substantial and sustained personal meaning and spiritual significance. *Psychopharmacology* (Berl) 187 (3): 268–283; discussion 284–292. https://doi.org/10.1007/s00213-006-0457-5. Epub 2006 Jul 7. PMID: 16826400. See also: hopkinspsychedelic.org

19. Aixalà, M.B. and Bouso Saiz, J.C. (2022). *Psychedelic Integration: Psychotherapy for Non-ordinary States of Consciousness*. Santa Fe, NM: Synergetic Press.

20. Jungaberle, H., Thal, S., Zeuch, A. et al. (2018). Positive psychology in the investigation of psychedelics and entactogens: a critical review. *Neuropharmacology* 142: 179–199 https://doi.org/10.1016/j.neuropharm.2018.06.034

21. Wusiman, D. (2023). Mushrooms make better leaders? Exploring psychedelic's impact on leadership mindset. Master thesis ESCP Business School, Evolute Institute; Wusiman, D.D. (2023). Research update: Can magic mushrooms make better leaders? – exploring psychedelics' impact on leadership mindset. 9 September. https://evolute-institute.com/personal-development-leadership/psychedelic-research-can-magic-mushrooms-make-better-leaders/ (accessed 17 October 2024).

22. Teboul, E. (2023). Interview with Dillfuzi "Daphne" Wusiman, 17 October.

23. Sampson, R. and Zelner, B. (n.d.). Participant interest. Connected Leadership Study. https://www.leaders.study/participant (accessed 17 October 2024).

Chapter 12

1. Forstmann, M. and Sagioglou, C. (2017). Lifetime experience with (classic) psychedelics predicts pro-environmental behavior through an increase in nature relatedness. *Journal of Psychopharmacology* 31 (8): 975–988. https://doi.org/10.1177/0269881117714049; Lyons, T. and Carhart-Harris, R.L. (2018). Increased nature relatedness and decreased authoritarian political views after psilocybin for treatment-resistant depression. *Journal of Psychopharmacology* 32: 811–819. https://doi.org/10.1177/0269881117748902; Watts R., Day C., Krzanowski J. et al. (2017). Patients' accounts of increased "connectedness" and "acceptance" after psilocybin for treatment-resistant depression. *Journal of Humanistic Psychology* 57: 520–564. https://doi.org/10.1177/0022167817709585; Carhart-Harris, R.L., Erritzoe, D., Haijen, E. et al. (2018). Psychedelics and connectedness. *Psychopharmacology* 235: 547–550. https://doi.org/10.1007/s00213-017-4701-y; Lerner M. and Lyvers M. (2006). Values and beliefs of psychedelic drug users: a cross-cultural study. *Journal of*

Psychoactive Drugs 38: 143–147. 10.1080/02791072.2006.10399838; Studerus E., Kometer M., Hasler F. et al. (2011). Acute, subacute and long-term subjective effects of psilocybin in healthy humans: a pooled analysis of experimental studies. *Journal of Psychopharmacology* 25: 1434–1452. 10.1177/0269881110382466.

2. Kettner, H., Gandy, S., Haijen, E. C. H. M. et al. (2019). From egoism to ecoism: psychedelics increase nature relatedness in a state-mediated and context-dependent manner. *International Journal of Environmental Research and Public Health* 16 (24): 5147. https://doi.org/10.3390/ijerph 16245147.

3. Luke, D. (2019). *Otherworlds: Psychedelics and Exceptional Human Experience*. London: Aeon Books Ltd.

4. Studerus, E., Kometer, M., Hasler, F. et al. (2011). Acute, subacute and long-term subjective effects of psilocybin in healthy humans: a pooled analysis of experimental studies. *Journal of Psychopharmacology* 25 (11): 1434–1452. https://doi.org/10.1177/0269881110382466. Epub 2010 Sep 20. PMID: 20855349.

5. Sample, I. (2016). LSD's impact on the brain revealed in groundbreaking images. *The Guardian* (11 April).

6. Carhart-Harris, R., Leech, R., Hellyer, P. et al. (2014). The entropic brain: a theory of conscious states informed by neuroimaging research with psychedelic drugs. *Frontiers in Human Neuroscience* 8. https://doi.org/10.3389/fnhum.2014.00020

7. Girn, M., Mills, C., Roseman, L. et al. (2020). Updating the dynamic framework of thought: creativity and psychedelics. *NeuroImage*, 213: 116726. https://pubmed.ncbi.nlm.nih.gov/32160951/; Baggott, M.J. (2015). Psychedelics and creativity: a review of the quantitative literature. *PeerJ PrePrints* 3: e1202v1. https://doi.org/10.7287/peerj.preprints. 1202v1

8. Mason, N.L., Kuypers, K.P.C., Reckweg, J.T. et al. (2021). Spontaneous and deliberate creative cognition during and after psilocybin exposure. *Scientific Reports* 11 (1): 8565. https://doi.org/10.1038/s41398-021-01335-5. See also Girn, M., Mills, C., Roseman, L. et al. (2020). Updating the dynamic framework of thought: creativity and psychedelics. *Neuro-Image* 213: 116726.

9. Gattuso, J.J., Perkins, D., Ruffell, S. et al. (2023). Default mode network modulation by psychedelics: a systematic review. *The International Journal of Neuropsychopharmacology* 26 (3): 155–188. https://doi.org/10.1093/ijnp/pyac074. PMID: 36272145; PMCID: PMC10032309.

10. Lehmert, K., Ambrozova, E., Pokorny, V. et al. (2021). Microdosing of psychoactive substances in business practice. *Businesses* 1 (3): 196–204. https://doi.org/10.3390/businesses1030014; Andersson, M. and Kjellgren, A. (2019). Twenty percent better with 20 micrograms? A qualitative study of psychedelic microdosing self-reports and discussions on YouTube. *Harm Reduction Journal* 16 (63). https://doi.org/10.1186/s12954-019-0333-3; Silver, L.S. (2020). Turn on, tune in, drop in: psychedelics, creativity and entrepreneurship. *American Journal of Management* 20 (3). https://doi.org/10.33423/ajm.v20i3.3104.

11. See Fadiman, J. (2011). *The Psychedelic Explorer's Guide: Safe, Therapeutic, and Sacred Journeys.* Rochester, VT: Park Street Press. ISBN 978-1594774027.

12. Hutten, N.R.P.W., Mason, N.L., Dolder, P.C. et al. (2020). Low doses of LSD acutely increase BDNF blood plasma levels in healthy volunteers. *ACS Pharmacology and Translational Science* 4 (2): 461–466. https://doi.org/10.1021/acsptsci.0c00099. PMID: 33860175; PMCID: PMC8033605.

13. Roseman, L., Ron, Y., Saca, A. et al. (2021). Relational processes in Ayahuasca Groups of Palestinians and Israelis. *Frontiers in Pharmacology* 12. https://doi.org/10.3389/fphar.2021.607529. Add also that they are expanding this research.

14. On this topic: Pokorny, T., Preller, K.H., Kometer, M. et al. (2017). Effect of psilocybin on empathy and moral decision-making. *The International Journal of Neuropsychopharmacology* 20 (9): 747–757. https://doi.org/10.1093/ijnp/pyx047. PMID: 28637246; PMCID: PMC5581487; Mason, N.L., Mischler, E., Uthaug, M.V. et al. (2019). Sub-acute effects of psilocybin on empathy, creative thinking, and subjective well-being. *Journal of Psychoactive Drugs* 51 (2): 123–134. https://doi.org/10.1080/02791072.2019.1580804; Dolder, P.C., Schmid, Y., Muller, F. et al. (2016). LSD acutely impairs fear recognition and enhances emotional empathy and sociality. *Neuropsychopharmacology* 41 (11), 2638–2646. https://doi.org/10.1038/npp.2016.82; Hysek, C.M., Schmid, Y., Simmler, L.D. et al. (2014). MDMA enhances emotional empathy and prosocial behavior.

Social Cognitive and Affective Neuroscience 9 (11): 1645–1652. https://doi .org/10.1093/scan/nst161. Epub 2013 Oct 4. PMID: 24097374; PMCID: PMC4221206; Carlyle, M., Stevens, T., Fawaz, L. et al. (2019). Greater empathy in MDMA users. *Journal of Psychopharmacology* 33 (3): 295–304. https://doi.org/10.1177/0269881119826594.

15. MDMA is classified as an empathogen, meaning it induces a heightened sense of emotional closeness, empathy, and understanding toward others. It primarily works by increasing the release of serotonin, dopamine, and norepinephrine in the brain, creating a flood of neurotransmitters associated with mood, pleasure, and arousal. This mechanism distinguishes it from classical psychedelics, which typically act on serotonin receptors, leading to altered perceptions and hallucinations. The empathogenic effects of MDMA result from its ability to enhance emotional processing and connection, setting it apart from the more perceptual alterations induced by classical psychedelics.

16. George, A. and Sol, W. (2023). Potential Benefits of MDMA-Assisted Conflict Transformation. Informed Couple Therapy: Transpersonal Roots and Future Promise. California Institute of Integral Studies, San Francisco, CA, USA. https://digitalcommons.ciis.edu/cgi/viewcontent .cgi?article=1075&context=advance-archive.

17. Ferriss, T. (2023). *My Healing Journey after Childhood Abuse (Includes extensive resource list)*, 14 September. https://tim.blog/2020/09/14/ how-to-heal-trauma/ (accessed 16 October 2024).

18. Lindenfeld, J. (2023). "It's ripped the world apart": David Bronner on how psychedelics could be a cure for capitalism. *Rolling Stone*, 6 May. https:// www.rollingstone.com/culture/culture-features/david-bronner- psychedelics-capitalism-1234730373/ (accessed 16 October 2024).

19. Wheal, J. (2021). *Recapture the Rapture: Rethinking God, Sense, and Death in a World That's Lost Its Mind*, 163. Harper Wave.

Chapter 13

1. World Economic Forum and AlphaBeta (2020). *New Nature Economy Report II: The Future Of Nature And Business.* https://www3.weforum .org/docs/WEF_The_Future_Of_Nature_And_Business_2020.pdf (accessed 29 October 2024).

2. World Economic Forum, Alphabeta, 2020.

3. SEIA (7 October 2020). Report: U.S. Corporate Solar Investments Swell to 8300 Megawatts, Grow 20-Fold Over Last Decade. The Solar Energy Industries Association. https://www.seia.org/news/report-us-corporate-solar-investments-swell-8300-megawatts-grow-20-fold-over-last-decade (accessed 29 October 2024).

4. World Economic Forum, AlphaBeta, 2020, p. 4.

5. Mackey, J., Friedman, M. and Rodgers, T.J. Rethinking the Social Responsibility of Business, Reason.com, 21 August 2020. https://reason.com/2005/10/01/rethinking-the-social-responsi-2/?print (accessed 29 October 2024).

6. Larry Fink to CEO, "A Sense of Purpose," Harvard Law School Forum on Corporate Governance and Financial Regulation, 17 January 2018, https://corpgov.law.harvard.edu/2018/01/17/a-sense-of-purpose/ (accessed 29 October 2024).

7. Waldron, S. (2021). *Corporate Social Responsibility is Not Public Relations: How to Put CSR at the Heart of Your Company and Maximize the Business Benefits*, 7. LID Publishing.

8. Axios (2021). The 2021 Axios Harris Poll 100 Reputation Rankings, 13 May 2021. https://www.axios.com/2021/05/13/the-2021-axios-harris-poll-100-reputation-rankings (accessed 29 October 2024).

9. Marcario, R., quoted in Diane Primo, Adapt: Scaling Purpose in a Divisive World (Weeva, 2022), Accessed March 28, 2024, https://purposebrand.com/books/adapt-book-scaling-purpose-in-divisive-world/ (accessed 29 October 2024).

10. Sisodia, R., Wolfe, D. B. and Sheth, J. (2014). *Firms of Endearment: How World-Class Companies Profit from Passion and Purpose*, 2. Pearson FT Press.

11. Tony's Chocolonely (2021/2022). Annual Fair Report, 6. https://online.flippingbook.com/view/400561186/6-7 (accessed 29 October 2024).

12. Riding, S. (2020). ESG funds forecast to outnumber conventional funds by 2025. *Financial Times* (17 October) https://www.ft.com/content/5cd6e923-81e0-4557-8cff-a02fb5e01d42 (accessed 29 October 2024).

13. Gallup (2023). State of the Global Workplace Report. https://www.gallup.com/workplace/349484/state-of-the-global-workplace.aspx?thank-you-report-form=1 (accessed 29 October 2024).

14. Edmans, A. 28 Years of stock market data shows a link between employee satisfaction and long-term value. 24 March 2016. https://hbr.org/2016/03/28-years-of-stock-market-data-shows-a-link-between-employee-satisfaction-and-long-term-value.

15. Business Roundtable Statement of the Purpose of a Corporation Two-Year Anniversary Post. Business Roundtable. https://www.businessroundtable.org/purposeanniversary (accessed 29 October 2024).

16. World Economic Forum. *Davos Manifesto 2020: The Universal Purpose of a Company in the Fourth Industrial Revolution. World Economic Forum Agenda.* 2 December 2019. https://www.weforum.org/agenda/2019/12/davos-manifesto-2020-the-universal-purpose-of-a-company-in-the-fourth-industrial-revolution (accessed 29 October 2024).

17. Winston, A. What 1,000 CEOs Really Think About Climate Change and Inequality. *Harvard Business Review.* 24 September 2019. https://hbr.org/2019/09/what-1000-ceos-really-think-about-climate-change-and-inequality (accessed 29 October 2024).

18. Deloitte. For Millennials And Gen Zs, Social Issues Are Top Of Mind—Here's How Organizations Can Drive Meaningful Change. *Forbes* (22 July 2021). https://www.forbes.com/sites/deloitte/2021/07/22/for-millennials-and-gen-zs-social-issues-are-top-of-mind-heres-how-organizations-can-drive-meaningful-change/ (accessed 29 October 2024).

Acknowledgments

I extend profound gratitude to the brilliant leaders who, with unwavering generosity, shared their stories and perspectives. Their insights have significantly shaped the direction of this book, offering invaluable lessons in conscious business and conscious living. I am honored to have the privilege of sharing their monumental wisdom.

I am especially thankful to Raj Sisodia for inspiring me with his work on conscious capitalism and for writing the foreword for this book. Your steadfast support and advocacy have meant so much to me.

My sincere thanks to Alexandra Feldner and Dr. Scilla Elworthy, cofounders of FemmeQ, for introducing me to the transformative concept of feminine intelligence. Their spiritual and emotional perspectives broadened my understanding and were pivotal in shaping my thinking.

I want to express my appreciation to Dr. Dominique Morisano, my mentor at the California Institute of Integral Studies in the Certification on Psychedelic Assisted Therapies, for her dedicated feedback and review of my chapters in this area.

I would also like to express my deep gratitude for Anthony Farr, who spent countless hours with me working through the chapters on the Allan & Gill Gray Foundation. Because I was not present for much of its history, his insights served as my window into the past, and his support was priceless. I couldn't have done it without him.

Heartfelt appreciation goes to Diane Eaton, whose tireless and generous editorial support played an indispensable role in crafting this book. Your dedication and expertise have been a guiding force, and I am profoundly grateful for your contributions. I also extend my deep gratitude to Randy Peyser at Author One Stop, Inc., whose remarkable efforts were instrumental in bringing this book to life and placing it into the hands of Annie Knight at Wiley. Without your exceptional work, this journey wouldn't have been possible.

To my publisher, Annie Knight at Wiley: your contagious enthusiasm and bright smile reassured me that this book was in the best hands. Your energy has been an inspiration throughout this process, and I knew from the start that you were the perfect partner to shepherd this work. I would like to extend my heartfelt thanks to the entire Wiley editorial team for their exceptional support and guidance throughout this journey.

Finally, my deepest appreciation goes to Allan Gray and the Gray family. Allan's profound influence has not only opened my eyes but enriched my heart with a deep understanding of values-based leadership, social entrepreneurship, and collective responsibility. His legacy extends far beyond what words can capture, and I am eternally grateful for his mentorship. I only wish he could have read this work.

Index

A

The Accounting Review, 111
AGOF (Allan Gray Orbis Foundation), 58–66, 78
al Bayati, Hamid, 106
Albertson's, 20
Allan & Gill Gray Foundation, 43, 82–85
Allan Gray Investment Council, 78
Allan Gray Orbis Foundation (AGOF), 58–66, 78
Altered states of consciousness, 149
American Accounting Association, 111
Anderson, Ben, 120–121
Apple, 54
Aquinas, Thomas, St., 53
Ardern, Jacinda, 106
Ardern, Jainda, 35
Artisan Partners, 124
Authenticity, 70–72
Awaken (Sisodia), 97
Ayahuasca, 98, 175, 181

B

Barnes, Andrew, 61–62
Batson, Daniel, 131–132
BBBEE (Broad-Based Black Economic Empowerment), 79
B Corporation certification, 115, 120–123
The Beam Network, 90–91, 97
BEE (Black Economic Empowerment) Act, 79

Behavioral economics, 12
Beiner, Alexander, 162, 180
Beltman, Henk Jan, 190
Ben-Shahar, Tal, 94
Berry, Thomas, 55
Bhutan, 103–107
BIA (B Impact Assessment) tool, 119, 121
The Big Short (Lewis), 20
B Impact Assessment (BIA) tool, 119, 121
B Lab, 115, 119–123
Black Economic Empowerment (BEE) Act, 79
Blackrock, 189
Bluebell Capital, 124
B Movement Builders (BMB), 121–122
Body work, 148
Boeing, 20
Both/And Thinking (Smith and Lewis), 39
Brain:
  hemispheres of, 27–28
  right, 30
Brand, Stuart, 151
Break open, 41–56
Breega, 65
Brin, Sergey, 152
Broad-Based Black Economic Empowerment (BBBEE), 79
Bronner, David, 152, 157, 180
Brown, Brené, 73–74
BRT (Business Roundtable), 191
Buffett, Warren, 20, 132

215

Built to Last (Collins and Porras), 187
Burnout, 14–15
Burns, James MacGregor, 31
Business Roundtable (BRT), 191

C

Campbell, Joseph, 96
CapitalG, 68
Capitalism:
   conscious, 108–109
   power of, 1
Capitalism and Freedom (Friedman), 15
Carasso, Isaac, 116
Carhart-Harris, Robin, 158, 172, 173
Carnegie, Dale, 66
Change, 149–150
Chemins de Traverse (Faber), 124–125
Chief, 68–71
Childers, Carolyn, 67–70
Childhood trauma, 177
Chopra, Deepak, 138
Chouinard, Yvon, 22
Chrysler, 20
Cicero, Marcus Tullius, 154
Citigroup, 20
Cleaver, Bruce, 192
Climate crisis, 6
Cognitive crafting, 92–93
Collier, Paul, 18
Collins, Jim, 187
Columbia Law School, 4, 42–43
Columbia University, 44, 94
Como Wellbeing Manifesto, 107
Compassion, 38
Complex problems, 141
Complicated problems, 141
Confino, Jordana, 4
Congruence, 46–52
Conscious capitalism, 108–110
Conscious Capitalism movement, 98
Conscious leadership, 2–4, 110
Consciousness, 36–37, 149
Controlled Substances Act (CSA), 156
Cook, Tim, 54
Corporate Social Responsibility is Not Public Relations (Waldron), 190
Council of Foreign Relations, 35

Courage, 70–76
COVID-19 pandemic, 93
Crawford, Bill, 144
Creativity, 171–175
Crick, Francis, 152
CSA (Controlled Substances Act), 156
Csikszentmihalyi, Mihaly, 173
Cuccinelli, Brunello, 109

D

Dalio, Ray, 21, 148
Danone Manifesto Ventures, 118
Danone North America (Danone NA),
   49–50, 115–120, 124–127
Darley, John, 131–132
Davis, Lorna, 49–50, 52, 93, 117–120
Davis Polk & Wardwell LLP, 43
Davos Manifesto, 191–192
DEA (Drug Enforcement Administration),
   156
Default mode network (DMN), 173
Deloitte, 89
De Saint-Affrique, Antoine, 126
Digital Age, 9–10
DMN (default mode network), 173
Doblin, Rick, 158
Donner, Jonathon, 95
Drive (Pink), 47
Drug Enforcement Administration
   (DEA), 156
Druk Gyalpo, 103–105
Duncan, Samantha, 42

E

Earth Law Center (ELC), 42, 54–55, 168–169
Economic systems, 9–10
Edmondson, Amy, 60
Eigeland, Chris, 61
Einstein, Albert, 28
ELC, *see* Earth Law Center
Elworthy, Scilla, 35, 49
Emotional mastery, 145–147
Empathy, 136, 175–176
Equality, gender, 32
E Squared, 64–65
Evolute Institute, 161
Exercise, physical, 148–149

F

Faber, Emmanuel, 96–97, 116–120, 124–127
Faith in Nature, 52–53
Farr, Anthony, 81–82
The Fearless Organization (Edmondson), 60
Feilding, Amanda, 163, 174
Ferris, Tim, 171, 177–178
Financial Times, 20
Fink, Larry, 189
FLC (Future Logistics Company), 63–64
Flow, 172–173
Flow Genome Project, 173
Forbes, 125, 192
Fordham Law School, 4
Frankl, Viktor E., 99, 185
Frederickson, Barbara, 137–138
Free markets, 21
Friedman, Milton, 15–17, 19, 183, 186
Future Logistics Company (FLC), 63–64

G

Gandhi, Mahatma, 26–27, 88
Gandy, Sam, 170
Gawdat, Mo, 38, 41–42
GE, *see* General Electric
Gelles, David, 19
Gender equality, 32
Gender stereotypes, 32
General Assembly, UN, 105–106
General Catalyst, 68
General Electric (GE), 19–20, 55–56
Gen Zers, 190, 192–193
Gerzema, John, 34
Gibran, Kahlil, 109
The Gifts of Imperfection (Brown), 73
Go1, 61–63
Good Samaritan Study, 131
Google, 41, 60, 152
Goop, 152
Gray, Allan, 43–45, 52, 58, 63, 70–71, 75–85
Gray, Gill, 58, 78
Great Recession, 20–22
Greed, 9–23
   and breaking capitalism, 19–21
   corporate executive, 17

and maximizing profits, 15–19
   and rational self-interest, 11–15
Griffiths, Roland, 157, 181, 182
Grof, Stanislav, 178
Grounding techniques, 144
Guggenheim, Karen, 42, 107

H

Happiness, 103–105
Harari, Yuval Noah, 134
Harvard Business School, 78, 95
Harvard University, 27, 94, 155
The Healing Organization (Sisodia), 98
Helene, Zoe, 160
Henderson, Rebecca, 109
Hero's Journey, 96–100
Hoffman, Reid, 79
Hoffmann, Albert, 154
Home Depot, 20
Hood, Chris, 61
How to Change Your Mind (Pollan), 157
Hughes, Chris, 25–27
Humility, 49
Hussein, Saddam, 106
Hutchins, Giles, 109

I

IBM, 41
Imperial College London, 172, 173
Independence, 135–136
Individuation, 37
Industrial Age, 9
Inner work, 47–49
Inspired Capital, 68
Intelligence:
   feminine, 5–6, 186–187
   masculine, 6, 187
   spiritual, 142–143
Interdependence, 135
Intuition, 38

J

Jakobsdóttir, Katrín, 106
Job crafting, 92, 94
Jobs, Steve, 60, 152, 153
Johns Hopkins University, 157

Index

Joly, Hubert, 137
Jotler, Steven, 173
Jung, Carl, 33, 37, 179

K

Kabat-Zinn, Jon, 133
Kahneman, Daniel, 132
Kaplan, Lindsay, 67–70, 72, 75
Kaufer, Katrin, 141
Ketamine, 152
King, Martin Luther, Jr., 26–27, 137
Kotch, Elizabeth, 152
Kraft Foods, 50, 117

L

Lagarde, Christine, 36
Lamont, Annie, 124
Lateral thinking, 172
Lawyers for Nature (LFN), 54
Leadership:
    conscious, 2–4, 110
    honing your, 129–131
    new era of, 193–195
    next generation of, 23
    potential of, 10–11
    power, 46
Leary, Timothy, 155
Left brain, 30, 55
LeGuin, Ursula K., 140
Lewis, C. S., 177
Lewis, Marianne W., 39
LFN (Lawyers for Nature), 54
Life Map exercise, 70–71
London Business School, 191
Love 2.0 (Frederickson), 137–138
LSD, 151–152, 154–156
Lubega, Melvyn, 57–66, 80

M

Machiavelli, Niccolo, 22
Mckenna, Terence, 155
Mackey, John, 108–110, 129, 152, 186, 191
McKinsey and Company, 90
Mandela, Nelson, 26–27
The Man Who Broke Capitalism (Gelles), 19
MAPS (Multidisciplinary Association for
    Psychedelic Studies), 158

Marcario, Rose, 190
Marin, Sanna, 106, 127
Masculine intelligence, 6, 187
Masculine mindset, 29–33, 73, 140
Maslow, Abraham, 45
Materialism, spiritual, 159
MDMA, 152, 156–158, 176
Medicines, psychedelic, *see* Psychedelic
    medicines
Meditation, 147–148
Merck, 156
Merkel, Angela, 36
Microdosing, 174
Microsoft, 41
Millennials, 190, 192–193
MIND Foundation, 160
Mindset:
    masculine, 29–33, 73, 140
    whole-brain, 56
Morales, Ana, 97
Morales, Bertha, 97
Morals, 13
Morgan, Flemming, 125
Mother Earth, 38
Mother Teresa, 188
Muir, John, 171
Mullis, Kary, 173
Multidisciplinary Association for Psychedelic
    Studies (MAPS), 158

N

NASA, 151
Native American Church, 181
Nature, 53, 169–171
Nespresso, 122
Nestlé Group, 122
Net Purpose, 42
New York Times, 16, 19
New York University, 4
Nixon, Richard, 51, 155
Nooyi, Indra, 112, 139
Nutrition, 148–149

O

#OneBillionHappy movement, 42
Oxford Research Group, 35
Oxford University, *see* University of Oxford

P

Paltrow, Gwyneth, 152
Parenting, 30
Parker, Quanah, 181
Parmelee, Michele, 193
Pascal, Blaise, 13
Patagonia, 190
Patriarchy, 32
PepsiCo, 112
Perel, Esther, 135
Perfectionism, 74
Philanthropy, 43–44
Physical exercise, 148–149
Pink, Dan, 47
Plato, 154
Pollan, Michael, 157
Polman, Paul, 94–96, 109, 111
Porras, Jerry, 187
Portas, Mary, 188
"Positive Lawyering" course, 4
Power leadership, 46
Prince, Chuck, 20
Princeton University, 131
Problems, complicated vs. complex, 141
Profits, 1, 21
Project Aristotle, 60
Psilocybin, 152, 172
Psilocybin Project, 155
Psychedelic medicines, 45, 151–165
    and connection to self, 176–179
    and creativity, 171–175
    and empathy, 175–176
    and higher connection, 179–182
    history of, 153–160
    leadership transformed with, 160–162
    and nature, 169–171
Psychological safety, 60
Psychospiritual experiences, 149, 167
PTSD, 158–159
Purpose:
    about, 88–89
    encouraging, in your people, 92–95
    and Hero's Journey, 96–100
    and why, 89–92

R

Rational self-interest, 11–13, 15–17
Reductionism, 140

Regenerative Leadership (Storm and
    Hutchins), 109
Regulation, 16–17
Reimagining Capitalism in a World on Fire
    (Henderson), 109
Relationship mastery, 134–139
Rhodes University, 78
Riboud, Antoine, 116, 128
Riboud, Franck, 116
Right brain, 30
Robbins, Tony, 90
Roosevelt, Franklin D., 8
Rowell, Falen, 151–152
Russell, Bertrand, 143

S

Sabina, Maria, 155
Safety, psychological, 60
St. Paul's Cathedral (London), 87
Salzberg, Sharon, 134
Sampson, Rachelle, 161–162
Sangwan, Neha, 135
Santo Daime, 181
Scharmer, Otto, 141
Self-discovery, 145
Self-interest, rational, 11–13, 15–17
Shakti, 37
Shaw, George Bernard, 193
Shiva, 37
Shulgin, Alexander, 156
Simon, Herbert, 141
Sinek, Simon, 89, 91
Sisodia, Raj, 97–99, 108–110, 152, 191
Smith, Adam, 11–15, 19, 105, 183
Smith, Terry, 112
Smith, Wendy K., 39
Social impact, 35
"The Social Responsibility of Business Is to
    Increase Its Profits" (Friedman), 16
Somatic awareness, 144, 148
The Soul of Leadership (Chopra), 138
Spencer, Octavia, 54
Spiritual intelligence, 142–143
Spiritual materialism, 159
Standard Bank London, 81
Starfish Greathearts Foundation, 81–82
Stealing Fire (Kotler and Wheal), 173
Stillness, 38

Stock prices, 16, 105
Storm, Laura, 109
Sturgeon, Nicola, 106–108

T

Taylor, Jill Bolte, 27–29
The Theory of Moral Sentiments (Smith), 12
Thinking Fast and Slow (Kahneman), 132
Three breaths, taking, 148
Thunberg, Greta, 189
Time Magazine, 69
Time mastery, 131–134
Tippett, Krista, 142
Tony's Chocolonely, 190
Tools of the Masters, 129
Toxic femininity, 7
Tran, Vu, 61
Transactional style, of leadership, 31–32
Trauma, childhood, 177
Trebeck, Katherine, 107
TRUE Model, 129–147
    emotions, 139–145
    relationships, 134–139
    time, 131–134
    uncertainty, 139–145
Trungpa Rinpoche, Chögyam, 159
Tutu, Desmond, 59, 70

U

ULDP (Unilever Leadership Development
    Program), 95
Uncertainty, 139–145
Unilever, 94–96, 109, 111, 112
Unilever Leadership Development Program
    (ULDP), 95
United Nations, 36, 105–106
University of Cape Town, 61
University of Maryland, 161
University of Oxford, 62, 105

V

Vanity Fair France Magazine, 124
Voltaire, 123

W

Waldron, Sangeeta, 190
Wallace, David Foster, 15
Wall Street (film), 17
Wall Street Journal, 174
"War on Drugs," 51, 156
Wasson, Gordon, 155
Wasson, Valentina, 155
Watson, James, 152
Wayne, John, 73
The Wealth of Nations (Smith), 11, 13
Weaver, Warren, 141
WEF, *see* World Economic Forum
Welch, Jack, 19–21, 27, 55–56
The Wharton School, 92
Wheal, Jamie, 173
Whole-brain mindset, 56
Whole Foods, 129, 186
Wholeness, 183–186, 188–189
Why, 89–92, 109–110
Williamson, Marianne, 146
Wilson, Grant, 42, 54
Winfrey, Oprah, 138
WOHASU, *see* World Happiness Summit
World Economic Forum (WEF),
    153, 186, 191
World Happiness Report, 36, 42, 105–106
World Happiness Summit (WOHASU),
    42, 97, 107
Wren, Christopher, 87–88
Wrzesniewski, Amy, 92–93
Wusiman, Dillfuzi "Daphne," 161

Y

Yang, 36–37
Y Combinator, 62
Yin, 36–37
Yoco, 61
Yousafzai, Malala, 192
Yue, Michelle, 97

Z

Zelner, Bennet, 161–162